Charles Ives:

The Making of The Composer

Antony Cooke

 Estrella Books

ISBN paperback
978-1-0-9834-216-6

First Edition 2020

Front Cover

(From top center, clockwise) Charles Ives's Yale graduation portrait [PD]; Center Church on the Green, New Haven, CT (Antony Cooke); George Ives, Ives's father
and Danbury bandleader [PD]; old Civil War etching [PD]; Horatio Parker around the time Ives knew him [PD]; First Congregational Church, Danbury, CT (Antony Cooke)

Dedicated with admiration and gratitude

to

Carol K. Baron

Contents

Chapter 1
Introduction

*T*he year was 1987; it will forever stand as the moment in time when efforts to rewrite Charles Ives's legacy would cover up what he achieved and how he did it, damaging his ascendency for decades; the energy squandered to foster one of the most unfortunate misrepresentations of any composer in the history of Western music is hard to overestimate. Differently directed, that effort would have allowed countless truths about the man and his music to be known, instead of being lost in the noise of redefining him. Despite recent research that has laid bare the wrongs, even the deliberate obfuscations, politicizations and redefinitions,[1] Ives stands unapologetically diminished in scholarship—seen as just one of many early twentieth century pioneers—his unique contributions remaining yet to be adequately or subjectively recognized and analyzed, even more, what lay behind them still misunderstood and under-appreciated.

The overriding purpose of this book, therefore, is to unearth as much as possible about all that led to one man's unique form of expression; it will, by default, illuminate greater truths to Ives's story and accomplishments. Is it naïve to hope that prospective music lovers who have been deterred from listening, and who might, otherwise, have been counted among his most ardent followers, finally will be brought into the fold? The truth cannot be suppressed forever; Ives, one day, will know full his acceptance as the true first 'Great American Composer,' the road he followed to the stars in near total isolation finally revealed. He was always, of course, no stranger to rejection, and wore it as a badge of pride for recording authentic

---

[1]Examples: Antony Cooke: *Charles Ives's Musical Universe* (West Conshohocken, PA: Infinity, 2015); *Charles Ives and his Road to the Stars*, second edition (West Conshohocken, PA: Infinity, 2016); Baron, Carol K, "Dating Charles Ives's Music: Facts and Fictions," *Perspectives of New Music*, 1990: 20–56; Budiansky, Stephen, *Mad Music: Charles Ives the Nostalgic Rebel* (Lebanon, NH: ForeEdge, University Press of New England, 2014).

experiences of his surrounding in sounds that neither listeners nor players could access as at the time. His composer peers, or performing musicians he invited to his house, rejected his music out of hand. To sustain his way forward took courage, and required his separation from the larger musical community. Just when it appeared he had finally been embraced by the academic musical community *of his own country*, internal political wrangling entered the fray that led to the notorious efforts after 1987 to debunk much of what he accomplished and almost everything about him.

Ives, a musical and business visionary, led a double life as an executive and composer. He pursued it with a passion that gave little thought for his personal wellbeing; his famous, yet oddly obscured health collapse in 1918, spoke to it. As well-known in the business community as he was *un*known as a composer, his acquaintances in either field often had no idea about his double identity. To this day, only a fraction of his life as a business executive is known—which explains, perhaps, the frequent and wholly inaccurate depiction of him as "an insurance salesman," even though Ives never *sold anything*! Although his life as a composer has been more widely explored, it has been no less widely misrepresented! A revolutionary in both fields, however, Ives rebuilt life insurance in America and became its greatest advocate, *simultaneously* and pre-emptively composing wholly authentic American music while pioneering techniques for which he still is inadequately credited, and that are usually associated with others!

Not depending on music for a livelihood allowed Ives to live in accordance with his aspirations and ideals—his success in business allowed him to fulfil his altruistic instincts, and an uncompromised musical avocation. His status as a non-professional composer was, in fact, preordained even before he attended Yale; its reputation then mainly as a business school was in keeping with the greater family's professional outlook. Likely selected by Lyman Brewster (a prominent lawyer, and Ives's illustrious uncle) even before Ives's father died unexpectedly, Brewster provided for his education, and subsequently secured for him a position in the life insurance industry.[2] Largely confirming the rejection of music for a career, it was only during Ives's time at Yale that the newly appointed dean of the school of music, Horatio Parker, would embark on a decades-long agenda to build the music program, in a move to compete with Harvard.

Soon after entering the insurance workforce, however, Ives would find himself embroiled in the infamous 'Bankers' Panic' scandal of 1907. Rampant speculation with investors' capital into unsecured stock market holdings triggered a widespread

---

[2] Stuart Feder, *Charles Ives: "My Father's Song," a Psycho-Analytical Biography* (New Haven, CT: Yale University Press, 1992) 57–58.

investigation that rocked life insurance to its foundations. In its aftermath, Ives and his friend in business, Julian Myrick, formed their own business (Ives & Myrick); Ives's own actuarial system would become the industry standard, its formula providing lifetime support of his insured dependents, and long-term survival of the company and adequate compensation for its employees. Ives's model was famously outlined in a 1912 pamphlet, finally retitled in 1920 "The Amount to Carry— Measuring the Prospect," and reproduced in *The Eastern Underwriter*.[3]

The little enthusiasm Ives received for his music, however, came from a small cadre of admirers, and most notably, his devoted wife, Harmony. The same personal philosophies, spiritual and social that guided his approach to business acted no less significantly in his music, even as it was met mostly with rejection. If Ives himself was a traditionalist at heart, his music advanced into another age, retaining, through his traditionalism through a bond with his time and place in history. In turn, he created a virtual recording unique to his American spirit and the times in which he lived, its vividness and perspective—from his early years and well into the bustling new century—captured as a living testament. Even before the new music of the twentieth century was a glint in anyone's eye, Ives already was composing quantities of highly predictive music that freely explored unchartered terrain. Expressing himself as he pleased, its *relevance*, rather than establishing any particular priority, being the driving force behind it. Musically, Ives already had taken on the reclusiveness that eventually defined his whole life once his cataclysmic illness struck him in 1918.

Ives's tenuous position in 'official' scholarship partly stems from an inability to understand how such remarkable musical priority could have emerged out of 'nowhere' at a time when no one in any of the major centers could do it. A product of unique circumstances, Ives's music was bound to generate skepticism, the unlikely teaching and influence he received from his father (George Ives)—a critical factor in the totality of the phenomenon—being questioned, too. Dismissing any suggestion that such unorthodoxy could have provided the foundation of his son's musical education, his music professor at Yale, Horatio Parker, has been credited instead. However, by the time Ives entered Yale, the die was already cast, if not yet, perhaps, fully enabled to realize his potential. What can only be described as musical archeology is required finally to clarify what Ives did during the waning years of the Romantic age, and whose talent and circumstances embraced the advancing and ebbing tides that shaped the continents of the new world musical order.

---

[3] Charles E. Ives, "The Amount to Carry—Measuring the Prospect," *The Eastern Underwriter* 21 (1Ives's life as a. businessman began 920): 35–38.

The 'Ives Legend'

The 'Ives Legend' is a term coined by the late Frank R. Rossiter in his ultimately depressing account of Ives's life and work. Summing up exaggerated biographies of the composer, the term has been borrowed in recent years to project Ives as unreliable, even dishonest and duplicitous.[4] However, Rossiter's original 'Legend' reflected mostly the summation of the late supporter, Henry Cowell, which featured a number of careless distortions and misunderstandings in the wake of his initial excitement of finding the long sought 'Great American Composer.' The 'Ives Legend,' as summed up, below, by Gayle Sherwood Magee[5] in its typical florid verbiage, indeed, was overdue for a more critical examination:

> Born in Danbury, Connecticut, in 1874, Ives received a brilliant and unconventional education from his father, George Ives, and amateur bandleader and musical visionary. Charles proceeded to Yale where his forward-looking compositions outstripped the limited vision of his instructor, Horatio Parker, an academician and one of the leading conservative composers. But after Yale, Ives realized that his compositions were too far ahead of their time to appeal to the narrow-mined contemporaries or to be published by conservative musical presses. So, in his own words, he "gave up music" and chose to work in insurance by day while continuing to write daring music in his spare time. After more than a decade of this double life, Ives had a heart attack in 1918 that ended his compositional career. From then until the end of his life, Ives cleaned up his works and introduced them to an audience through a growing group of young American and European-American modernists such as Henry Cowell, Bernard Herrmann, and Nicolas Slonimsky. With their support, Ives emerged from his self-imposed exile, gaining wider admiration that peaked with the awarding of the Pulitzer Prize in 1947 for his Third Symphony. Having proven the value of his work decades after it was first conceived, Ives's reputation as the ancestor of modern American music was secured, and his years of isolation and neglect vindicated.[6]

---

[4] Frank R. Rossiter, *Charles Ives & His America* (New York, W. W. Norton & Company (February 11, 1975), *xii.*

[5] Gayle Sherwood Magee, *Charles Ives Reconsidered* (Urbana, IL: University of Illinois Press, Music in American Life Series, 2008).

[6] Magee, *Charles Ives Reconsidered*, 2.

4

Such uncritically and casually recounted accounts of Ives's life and work still were prevalent as recently as 1970, as further illustrated by the excerpt from the newsletter of the Historical Society of Bloomfield, NJ, the township in which Ives held his first position at Old First Presbyterian Church after graduating from Yale:[7]

> Most of Ives's music is sprinkled with snatches of religion, patriotic and folk tunes popular at the turn of the century. Ives. . . went into the insurance business to avoid "starving on dissonances" and became a very wealthy businessman. . . . His music was an avocation until his retirement in 1930. He worked in a visionary's isolation, turning out a steady stream of revolutionary works that presaged the atonal experiments of Schoenberg and Stravinsky. . . . His works were neglected because Ives insisted that he receive no royalties. . . recognition never came to him during his lifetime. It did not bother Ives; he explained, "whether he be accepted or rejected, whether his music is always played or never played—all this has nothing to do with it—it is true or false by his own measure. . . .

Equally glib and careless accounts of Ives's life have propagated myths that persist in spite of themselves—and foster others in turn. For example, it is often claimed that Ives never intended to complete the *Universe Symphony*, although Ives, himself, stated otherwise.[8] Stuart Feder used

Old First Presbyterian Church, Bloomfield, NJ

---

[7] Marguerite M. Elliott, "Charles Ives in Bloomfield: Organist at 'Old First.'" *The Town Crier*: Official Newsletter—The Historical Society of Bloomfield (Bloomfield, NJ) 1, 5 (January 1970), 2.

[8] Charles E. Ives. *Memos*, ed. John Kirkpatrick (New York: W.W. Norton & Co., 1972), at 106.

that particular myth to support his argument that Ives was mentally incompetent when he wrote the sketches to sustain a portion of his argument.[9] Less clearly determined, the 'Legend' sustained the likely incorrect claim that Ives, originally, had intended to become a full-time professional composer. Because his father (George Ives) wished him to avoid the struggle he had endured, Ives probably never seriously entertained the prospect, despite one fleeting attempt to do so (the 1901 New York premiere of *The Celestial Country*).[10] Moreover, Yale was no place to which an aspiring musician would have been drawn in 1894 (Ives's first year there as a freshman). In that year, Horatio Parker had only just been appointed Dean of the Yale School of Music, and had not yet begun to build it into the leading musical institution it was to become. Attending Yale, then, as primarily a college for *business*, would continue the greater Ives family tradition of 'professional' careers, such as lawyers, bankers and industrialists.

If Ives never had intended to follow music for a career, perhaps it explains Parker's failure to recognize the latent talent he was nurturing: why expend his efforts on a music hobbyist? Nevertheless, it appears that Ives still was not ready to completely abandon the idea. 'Testing the waters' in 1902, Ives paid for and staged his thoroughly Parker-inspired early post-Yale cantata, *The Celestial Country*, in New York City. Such relatively conventional music makes clear that he knew the public would not embrace anything radical (even though he claimed to have thrown in some wildly avant-garde organ dissonances at the performance), and also in deference to his father's discouragement of incorporating unconventional 'experiments' into actual works of music.[11] Although *The Celestial Country* features words that Ives (incorrectly) thought had emanated from the same source—the poems by Bernard of Cluny Parker had featured in his cantata of 1892, *Hora Novissima*.[12]—the link in Ives's mind to Parker's musical success is clear, although the style of Parker's cantata was an unlikely artistic choice. It least in Ives's mind, it was a necessary compromise to make for a possible career as a composer. With *The Celestial Country*, Ives was ready to test career opportunities in America, no better exemplified by Parker—composer-organist, choral-director, and teacher—whose own career was as successful as that of any American musician to date.

---

[9] Feder, *"My Father's Song,"* 292–306.

[10] Ibid., 121.

[11] Ives, *Memos*, 115. Also, Feder, *"My Father's Song,"* 114.

[12] As the work that Ives used as a model, *Hora Novissima* is the only work by Parker still reasonably well known, and which had propelled him to fame—even to his new position as Dean of the School of Music at Yale.

Ives's Life and Times Rewritten

For much of the listening public, Ives's image remains largely unscathed—and surprisingly close to that of the now cliché-ridden 'Ives Legend.' In the face of the unrelenting thirty-year history of falsehoods and re-appropriated 'facts,' such news might be welcome, though the truth would be better. More likely, it is due to the unbridged 'gap' between scholarship and the public, most of the latter unaware of its stance. Magee considered Ives's acceptance by the public entailed three stages: rejection, neglect, and final embrace.[13] However, the greater rejection has come from the musicological community rather than the public; there is plenty of blame to go around for the 'neglect,' especially during most of Ives's lifetime; the final 'embrace' is yet to take place in musicology, the correct history needing to be memorialized before the reinvented Ives is spirited away forever. The misappropriations of reality are not entirely the fault of latter-day revisionism, however; aside from the (*albeit, unsourced*) direct statements by Ives himself, their wholesale dismissal is unwarranted, because more than a grain of truth can be found within them; indeed, a good deal of the perceived flaws in the 'Legend' actually *did* take place. To summarize:

- In 1987, Maynard Solomon, in an article now generally derided as one-sided (though tacitly upheld in scholarship) and inaccurate, accused Ives of falsifying the dates of his compositions in order to appear more prophetic than he really had been.[14] The bombshell article spawned the beginning of the alternative, new portrait of Ives, enabling 'reality' to be replaced with 'palatability,' diminishing a noble human being and musical visionary, whose contributions to American culture are immeasurable. Taking Carol K. Baron's lead in refuting the arguments Solomon had raised with a forensic dating system,[15] the author was readily able to validate Baron's work and add further weight to the fallacies of Solomon's hypothesis.[16]

---

[13] Magee, *Charles Ives Reconsidered*, 1.

[14] Maynard Solomon, "Charles Ives: Some Questions of Veracity," *Journal of the American Musicological Society*, 40, 3 (Fall 1987): 443–70. Solomon's article since has been used as the basis to relate Ives's entire catalog, and subsequently, and is at the core of modern Ives scholarship (see later), despite having been convincingly disproved (see below, n.15 & n.16).

[15] Carol K. Baron, "Dating Charles Ives's Music: Facts and Fictions," *Perspectives of New Music* (Winter issue, 1990): 20–56.

[16] Antony Cooke, *Charles Ives's Musical Universe* (West Conshohocken, PA: Infinity, 2015), 517–56.

- Gayle Sherwood (now Gayle Sherwood Magee) was an early entrant into the new Ives scholarship with articles (under her former name, Sherwood), and later, her 2008 book (*Charles Ives Reconsidered*, as Sherwood Magee)[17] that extended the cases she had originally made.[18] With another theory for Ives's illnesses,[19] Ives became a victim of a pseudo-psychological non-existent disease ('neurasthenia'), often fashionably applied in Ives's day to real ailments that could not be properly diagnosed. Magee's hypothesis was contrary to the facts of what really befell him, and to the facts that document what really befell him. It was not a heart attack, and probably at no other time was such an event ever a factor in his health.[20]

- As the standard explanation of the illness that negatively impacted and cut short his work, the fact that the documents to refute the 'heart attack story' always have been readily available renders all other modern theories about the nature of his primary illness suspect.[21] Moreover, what befell Ives in 1918 did not "end his career," although it would lead to lead to its ultimate cessation in the middle of the next decade.

Remarkably, *it was Ives himself* who was responsible for promulgating the 'heart attack' myth to dispel any notion he was doomed after the appalling prognosis at the time of his actual illness: diabetes. Even after the date (c. 1926) that Ives officially ceased composing, he still undertook some occasional composition projects, including the full scoring of *Washington's Birthday*, adapting *Putnam's Camp* for the chamber orchestra version, putting together the

---

[17] *Op. cit.*, n.5.

[18] *Op. cit.*, n.3.

[19] Gayle Sherwood Magee, "Charles Ives and 'Our National Malady,'" *Journal of the American Musicological Society,* 54, 3 (Fall, 2000): 555–84. Despite raising this summation of what had survived years of re-telling, Magee proposed an alternative, medically debunked, explanation to replace it, tying her 'diagnosis'—neurasthenia—to Ives's mythical and infamous cardiac issue with the term, 'cardio-neurasthenia' (*Charles Ives Reconsidered*, 84– 85). Magee already had undermined her case by revealing that the supposed ailment was an imaginary disease (74–84)!

[20] Stephen Budiansky, "Ives, Diabetes, and His 'Exhausted Vein' of Composition," *American Music*, 31, 1 (2013): 1–25.

[21] Among the more egregious of all accounts is the editorial comment in the *Descriptive Catalogue of the Music of Charles Ives* by James B. Sinclair (New Haven, CT: Yale University Press, 1999), 45, in which it is stated that his illness was "an emotional breakdown that took a serious toll on his heart." The timing of the publication of Sinclair's catalogue (1999) points to what might be the source of Magee's 'neurasthenia diagnosis' in her article, "Charles Ives, and 'Our National Malady'" (2000), and book, *Charles Ives Reconsidered* (2008).

8

second edition of the *Concord Sonata*, and updating the song, *He is There!*, to become *They are There!* as a patriotic call to arms in World War II.

- A continued effort has been made to deny Ives the musical background he received under his father, George Ives, whose influence and significance in Ives's early education has been re-portrayed as inconsequential—a mere small-town band musician. In *Charles Ives Reconsidered*, Magee used the less-than-flattering term, 'amateur,' for George no less than a dozen times in the first chapter, alone. Jan Swafford, however, put a better perspective on the lot of musicians through the ages, most of whom had made their "living on a little bit of this and that."[22] Thus, the role they played did not necessarily render them amateurs, with all its implications, by default. *Lack of opportunity* meant that George Ives, no less a thorough musician than countless others in his day, would struggle to make ends meet. Being a musician in nineteenth century America was precarious; in the wake of the Civil War, music was seen as a pastime in a time when rebuilding and advancing through industry and commerce was at society's focus. Few individuals would even contemplate music as a career. Although George Ives made a better run at it than most, he often needed to 'prop up' his earnings, which necessitated working sometimes as a part-time bookkeeper. His single-mindedness to remain first and foremost a musician, however, allowed him to retain his pride, until, tragically, he lost it to the disillusionment of later years when his musical opportunities all but evaporated.[23]

- It has been proposed that Transcendentalism was adopted by Ives only in mid-life, a position originally proposed by J. Peter Burkholder, perhaps first to question the long-standing acceptance of Ives's family background and philosophy.[24] Nicholas E. Tawa even proposed that perhaps Ives's Transcendentalism emanated from Parker, rather than Ives's family. Horatio Parker, in both of these texts, not only is made to be Ives's primary musical influence, but also to his core philosophies, and someone no less *radical* as a composer than Ives himself! Parker's influence, thus, was elevated far beyond his staid reluctance to engage Ives on a more personal level.[25]

---

[22] Swafford, *Charles Ives: A Life with Music* (New York: W.W. Norton, 1996), 38.

[23] Ibid., 70; see also, Feder, *"My Father's Song,"* 86.

[24] Burkholder, *The Ideas Behind the Music*, 22.

[25] Nicholas E. Tawa, "Ives and the New England School," in *Charles Ives and the Classical Tradition*, ed. Geoffrey Block & J. Peter Burkholder (New Haven, CT: Yale University Press, 1996), 54. See also Carol K. Baron, "Efforts on Behalf of Democracy by Charles Ives and his

- At Yale, Ives did not "outstrip" Parker.[26] No public rivalry between student and celebrated professor took place being during these years. Parker (despite being less of a slave to dogma than Ives projected), stifled student compositions that fell outside the norms of the day. Ives discovered Parker's low tolerance early on; the unconventional ending of his song, *At Parting*, written in his freshman year, provoked Parker's stern rebuke. Ives learned quickly not to show him anything that bent the 'rules.'[27]

- Ives's greater family had no intention of encouraging, even more, after George Ives died, supporting another 'starving artist.' Ives did not eschew a career as a composer because he considered his compositions were 'too far ahead of their time' to be accepted by his contemporaries or publishers. He did realize, however, even as a composer of relatively conventional, accessible, works—as exemplified by the cool reception accorded his self-funded premiere of *The Celestial Country*—that the lot of an aspiring professional composer in America was precarious; it would be his only serious attempt to launch such a career.

Ives shared many of the same musical ties with his predecessors. He heard the same music in churches, at community festivals, open air band performances, dances, and the ever-present popular songs of the day. It is harder, however, to overstate how greatly contrasting was the effect of them on Ives relative to his contemporaries, in which universally shared circumstances did not result in a shared response.[28] Ives was no more in step with other contemporaries than he was with other composers abroad. During the great American population expansion in the wake of the Civil War (more than doubling by 1900), it is hardly surprising that the predominant German immigrant influx brought their cultural heritage with them—already dominant throughout Europe, it would effectively colonize America's culture, too.

Despite the independent spirit of the American people, its composers remained in the shadows of the European masters, and typically spent time abroad to complete musical their education. The music of the best of these composers, by and large,

---

Family: Their Religious Contexts," *The Musical Quarterly*, 87, 1 (2004): 6–43. In this article, Baron clearly showed that Ives and his family indeed *were* steeped in a rich Unitarian-Congregationalist tradition. It is inconceivable that Ives was raised in isolation from what was second nature to his family.

[26] *Op. cit.*, n.5.

[27] Ives, *Memos*, 116.

[28] See, for example, Nicholas E. Tawa, "Ives and the New England School," in *Charles Ives and the Classical Tradition*, 61, 72

seems strangely awkward and derivative, lost in its search for an identity, yet, it is no less a part of the larger Western culture; American music shares the same roots. It should never have surprised musicologists that Ives's music retained thoroughly Western foundations, even as it discovered the uniquely American qualities and methodologies that allowed its unique voice finally to be heard. The search to define American musical culture can be found in an article by Douglas Shadle,[29] which details how even the New York Philharmonic had been a thoroughly Germanic organization at the time. It was run by people determined to maintain its cultural trans-Atlantic legacy. Such political considerations in music, thus, are behind Ives's resentment of the ready acceptance of German musical dominance in America, rather than the implication of racism. The onslaught of World War I further solidified Ives's fears that America might become a trans-Atlantic province.

Ives's early music often seems to emanate from the same cultural corners as that of his predecessors; despite their struggles to find an American voice in their efforts, they could only exert their independence from the status quo to a limited degree. It seems until Ives shattered it— from his perspective *looking out* to the American landscape from a provincial city—virtually all other American composers were *looking in* to cramped city quarters and the musical traditions as practiced in them. The chasm between what he and they did is so wide that, initially, it might seem to be a fluke, or, due to something more in line with the stance of American musicology—that Ives was the product of the same formal musical system (in this case, his teacher at Yale, Horatio Parker) as other composers—which was, in fact, as far from the reality as it could be. Relevant comparisons are hard to find, especially, across the Atlantic, as the later evolutions of similar twentieth century innovative techniques came about in the form of various 'schools' of methodology, each the primary foundation for entire compositions. As a free-spirited 'Connecticut Yankee,' Ives utilized whatever technique(s) he had devised for any given composition that expressed his meaning best, thus, making almost any comparison irrelevant. Ives's predictive innovations are demonstrable.[30]

Perhaps most galling of all the acts of redefining Charles Ives has been the incredulous skepticism that a 'mere' provincial domestic composer had 'upstaged' his European counterparts so precipitously that it was necessary to *redate* of his

---

[29] Douglas Shadle, "Louis Moreau Gottschalk's Pan-American Symphonic Ideal," *American Music* (Winter 2011): 443–71.

[30] Antony Cooke, *Charles Ives's Musical Universe* (Conshohocken, NJ: Infinity, 2015), 517–56.

compositions to fit a musicologically approved timeline.[31] The significance of this development, often accepted by some as irrelevant in relation to the quality of Ives's music, is the denial of the recognition he deserves *as the pre-eminent musical visionary of the twentieth century.*[32] The upshot of the new dates has resulted in the placing of Ives's works ever more *forward* in time, contradicting the composer's lists, and even more significantly, replacing the meticulously researched and detailed catalog of his life's works by John Kirkpatrick,[33] by *A Descriptive Catalogue of the Music of Charles Ives* by James B. Sinclair.[34] Sinclair boldly claimed that his catalog was one Kirkpatrick, himself, would have embraced as the last word on the subject![35] With the omission of much information from conversations with Ives that Kirkpatrick so diligently recorded, and substituting (not merely adding) other details far less relevant, did Sinclair deem them more important?

Admittedly, Sinclair's catalogue is a well-organized and presented reference source, with musical excerpts of virtually every work, additional commentary about premieres, publications, etc. However, Sinclair chose to omit many significant details from Kirkpatrick's catalogue, while adding revised dates for every work—though the

---

[31] John Kirkpatrick, *A Temporary Mimeographed Catalogue of the Music Manuscripts and Other Related Materials of Charles Edward Ives* (New Haven, CT: Yale University, 1960).

[32] Gayle Sherwood Magee, *Charles Ives Reconsidered* (Urbana, IL: University of Illinois Press, 2010). Also, Gayle Sherwood, "Questions and Veracities: Reassessing the Chronology of Ives's Choral Works," *The Musical Quarterly*, 78, 3 (Autumn 1994): 429–47. Even if one were to accept that the dates of some music manuscript paper can be ascertained accurately (most cannot), the width of the overlapping ranges is not close enough to help the objective researcher in any meaningful way. The evidence for the writer's conclusion can be ascertained by the very examples that Sherwood cited in her article, and which one can assume, were considered among the best upon which to build the case. The overlapping of critical dates in the timeline during Ives's most productive years is no less spurious than the un-named, uncorroborated sources upon which Sherwood based her positions.

[33] Kirkpatrick, *A Temporary Mimeographed Catalogue*. Kirkpatrick surely did not mean to imply that the *contents* were temporary, or in any way of a makeshift nature! They did, however, require better organization and presentation than his modest mimeographed documentation.

[34] James B. Sinclair, *A Descriptive Catalogue of The Music of Charles Ives*. With a copy of this document even having made its way onto a bookshelf in Ives's recreated studio at the American Academy of Arts and Letters in New York City, it seems almost a gesture of desecration of Ives's own temple—in the writer's view, hardly the 'finalization' of Kirkpatrick's catalogue—its somewhat unfortunately and naïvely worded title having invited precisely what happened: John Kirkpatrick, *A Temporary* [author's emphasis] *Mimeographed Catalogue of the Music Manuscripts and Other Related Materials of Charles Edward Ives* (New Haven, CT: Yale University, 1969).

[35] Sinclair, *A Descriptive Catalogue*, xvi.

12

many inconsistencies and contradictions among them stand as testament to the two-plus decades of revising Ives's life and work at the time (1999). That it reflects, too, the mutual efforts of those people most responsible for the redefinition of the composer renders its dedication to Kirkpatrick all the more sardonic. Its substitution does not compensate for the loss to scholarship of so much of the valuable detail that Kirkpatrick labored to include. For that, one has to know about and manage to obtain the rare original work by Kirkpatrick, effectively banished from all future prying eyes as if it never had existed.

With George Ives's role as his son's most important teacher also being redefined, even dismissed,[36] Magee's seniors, J. Peter Burkholder, and James B. Sinclair all have played various roles in the revised history,[37] following the trail already well laid and forever part of Maynard Solomon's own legacy. Solomon, however, soon would have an equally ambitious rival, Stuart Feder, a musically trained psychiatrist qualified in all the ways that Solomon was not. Although Feder rejected Solomon's charge that Ives was dishonest, he set out to build the same fundamental case that Ives was not a reliable source of information—except, the cause, instead, became psychiatric issues.[38] Extending that hypothesis into part of Solomon's—a near-psychotic dependence by Ives upon his father—Ives was portrayed so *mentally* compromised in his later years that he was incapable of the deliberate deception of the scale that Solomon proposed! Regardless, the intended premise of Solomon's primary case—that Ives's legacy and priority was not true—was tacitly *upheld*, and notably, its perpetration has been continued at the highest levels by the guardians of Ives's legacy. However, Feder upended his own and Solomon's case by bringing up Carol K. Baron's research, which easily demonstrated the fundamental argument that Ives had falsified the dates of his compositions—according to *any* proposed theory—was, in itself, utterly false.[39]

The projection that George's role in Ives's musical education had been exaggerated is entirely in character with the 'amended' Charles Ives. Burkholder, in outlining the rationale for his book over the course of two chapters, *The Ideas Behind the Music* (20–41), Ives emerges as shallow, even opportunistic. Ironically, in the

---

[36] For example, see Magee, *Charles Ives Reconsidered*, 5.

[37] Magee, *Charles Ives Reconsidered*, 4. See again, also, n.20 in relation to Ives's 1918 illness; long in available documentation, Ives illness (diabetes) is sidestepped.

[38] Feder, *'My Father's Song.'*

[39] Ibid., 351–57; see too, Cooke, *Charles Ives Musical Universe*, 516–67, in which Baron's system was explored further in detail across the spectrum of his compositional output, and validated without reservation.

face of what has turned out to be a thirty-year span of revising Ives's life, Burkholder seemed unintentionally prophetic, too, having remarked two years before Solomon's sensational article that Lawrence Gilman's "indiscriminate attribution" of Ives's esthetics to those discussed in his famous writing, *Essays Before a Sonata*, "deprives Ives of his history."[40] Burkholder's later volume, *All Made of Tunes: Charles Ives and the Uses of Musical Borrowing*, attempted to break new ground, but instead, misappropriated the purpose of quotations by failing to differentiate between the few (usually early) works that *were* built around quoted melodies (and even then, sometimes just melodic fragments), versus the vast majority of more mature examples in which the quotes exist as isolated glimpses of memory, existing entirely outside the larger independent musical structure.[41]

It is hard to argue that Solomon's and Feder's work did not amount to a two-pronged assault on the legacy of John Kirkpatrick, too—at least as much as that of Ives. Kirkpatrick, having no formal, traditional grounding in musicology, had become a target, and would become at the focus of a movement, led by H. Wiley Hitchcock, then the 'dean of American musicology,' to supersede his role atop Ives scholarship. Kirkpatrick's unconventional approach and forceful style were considered untenable, despite his unique insights into Ives and his music, and his supreme achievement in musicology: the legendary catalogue. That Ives's true legacy was offered up on the altar of 'proper' musicological protocol seems not to have mattered.[42] Both Feder and Solomon were at the right place, at the right time. Although musicology had denied Solomon's original assault upon Ives's legacy, now, with the new dates assigned Ives's catalogue, what he had proposed was *tacitly validated*, the desired objective, after all—to remove Kirkpatrick and his influence in Ives scholarship—achieved.

Just before the publication of Solomon's article, J. Peter Burkholder, in *Charles Ives: The Ideas Behind the Music*, attempted to bring clarity to Rossiter's unexpected conclusions, appearing genuinely surprised to 'discover' that s Ives' music had roots in Western culture and traditions, even that he, an Ives scholar, found it was perplexing to know how to listen to, or appreciate, his music.[43] What could

---

[40] Burkholder, *The Ideas Behind the Music*, 5.

[41] J. Peter Burkholder, *All Made of Tunes: Charles Ives and the Uses of Musical Borrowing* (New Haven, CT: Yale University Press, 2004).

[42] Drew Michael Massey, "An Unobtrusive Minister of Genius: John Kirkpatrick and the Editing of Contemporary American Music," Ph.D. diss., Harvard University, 2010: 211–14.

[43] J. Peter Burkholder, *Charles Ives: The Ideas Behind the Music* (New Haven, CT: Yale University Press, 1985), ix.

Burkholder possibly have meant if he still wished to be taken seriously in his evaluations of Ives and his music? These words seem to be oddly disqualifying. Although it is regrettable that Ives did not have more opportunities to be able to offer more insights into his music, it is no less so that he lived before technology might have provided useful 'mock-ups' and other ready solutions for some of the more intangible sonic challenges. Meanwhile, Ives's music is unlikely to sound precisely as he had in mind without performers taking the necessary extra trouble to understand his intentions. However, such individuals are hardly run-of-the-mill. Regardless, not to be able to go about preparing a work by Ives, say, as one would a Beethoven symphony—on top of any financial restraints (the same restrictions Ives, himself, addressed)—are, of course, a part of the problem, too. Ives's music is sufficiently challenging to require more rehearsal time than most organizations can afford.[44]

Because Ives's tacit detractors have questioned his skills as a composer and the accuracy of his notation, it should be emphasized that Ives was a thoroughly grounded and schooled musician, who did not jot things down onto the page with no idea about their effect; his early symphonic compositions speak clearly to his expertise. More aware of the sound of his music than anyone, it is true that the lack of performances seldom allowed him the luxury of adjusting his scores; even the great (and ultimate orchestrator), Gustav Mahler, constantly readjusted his scores after each rehearsal or performance. And surely, *would not* Ives's copyists, who took pride in their precision and care to copy precisely, always checking questionable notation with the composer, be taken aback to read of the low regard such comments imply?[45] Most concerning in Ives's more complex excursions, however, is practicability and balance. It is instructive to realize that after he heard the *Scherzo* movement of his Fourth Symphony (in a rare reading of his more complex music), Ives wrote extensive notes for future conductors, based on his reservations about balance, though *he did not change any notation.*[46]

---

[44] The celebrated conductor-composer José Serebrier shared with me an interesting anecdote about the first performance of Ives's Fourth Symphony in 1965 under Leopold Stokowski, in which he had been the second conductor. It took six months of arduous rehearsals to put a coherent performance together with some of the best instrumentalists in New York. Subsequently, different orchestras suddenly needed less rehearsal time, which continued to decrease. Somehow the difficulties dissolved over time through some unknown process.

[45] *Op. cit.*, n.37. See too, Vivian Perlis, *Charles Ives Remembered: An Oral History* (Urbana, IL: University of Illinois Press, 1974), 188. An instruction Ives wrote to his copyist, George Price on the score of *The Fourth of July*. "Mr. Price, Please don't try to make things nice. All the wrong notes are *right*. Just copy as I have. I want it that way." Ives was extremely particular in matters of notation.

[46] Charles E. Ives, "A Conductor's Note," *New Music* (January 1929).

Contrary to the common perception that he had worked 'in a vacuum,' Ives actually was able to physically hear much of his music. As a prodigiously gifted pianist and organist, there was hardly composition conceived away from the keyboard. Adding his own singing while he played, he was clearly less limited than might be supposed. It should surprise no one that many of Ives's compositions began, or also ended up, in song form. Offering unique insights into his compositional process, they are infinitely more instructive than any words about them he was willing to share. However, he did physically hear quite a lot of his music. Aside from the benefits gained from his many well-known musical experiments during his college days with groups of friends (who thought they were participating in 'stunts' purely for fun). [47]

Ives's years as a church musician also likely offered him the opportunity to hear some of his more adventurous choral works in informal rehearsals, at least, if not necessarily during services. Later, Ives was known, too, to invite small groups of musicians for private readings of some of his music that, again, enabled him to hear the practicality of his ideas firsthand. Many of the small works he wrote for that purpose ended up as collections: sets for theater or chamber orchestra, and assorted small ensembles. Although performances of his larger works took place long after their composition, and came too late to influence their design, Ives's various combined practical experiences, therefore, should not be overlooked, and surely were highly instructive to him.

Regardless of the manner in which it has arisen, a 'correct,' even 'sanitized' Ives has emerged, more in line with the comfort zone of present-day American musicology. Emerging as just another twentieth century composer during the great transition out of the Romantic age, he is not in any particular way distinguishable from his European counterparts. The reality is quite different, however. One who expressed something wholly unique, and who ventured into hitherto uncharted waters well before his contemporaries ever considered setting sail, Ives single-handedly became the 'Great American Composer' of whom his predecessors had dreamed. In spite of the discomfort American musicology has in recognizing that, not only did it happen, but also that it *only* could have taken place in the unique environment in which Ives was raised and educated. To ignore the reality implies a willingness to do so, the search for insights and truth happily replaced by an agenda to redefine it in ways that better fits the accepted mold, and ignoring the substance of all he achieved.

---

[47] Ives, *Memos*, 39–41.

16

The dawn of a dubious age

If American musicology needed to redefine Ives and his music, why does it matter to us? We can still hear it as written. It matters because any such whitewashed view of Ives and his work diminishes him, and even more, eradicates any chance to understand the real components of his musical makeup. Ives cannot be fully appreciated when taken out of his place and time.

Most directly responsible for what led to a new stance on Ives took place in 1969. Composer Elliott Carter recalled to Vivian Perlis that he had witnessed Ives "jacking up" the dissonance while re-scoring *Putnam's Camp* for chamber orchestra in 1929.[48] This entirely erroneous assessment, coming from one who, if disturbed by what he saw, ought to have sought clarification from the composer who was there next to him before sounding the alarm on something he neither understood, nor cared to look into. Had he examined the 'before' and 'after' scores, he would have realized his error. Regardless, the 'sound bite' that he recited to Perlis effectively began the revolution in Ives scholarship, and a jaded view of Ives. Although Ives had mentored Carter—the son of one of Ives's clients—Carter cheerfully betrayed his old friend. If there is any excuse for Carter's actions, are they, perhaps, better understood in the context of his lifelong discomfort in accepting Ives as 'The Great American Composer,' he (Carter), who had done everything the 'right' way, even completed his studies in Europe according to the prescribed manner, still was struggling for *his* full measure of 'earned' recognition? Unfortunately, Carter's attitude of entitlement—even superiority—was now the epitome of the 'establishment'; Ives and other 'outsiders' could not be admitted to their pantheon of 'legitimate' composers. Carter's shortsighted competitiveness were at odds with the person whom, at one time, had looked up to Ives.

Carter's behavior fitted a pattern; in the aftermath of his scathing 1939 review of the *Concord Sonata*,[49] aware of the discomfort he had caused, never again could bring himself to visit Ives. Following up with efforts in print, and later, with compositions dedicated to Ives, he could not hide his resentment, and continued to find reasons to criticize Ives almost to the end. Jan Swafford summed up their awkward relationship succinctly: "Carter . . . would pay back his mentor with a

---

[48] Vivian Perlis, *Charles Ives Remembered* (Urbana, IL: University of Illinois Press, 1974), 138. See, too, Antony Cooke, *Charles Ives and his Road to the Stars*, second edition (W. Conshohocken, PA: Infinity, 2015), 235, for a detailed breakdown of what, actually, had taken place.

[49] Elliott Carter, "The Case of Mr. Ives," *Modern Music* (March-April, 1939): 172–76.

17

baffling mixture of admiration, advocacy, and cold repudiation."[50] Regrettably, the damage done by Carter was amplified by the publication of the first major attempt to "make sense" of the Ives phenomenon: Frank R. Rossiter's 1975 book, *Charles Ives & His America*, and its less-than-rapturous appraisal of the composer.[51]

George Ives's Enduring Role

George Ives was an independent soul, defying the near-certain negative odds of daring to go it alone and chasing a musical career. In his day, immediately following the Civil War, the chase was difficult enough anywhere in America; it was near impossible in a provincial town. His unconventional career choice also reflected his unconventional attitude toward music. According to his son, George's interest in acoustic phenomena extended to experiments with various contraptions, even glasses and pianos tuned in microtones.[52] Reportedly, George tried to analyze the tuning of church bells (their complex overtones much better understood today),[53] and tested the echoing sound of his cornet as it wafted over bodies of water. His own 'legend' and infinite curiosity, however, was most famously demonstrated by the much-referenced fascination with the polytonal dissonance of deliberately leading his band into sonic conflict with another on Main Street.[54]

Ives's good fortune of having daily contact with a musically forward-looking father was not reflected in the lowly social status in which George was held in his home town. In Danbury, a 'mere' musician—not being a member of the business-oriented 'professional class'—ensured that he would never be considered a pillar of the 'elite.' The image has reinforced negative stereotypes that imply his skills ought not to be taken seriously, either.[55] As a consequence, Charles's background prior to attending Yale has been treated as inconsequential, lightweight, even spurious, when, in fact, there is considerably more to it—and to George—than has been recognized

---

[50] Swafford, *A Life with Music*, 334.

[51] Rossiter, *Charles Ives & His America*.

[52] Nicolas Slonimsky, *Music of the Modern Era*, 3 (New York: Routledge, 2005), 168.

[53] Ives, *Memos*, 44–45.

[54] Vivian Perlis, *Charles Ives Remembered* (Urbana, IL: University of Illinois Press, 1974), 16.

[55] For example: Magee, *Charles Ives Reconsidered*, 10; 17–22; 184 n.13.

in scholarship, and that warrants re-examination.

George's struggles have been a conveniently used, however, to subtly diminish Charles Ives's early musical training. The case has been made that, as a prodigy organist, whatever knowledge of the classics gained during his Danbury years was mostly as a result exposure to organ literature, rather than to his father. George, tagged for "hard work" over accomplishment, was effectively marginalized to clear the way to rewrite his role in Charles Ives's musical development.[56]

George's lot, however, at one time, looked promising. For a brief time, he enjoyed a period of relative success as a

St. Peter's Catholic Church, Main Street, Danbury, which became the sponsor of George Ives's band.

local musician, finding many ways to secure employment. Feder, in attempting to clarify George Ives's musical career, remarked that at the beginning of the decade (1880s), for a time, his situation almost equaled that of many other professionals, "*anywhere*."[57] Although he would always struggle financially,[58] George was far from the 'amateur' of revisionist projection.[59] Aside from being in constant demand as a performer and bandleader, he had attracted a substantial class of private students. [60] As such, George had been the piano teacher of many of the town's children

---

[56] Magee, *Charles Ives Reconsidered*, 10.

[57] Feder, "*My Father's Song*," 86.

[58] Ibid., 77, 78, 85.

[59] Magee, *Charles Ives Reconsidered*, 11–27.

[60] Swafford, *A Life with Music*, 36

(illustrating that some of Ives's training on the keyboard must have come directly from his father), as well as teacher of the violin, cornet, and music theory.[61]

By 1879, George's directing jobs also included the St. Peter's Catholic Church Band, the Bethel Cornet Band and, the Bethel Citizen's Band, the Ives Band and Orchestra (his own), the Norwalk Band, the Danbury Cornet Band, and the Danbury High School Band.[62] It is clear, too, that the young Charles Ives had no shortage of exposure through to large quantities of music through George from the start, together with his expertise and musical philosophy. He also was well accustomed to disparate ethnic groups comprising these organizations, including many of the immigrant populations that had swelled Danbury's industrial workplaces. The inclusive values instilled in him from George's own father, George White Ives—one of the most influential leaders in the history of the Danbury community—made it entirely natural to see all peoples as one. Consequently, we can be sure that George handed down these values, too, to his sons, Charles and Moss. Beloved as the greater family was throughout Danbury's population, the seeds of intrigue were sown early on for them, as Swafford noted.[63] Such intrigue is typical when large, long established and prominent families have taken on identities that seem as large as the towns in which they live; another word to describe the phenomenon is 'gossip'; generally speaking, it is the harmless whispering behind closed doors, and not meant to cause harm. It is unfortunate that these very seeds of gossip in Danbury have germinated in modern Ives scholarship to paint George as little more than an eccentric failure—the 'town crank.'

Swafford, however, already had described George's standing in Danbury—far better than generally acknowledged in recent scholarship—his time and place in history in nineteenth century post-Civil War rural and semi-rural America not being easy.[64] The priorities of Danbury's citizens were more aligned with the emerging boom of the American miracle years than recreational activities, for which few had the luxury of time. Although the townspeople might have enjoyed, even admired,

---

[61] Swafford, *Charles Ives: A Life with Music*, 35.

[62] Feder, *"My Father's Song,"* 78. On this page, Feder quoted a passage from the *Danbury Evening News* in 1879 that surely contributed to the tales of delight George had famously derived from the effect of clashing independent bands on Main Street, also recalling a similar, if less spectacular, event in 1873, when the sounds of the marching Newtown Cornet Band conflicted with Ives's own Cornet Band. Indeed, on the next page, Feder perceptively deduced that the spatial aspects of Charles Ives's music were directly related to it.

[63] Swafford, *A Life With Music*, 15.

[64] Ibid., 14.

what George did, music, nevertheless, was seen more as a hobby rather than a profession—a common stigma that many professional musicians in America experience even to this day, and not just in provincial towns, either.

Elmwood Park, in Danbury, CT:
site of many of George Ives's band concerts

Stuart Feder summed up the lot of the relative few in America whom had tried to forge a living from music. Most, finding little success or solace, would need to supplement their earnings in any other way they could.[65] If George's opportunities were not on a par with those he might have enjoyed in a major city, and where he would have been woefully out of place, it was not likely due to shortage of ability. Nevertheless, Swafford, summed up George's professional lot, explaining how his career choice had created boundaries to his options in life.[66]

George, as something of an entrepreneur; had maximized all his possible prospects, taking advantage of every conceivable opportunity available in the area. It makes an impressive resumé, although it is revealing that most of his jobs were more

---

[65] Feder, *"My Father's Song,"* 25.

[66] Swafford, *A Life with Music*, 66.

entertainment-oriented than genuinely artistic. Swafford listed many of the venues for which he had provided the music in various ways, including parades, open air concerts, bandstand, opera house productions, social events, weddings, religious settings, camp meetings, camp-outs, grand openings, dances (as reflected by Ives years later in *Washington's Birthday*), festivals and variety shows, even horse races and ball games.[67]

Eventually, however, changing times left what George had to offer behind, and as his opportunities dwindled, he found himself taking part-time work as a bookkeeper, which was a major source of humiliation for him. Thus, he would join the ranks of most other musicians in nineteenth century America, and share in their disillusionment, resentment, and frustration. Poor, disrespected, and depressed was the usual sorry condition most experienced from trying to exist solely by the fruits of their musical labor.[68] Not everyone was oblivious to George's value to the community, however; many townspeople *did* appreciate what he did, even if they struggled to regard music making as a 'profession.' An article of appreciation appearing in the New York periodical, *Herald*, of January 5, 1890, stated that George had "probably done more for instrumental music than any other man' in the most musical town in Connecticut."[69]

Horatio Parker

As the new school of thinking has tried to build a case that Horatio Parker was primarily responsible for Ives's musical outlook and basic training, rather than his father, George Ives—a mere 'amateur' bandsman, who had provided Ives only limited musical and technical skills[70]—there is mutual agreement that Parker offered the young composer the best of his European schooling. However, it cannot be claimed that Parker's teaching was the major source of Ives's skills. Jan Swafford, however, saw the reality: Ives's musical education might have been 'completed' under Parker, but was not initiated by it.[71]

George Ives's teaching is often dismissed as lacking in thoroughness. There can be no doubt that he approached it with an infinitely more relaxed attitude than Yale's

---

[67] Swafford, *A Life with Music*, 36.

[68] Feder, *"My Father's Song,"* 67.

[69] Swafford, *A Life with Music*, 37.

[70] Magee, *Charles Ives Reconsidered*, 16.

[71] Swafford, *A Life With Music*, 65.

stern taskmaster, Horatio Parker, who, in turn inherited it from his own mentor in Munich, Josef Rheinberger.[72] That Ives's training under his father was of limited consequence has not met with universal agreement, because George certainly was more than up to the task. Carol K. Baron argued that his own notebooks showed, not only a sound and thorough musical grounding, but also, that it was at "*an advanced level*" [author's emphasis].[73] If George lacked the background to teach the young Ives to compose large musical forms—such as symphonies, sonatas and string quartets, even advanced orchestration—that part of his training *does* point to Parker's contribution,[74] the demonstrable lack of such works among Ives's surviving early efforts speaking to it.

Regardless, how can it be argued that Charles had *not* been exposed to many of the great masterworks during the years of his Danbury upbringing, when especially, in his capacity as a church organist, he would have played transcriptions of large quantities of the standard symphonic and other literature? Such music was part of an organist's staple, and Ives, one of the brightest young stars in the region (a truism that has not been challenged), would have been well versed in all aspects of European music long before 1894. What proportion of Ives's compositional sophistication really *was* due to Parker, rather than merely the exposure to music new to him each passing year? If Parker's influence was substantial, specifically, can it be demonstrated? A superficial examination of Parker's works from the 1890s, and before, reveals a predominantly choral and vocal composer. Could Parker alone have endowed Ives with the accomplished orchestration featured in his First Symphony? And bearing in mind that Parker was primarily an organist, rather than a pianist, where did Ives's extraordinary flair for virtuosic piano writing come from? Is there anything comparable among Parker's compositions?

In light of the confusion generated by conflicting appraisals of Parker's role in Ives's musical education—no less than by Ives himself—what he gained from Parker no doubt was significant. Ives's admiration of many aspects of his musicianship and teaching is evident, although he considered Parker to have been limited by his strict adherence to "The German rule."[75] Ives's comment carries more implications than might be obvious, although it is probably a fair assessment, the more radical

---

[72] J. Peter Burkholder, "Ives and Yale: The Enduring Influence of a College Experience," *College Music Symposium* 39 (1999), 27–42: 38.

[73] Carol K. Baron, "George Ives's Essay on Music Theory: An Introduction and Annotated Edition," *American Music* (Fall, 1992): 278, n.16.

[74] *Op. cit.*, n.66.

[75] Ives, *Memos*, 100.

tendencies even that Parker demonstrated during his youth largely constrained even in his most 'modern' compositions. He had the "pedantic" Rheinberger to thank for that (so described by *Parker's* former teacher and earlier Rheinberger protégé, George Whitefield Chadwick), whose uninspired, formulaic approach to composition has long left his own works largely redundant.[76] Here was the personification of "The German rule," to be handed down through successive generations, stultifying and creatively formulaic, and ensuring that no American ever would have an original spirit.

With German musical culture no less dominant in America than in Europe, the large influx of immigrants treasuring their tradition and legacy had stood, almost exclusively, atop a musical evolution dating back to the time of J.S. Bach. It was when American composers were desperately trying to formulate music to reflect their own culture, their position having been, essentially, one that had been little more than a derivative colonization of the original. As Ives became the breakaway figure, still admiring the music from across the Atlantic—which can be appreciated by his ease in quoting fragments of it, and maintaining the larger musical precepts of German composers—he wrote *American* music that directly reflected his environment, and separated the New World from the Old.

Not everyone who had studied with Parker was uncomfortable with his approach. They would not, however, become the trailblazers of a uniquely American music. Ives was cut from an entirely different cloth, his music ultimately rejecting the concept of having one's instincts overridden by restrictive 'rules,' while not rejecting their guiding principles. Although Parker, himself, also bent the 'rules' on occasion in his own compositions, little of even his, or that of his other disciples' most avant-garde work could be considered progressive or particularly unusual to modern ears. A casual examination of *Mona*, one of Parker's most ambitious projects, and known for its diffuse, chromatic harmonies and unlikely angularity of melodic line, reveals, nevertheless, a lingering strong conformity to late Romantic models, with its arpeggiated accompaniments, metric outlines, overall adherence to conventional chords, phrase structures and musical proportions, horizontally and vertically. These attributes ensured that Parker's music never stepped far from the boundaries of the old European order. Neither did the contributions of his contemporaries and students. Tawa considered that many American composers forgot about their own audience as they strove, first and foremost, to join the

---

[76] Bill F. Faucett, *The Life and Music of the Pride of New England* (Boston, MA: Northeastern University Press, 2012), 68.

international clique of composers.[77] Ives wrote very much for an audience that did not yet exist.

The Ives problem

Still perplexing to many scholars has been the phenomenon of progressively original music coming from 'out of the blue.' To these researchers, it is inconceivable that a young man growing up in a provincial American town, far from daily exposure to the sophistication of big city culture and its educational opportunities, could possibly have devised so many new musical techniques—which, only later, would be claimed, unwittingly, by others as their innovations. The writer, however, sees it differently—not as an unlikely isolated phenomenon, but rather, one that was *inevitable*. American culture, linked to the European culture from which it had arisen, nevertheless, had evolved to take on many unique trans-Atlantic attributes that, by default, could no longer wholly reflect its ancestor. Music in America, effectively, was yet to emerge from the wilderness of its own surroundings. Ives's purpose, rather to than supplant the predominant musical culture, was to define his own by any means at his disposal. The connection of Ives's music to the larger Western culture still seems to surprise many musicologists. It should not. All art is the product of its roots and the unique circumstances of its creator. Should it be surprising that Ives's music would be tied to it, too? Who would argue that Ives's thoroughly Western roots make his music less American, revolutionary or unusual? Ives's innovations preceded those of his European counterparts. Technically, the ways in which he did so, again, set him apart; as a means to an expressive end, they did not feature any particular philosophical approach to musical composition. Ives's straddled interesting times they maintained elements of the *Romantic* tradition, yet pushed music far into the emerging age from virtually every standpoint, his ability to cross through multiple pathways the reason why his music sounds so different to music from across the Atlantic.

Facts, not Fiction

If there is an upside to the many alternative theories and explanations that have arisen in Ives scholarship, it is that multiple positions on the same issues have revealed the contradictions between them that struggle to maintain credibility under a little careful scrutiny. Consequently, the real Ives begins to emerge. It is also true—and fortunate for us—that more realistic portrayals of Ives, his life and music also have come into

---

[77] Nicholas E. Tawa, *Serenading the Reluctant Eagle: American Musical Life, 1925–1945* (New York: Schirmer, 1985).

being during this period; prominent among their protagonists, Carol K. Baron, Kyle Gann, Philip Lambert, Jan Swafford, and Wayne B. Shirley waved red flags early in the emerging musicological dilemma.[78] However, their research—known and respected in scholarship—has suffered the fate of being largely 'swept under the rug'—like unwelcome news.

It remains imperative in the present climate of revised histories, therefore, to uncover as much as possible about all relevant parts of Ives's musical makeup, and what was behind them, before it is too late to affect a change of direction. Parts of it are slowly disappearing, too, including the private sale and remodeling of Ives's West Redding home (rather than allowing it to become a protected landmark), not to mention the unexplained 'disappearance' of immensely important items of record that Carol Baron uncovered in his study, which, otherwise, would have done much to expose some of the incorrect assertions with which modern musicology has mischaracterized Ives.[79] American scholarship has spent some of its best energies in accommodating a unique story into a preconceived narrative, rather than seeking a true understanding of Ives's work. The problem is amplified, of course, by the partly ambiguous record (no contemporary resident historian in the youthful Ives's hometown would have seen the need to record much in relation to someone's 'pastime'), the lack of greater recorded detail only contributing to the cultivated climate of distrust of the composer.

Another dilemma for American Ives scholarship—aside from its discomfort with John Kirkpatrick's position at the top of it—might have been Ives's political leanings and views. True to the values of his upbringing, Ives's caring about the plight of the working laborer might have been seen as just as extreme as his music.[80] Could it be that not all parties could comfortably accept them in a figure chosen to represent

---

[78] Carol K. Baron, *op. cit.*, n.14.

[i] Also, Kyle Gann, "Poisoned Musicology": *PostClassic*, *Kyle Gann on music after the fact*, 24 March 2014, https://www.artsjournal.com/postclassic/2014/03/poisoned-musicology-2.html. [ii] Also, Philip Lambert, *The Music of Charles Ives* (New Haven, CT: Yale University Press, 1997); [iii] Also, Jan Swafford, *Charles Ives: A Life with Music* (New York: W.W. Norton & Co. 1996); [iv] Also, Wayne B. Shirley, "The Second of July," in *A Celebration of American Music: Words and Music in honor of H. Wiley Hitchcock*, ed. Richard Crawford, R. Allen Lott, Carol J. Oja (University of Michigan Press, Ann Arbor, MI, 1990).

[79] Carol K. Baron: New Sources for Ives Studies: An Annotated Catalogue. https://www.stonybrook.edu/commcms/music/people/faculty-and-staff/affiliated_scholars/carol_baron. A source I am not at liberty to name, when the discovery of these materials was revealed to him, is said to have exclaimed, "I should have burned them years ago!"

[80] See again Baron, "Efforts on Behalf of Democracy," 2004.

the 'Great American Composer'? Is it also possible to ascribe *too* much attention to George Ives and Horatio Parker, the two primary figures in Ives's musical education, when it is clear they represent only part of the picture? Ives's unmistakable musical identity is a composite blend of many parts. As such, a new examination and appraisal of all that is reasonably known, or potentially knowable, is long overdue. An affirmative assessment of Ives's profile—instead of the decades-long deflation— would go a long way to restore the sense of wonder many of us felt in 'discovering' Ives in the spring-times of our years, and would go a long way to undo the damage done in the process. Moreover, though, the listening public could use more scholarly insights into Ives's music itself, beyond merely pointing out quoted fragments of tunes that enlighten few people about the music itself, or even reasons for the quotes themselves.

Chapter 2

Auspiciously Humble Beginnings

"He had no patrons to please or publishers to satisfy, and his music reflects all the idiosyncrasies and paradoxes of a composer who answers only to his own whims and agendas."

Philip Lambert, *The Music of Charles Ives*
(New Haven, CT: Yale University Press, 1997)

*C*harles Ives was a product of America's coming of age—a time of the great awakening of its potential—following the 'trial by fire' of a deadly, brutal, and bloody civil war, and the end of the age of innocence. Although the upheaval to the existing social order would take decades to settle down, the 'can-do' spirit of the nation already had emerged. Danbury, Connecticut—the provincial town in which Ives was raised, would soon typify the country's evolution from an agrarian nation to an industrial and international superpower. This pivotal period in the transformation of American life provided a vast resource of societal interactions and impressions; Ives recalled them in his music, while advancing most of the twentieth century's new methodologies well ahead of his European counterparts—in addition to leaving a musical time capsule that allows us to relive these times, when a newly vibrant American culture became all-defining.

Ives's parents, George and Mollie, even in Danbury, were hardly typical residents, especially relative to the prominent members of his extended family. George was the odd-man-out; the local bandmaster and music teacher, his heart had not led him to one of the 'respectable' professions. Remarkably little is known about Ives's mother, Mollie, who seems to have been a near invalid during all of Ives's years in Danbury; members of the family were virtually silent about her. George's hard work and enterprising spirit, however, ensured that the family was provided for and that his musically prodigious son would inherit his knowledge. Under George Ives's care, Charles was schooled in theory, harmony and counterpoint, and, it seems, initially in keyboard skills as well; when Charles outgrew any part of George's own expertise, only the best music teachers in the area were considered good enough.

George also introduced his son to good music as much as possible, even taking him into New York City to hear symphonic concerts at Carnegie Hall.[81] Charles, in turn, would be recognized early as a prodigy in Connecticut, making a name for himself on the organ; by his early teens, he held regular church positions in Danbury. In this environment, he was introduced to additional repertoire of musical literature; organists in Ives's day were expected to play transcriptions of many types of composition, even symphonic works. By the time he was ready for college, it is hard to make the case that Ives was not already an accomplished and broadly educated musician.

Danbury: Idyllic town of Ives's upbringing?

By the late nineteenth century, Danbury had established itself as the center of the American hatmaking industry, and, as such, largely being transformed into an industrial rather than a sleepy provincial town. Well outside any nineteenth century metropolitan area, it was an unlikely location from which a great composer would emerge. Danbury society, typical of such communities at the time—barely aware of the finer arts—offered relatively few opportunities for a musically gifted youngster. Instead, it would provide another kind of foundation—a vast, authentic resource of Americana that inspired the creative and revolutionary explosion in Charles Ives's

---

[81] In his years after college, it was here that Charles would attend concerts of the New York Philharmonic conducted by Gustav Mahler, its director from 1909–11. It is a remarkable historical connection to contemplate.

music, the new technical resources he pioneered expressing many colorful images of life in America during the late nineteenth century, its festivals and pageantry.

In hindsight, however, it is clear that life for many other residents in Danbury was not quite so idyllic as it seemed to the young Ives. Consisting of two fundamentally separate populations: the longstanding members of families who had lived and worked there for generations, and a 'shadow' population of recent émigrés to the United States, who filled the growing employment opportunities in Danbury's hatmaking industry.[82] The latter had little in common, culture, language—although, due to the philanthropic lead by Ives's grandfather, George White Ives, they were, nevertheless, welcomed into the social 'mix' with the 'locals,' and able to participate in virtually every part of Danbury life and culture. Regardless, it is difficult to know if the locals saw them more as part of a temporary working population or long-term fixtures.[83]

As an adult, Ives gradually would become aware of an incongruity forged by the very industry that nurtured his town; it had sheltered him from adversity, but not the hatting industry workers. Because few industries operated under proper regulations or fair labor practices, building an equitable balance between the 'few' (the factory owners), and the 'many' (the factory workers), was hardly realistic; they were treated as if they should feel fortunate just to have employment. Thus, what became Ives's political and social outlook reflected his keen sensitivity to the struggles of the 'masses,' no less than his charitable philanthropy was the inspiration behind many of his mature compositions and writings. They were also the product of a unique blend of the religious and Transcendental values that the generations of his greater family had instilled in him from birth.

In 1996, In his book, *Charles Ives: A Life With Music*, Jan Swafford captured the essence of Ives's time and place better than can be found in any other source—it is a picture that leaps to life off the pages.[84] Along with many insights into Ives's early musical training, Swafford left no stone unturned, even providing some tantalizing leads to the darker side of Danbury's post-Civil War boom. Relating the serious ill effects that the hatters experienced from exposure to the mercury, Swafford

---

[82] Hatmaking was a terrible way to make a living; a poisoned workplace (from the mercury used in the pelting process) ruined the health of its workers and polluted the entire region. It is hardly surprising that new immigrant labor, struggling to find employment, would fill these places. If the 'locals' were not aware of the actual downsides of working in hatmaking, they knew, nevertheless, to avoid it.

[83] Swafford, *A Life With Music*, 10.

[84] Ibid., 9–15.

exposed the town's Achilles heel. Even young workers in their twenties experienced the infamous 'hatters shakes,' together with the accompanying incoherence, drooling, and sometimes insanity, too. Often confused with drunkenness, typically, both mercury *and* alcohol were responsible. The factory workers drank to relieve their plight and many health problems, and eventually Danbury would become known for its many taverns—and drunks. Although this depiction does not coincide with Ives's rosy memories, his comments in the program notes to *The Fourth of July* seem to hint at it: "more drunks the usual" suddenly makes obvious what Ives witnessed almost daily, even if he was still not yet aware of what the reality meant.

Remnant of Danbury's 'glory' days

The last surviving factory building from the hat making industry
P. Robinson Fur Cutting Company, Old Mill Road, Danbury, CT
Image courtesy of "Carinlisa"

It seems surprising and inexplicable, in hindsight, that Ives, or members of Danbury's long-established professional population, could remain unaware of the cause of the terrible toll, even the specific symptoms exacted on the hatting workers from the conditions in which they worked. There is virtually no mention of it by Ives, or in any recorded document prior to the turn of the twentieth century. Ives, in fact, never referred to the city's curse at all. Perhaps too young at the time to comprehend these profound social issues, a more realistic appraisal of the anomaly, however, might be that the long established families were unable to acknowledge what they

32

knew deep down in their beloved Danbury. Ives spent the second part of his life working tirelessly toward the common good, extending a helping hand to countless people and causes—notably, in total anonymity.[85]

Over the years, the 'Danbury Shakes,' however, would become synonymous with the town, just as the same disastrous consequences had resulted earlier in felt manufacturing in other hatmaking centers in Europe.[86] Nevertheless, the spirit of the times seems to have been the hallmark of post-Civil War boomtown Danbury. The colorful, tradition-rooted culture had defined generations and fueled the optimism of its descendants, rather than the ugly downside to its thriving industry. Charles Ives lived that spirit and caught it in his music. However, the day would come when the consequences of unregulated manufacturing in a booming age was unavoidable; influencing Ives, he chose to live his life in a manner that placed capitalistic venture alongside philanthropic compassion; his words and music came to express solidarity with the oppressed masses. Ives's years in Danbury bequeathed him a remarkable blend of attributes, his thoroughly New England individuality and musical identity abundant at every turn; his perspectives about America and all that it meant to him evident in his work were fueled by the wave of energy sweeping the nation. Sadly, with the real Charles Ives increasingly lost in the smoke and mirrors of revisionist scholarship, he is scarcely recognizable. Although there are many facets of Ives's background that lack formal records, many shreds of information and clues remain yet to be integrated and collated. Putting together the many pieces in the jigsaw puzzle into one place allows a more accurate assessment of what transpired.

Ives's direct musical influences extend, unsurprisingly, not only to the established European masters, but also to music not usually considered suitable for inclusion in concert music: the vernacular music of the people. There were many forms that such music took: hymns and religious songs, the music of his father's bands, Civil War tunes, folk and popular tunes, ultimately, even minstrel music and

---

[85] See again, Carol K. Baron, "New Sources for Ives Studies: An Annotated Catalog," https://www.stonybrook.edu/commcms/music/people/faculty-and staff/affiliated_scholars/carol_baron. The documents revealed the broad extent of Ives's political interests and social awareness even very late in life; he was a benefactor to countless musicians, most notably, Nicolas Slonimsky, Lou Harrison and John Cage; Ives freely gave funds toward anyone in need, such as John Becker, and even his employees. See Perlis, *Charles Ives Remembered*, 63, 66, 182; see, too, Tom C. Owens, *Selected Correspondence of Charles Ives* (Berkeley, CA: University of California Press, 2007; 203, 206, 250, 252, 277, 282, 352, are among many pages that refer directly to Ives's generosity.

[86] See Alison Matthews David, "Mercurial Styles, Persistent Toxins: Materiality, "Mad" Hatters, and Mercury Poisoning in the Felt Hatting Trade," *Russian Fashion Theory: The Journal of Dress, Body and Culture*, 21 (Autumn 2011): 13-38.

33

Ragtime. In this light, Ives's placement in the heart of provincial America during the years following the Civil War—and in the region of the country primarily responsible for much of what defines the nation—illustrates why he cannot be forced into the straightjacket of a conventionally raised or trained composer.

Old Main Street, Danbury

Scene from Danbury's prime
Image AC

One can find direct links, as well, to the work of a number of domestic composers who, before Ives, had tried—largely unsuccessfully—to define an American 'voice' in music. The difficulties in finding an authentic musical identity were substantial, because the huge numbers of new immigrants during these years brought their musical cultures with them. In this way, Americans suffered a sense of inferiority, and feared anything they might produce would never compare with it favorably. The mindset explains why it was seen as almost a prerequisite for American composers to complete their training abroad. Thus, the European masters, who had developed their own art music abroad, already had a foothold in America, effectively colonizing it, by default. Their music, predominantly, too, a German art form, combined with Germany finding itself at the center of two soon-to-be-unleashed world wars, the prospect of *total* colonization is at the heart of Ives's occasional slight of German musicians (even when not specifically named as such), rather than bigotry, which does not represent him at all.

34

Ives's vernacular roots

At the forefront of the many types of vernacular music that influenced Ives were the hymns on which he was raised, learned as a church organist, even those that had touched him greatly during the many camp meeting services at which his father directed or performed. Hymns came in distinctly different formats: those of the 'higher' old established churches, versus those of the newer evangelical churches (which included camp meetings). Of the former, the tunes to which various texts were set are likely to be known by names other those than relating to the words, often directly linked in some way with the figure who wrote the melody. Names, such as *Bethany*, *Federal Street*, *Woodworth*, *Martyn*, and *Nettleton*, are largely how these hymns are most easily identified, many having been in existence since the earliest days of the republic, and even before. The phenomenon of evangelicalism belongs to more recent times in America, becoming established during the nineteenth century in 'camp meetings' as a means of bringing religion to rural populations, in which congregants would, literally, camp for a period of days to participate in a type of religious festival. The hymns sung often had recent origins, with a distinctly evangelical quality, and usually are known by specific names that related only to one melody, written exclusively for the words, such as: *There is a Fountain*, *Happy Land*, *The Beautiful River*, *Beulah Land*, and *In the Sweet Bye and Bye*.

Regardless, even from the earliest times, the melodic die was partially cast by past precedent. Locally-sourced folk tunes, handed down by the original Anglo-Celtic Plymouth settlers, ensured that many melodies had trans-Atlantic roots, even as their structures and idioms had slowly evolved. As perhaps the most prevalent music in nineteenth century New England society, it is hardly surprising that the melodic and harmonic choices of its 'classical' composers would be subconsciously influenced by them, too. The distinctive Americanism of many of these tunes is the direct result of subtle 'reshuffling' or 'reshaping' details that gives the tunes an entirely different character. H. Wiley Hitchcock noted the common emphasis of the *subdominant* in relation to the hymn tunes and folk melodies close to the core vernacular quotation in Ives's music.[87] Nicholas E. Tawa, in "Ives and the New England School," offered further details and was struck by the unusual frequency of the subdominant, submediant and median harmonies, and the frequent avoidance of dominant harmonizations of melodic lines in Ives's music.[88]

---

[87] H. Wiley Hitchcock, *Ives: A Survey of the Music* (London: Oxford University Press, 1977), 34.

[88] Nicolas E. Tawa, "Ives and the New England School," in *Charles Ives and the Classical Tradition*, ed. J. Peter Burkholder (New Haven, CT: Yale University Press, 1996), 52, 62–63.

Only on occasion did Ives utilize existing melodies as a creative foundation in these works, the tendency to do so, contrary to common perception, not true of his music in general. Among instances when he actually did build his music around an existing melody (the first movement of First String Quartet, for example), it is strongly rooted in hymn tunes; even more strikingly, the methodology is most uniquely incorporated within the remarkably creative Third Symphony (largely sketched and complete by c.1904), in which the materials are transported into previously unheralded territory.[89] This type of compositional technique is not dissimilar to Bach's chorale preludes, for example, in which their most remarkable qualities lie outside the tunes themselves. Regardless, Ives seldom utilized more than just a part or fragment of the melody, usually serving as no more than flashes of memory on top of his own innovation.

Nevertheless, actually locating *original* themes by Ives fitting the attributes Tawa cited, is not necessarily easy, even a prevalent trait. As Ives matured, his melodies took entirely different, freely conceived forms with vaguer tonal restraints, often largely atonal. Consequently, Ives's early works (pre-Yale) reveal the traits Tawa cited the most. However, some of these compositions quote extended diatonic sources as their primary material, or derivations of them, so they are not necessarily characteristic of Ives's own melodic structures. Works composed during his college years and for a few years after, provide, perhaps, the best places to survey, although his musical roots can be traced, nevertheless, and show up in various guises throughout his entire output. For example, the first four-bar phrase of the 1920 song, *Charlie Rutlage* (No.10 in *114 Songs*)—the unlikely Western location and date, to be sure—seems to ghost the first phrase of the hymn melody *Dorrnance*. Because, as Carol K. Baron so aptly pointed out, simple diatonic melodies share common features, which, over countless examples, become variously interchangeable, so precisely which tune is reflected in another is entirely subjective, although our interest

---

[89] It is only in works, such as these, that the premise that Ives's music is built upon a *foundation* of such tunes—an argument that J. Peter Burkholder promoted in his book, *All Made of Tunes*—has an element of merit. However, ascribing the premise to Ives's music in general still is no more appropriate than it is to do so, say, to a Bach Chorale Prelude. Such works used only the basis of these tunes as a starting springboard to truly original composition; such tunes do not constitute the primary melodic material, which, typically is far more diffuse and peripherally connected. As an example, Baron conclusively (review by Carol K. Baron, *Journal of the American Musicological Society*, 53, 2 [Summer, 2000]: 437–44) illustrated that the quoted melodies in the First Violin Sonata were, in fact, only secondary to the primary themes; of the first movement, the primary theme is "abstract, emphasizing Fifth- and whole-tone- cycles," and was stated clearly throughout.

here is in detecting melodic and harmonic characteristics, rather than melodies, themselves.[90]

Such melodies do, however, appear in the *Concord Sonata*, and it is necessary to remind the reader—as will be obvious in this instance—they do so *only* in diatonic and related lines, in this instance as the 'Pentatonic' and 'Lyrical' melodies of the first movement (*Emerson*), for example. The author already has demonstrated how the 'Human Faith Melody,' so dominant a feature in the sonata that it appears as the strategic anchor to all four movements, is strongly linked, even derived from, the hymn, *Bethany*.[91] Further examination reveals that, not only is it entirely diatonic to one key, but also avoids for its entirety, any harmonization by the dominant chord. Earlier works show the feature much more, however. The Second Symphony is notably full of this tendency—even more than the First. If more pronounced than in most of Ives's compositions, it is simply because of the large vernacular resource at its heart; the work was drawn from many of his early materials, after all.[92]

Characteristic 'New England' melodic and harmonic structure is clearly detectable in Ives's 1901 song, *Elégie* (one of the eighteen so-called "German songs"). In A1-B-A2 form, over its entire fifty-eight-bar duration, the dominant chord only appears convincingly in a true cadential capacity at the end of the B section. Otherwise, the single instance of dominant harmony occurs once on the first page, and not even at a pivotal juncture at that, being used more in a transitional sense within a larger harmonic scheme. This design mostly features various alternations of tonic and flatted leading tone harmonies. Should the middle (B) section of the three-part structure appear, superficially, to be more harmonically (and rhythmically) active, careful examination shows it consists of somewhat more elaborate variations of another static harmony (I–III), which serves to gradually lead back to the concluding (A2) segment of the song. It does so through the only portion that features an element of more traditional harmonic progressions, as well as through the one true perfect cadential point (C7) at m.43, approached and anticipated by another dominant harmony (G7) in the previous bar. Ives colored this definitive moment, in returning to the opening tonality (F) mid-bar, by blending into it a gentle E7 chord—one of his standard techniques, in which tones just outside the predominant tonality create

---

[90] Baron, review, *Journal of the American Musicological Society*: 53, 2 (Summer, 2000): Burkholder, *All Made of Tune*, 439.

[91] Cooke, *Charles Ives's Musical Universe*, 276–78.

[92] For this reason, alone, the symphony resembles the tenor of Dvořák's *New World Symphony* much more closely than it does Ives's first symphonic excursion, despite the commonly accepted position to the contrary from some circles of scholarship. See analysis discussion, First Symphony, Chapter 6.

startling new coloration.[93] However, one can overstate any avoidance of the dominant in Ives's harmony; as often as not, he seems to march to no particular drum, and certainly not necessarily at any particular point in his compositional timeline. His songs, as a wide reference source of his compositional range, reveal more about what is harmonically unique in his choices than they do to obvious links to his vernacular heritage.

Tying Ives further to his European cultural heritage, Keith C. Ward, in "Ives, Schoenberg, and the Musical Ideal," remarked, too, upon both Ives's and Schoenberg's usage of 'cells,' which really is only another term for the development of motifs, small cycles, or other compact ideas, often in systemized fashion.[94] Although, as utilized in Ives's and Schoenberg's work, these 'cells' are handled in original ways, actually, the technique, conceptually, hardly is exclusive to these composers—nor even especially unusual in Western music, itself. A mainstay of Bach's compositional technique, the music of Beethoven, and reaching, perhaps, its apex in the leitmotifs that lie at the heart of the music of Wagner, even that of Mahler, without the development of these germinal ideas in composition, extended works of music would be virtually possible. Even extemporization relies to a substantial degree on the same technique.

Musical Beginnings

Charles Ives's musical curiosity and early experimentation first manifested itself in his efforts to emulate the sound of drums on the piano;[95] George, observing the five-year-old youngster recreating the sound of 'street beat' he had heard in the town band, sent him to his old wartime friend and bandsman colleague, Charles Schleyer, (Feder spelled the name, Slier) for drum lessons.[96] It seems fairly safe to assume that George Ives was Charles's first piano teacher, although the matter is not mentioned anywhere. The supposition is all the more likely, because Carl Foeppl (George's teacher in New York City before and after the Civil War) was himself a pianist, and is thought likely to have taught George the piano, too. At some point later on, however, George engaged Ella Hollister to become Charles's first designated

---

[93] Antony Cooke, *Charles Ives's Musical Universe*, analysis of *Thanksgiving*, mm.130–37, mm.219–20.

[94] Keith C. Ward, "Ives, Schoenberg, and the Musical Ideal," in *Charles Ives and the Classical Tradition*, 96.

[95] Ives, *Memos*, 42.

[96] Feder, *"My Father's Song,"* 89.), who was the local barber. Also, Henry & Sidney Cowell, *Charles Ives and His Music* (London: Oxford University Press, 1955), 24.

38

keyboard teacher.[97] It is not known, however, who, initially, taught him the organ (especially in light of the specialized pedal technique required), although it seems reasonable to assume that it was Miss Hollister, too. As the organist at the Disciples Church in Danbury, it is likely she would have instructed him on the instrument, especially in regard to the skills needed to play the organ pedals.[98]

In the later 1880s, young Charlie also studied briefly with the organist, Hans Raasch. The encounter was not successful; George would abruptly cease the arrangement after a disagreement about the merits of Wagner's music![99] The occasion demonstrates that George, with well-founded, strong opinions on music and its protagonists, was hardly the musical hayseed of revisionist myth. As Charles's interest in musical matters grew, George lavished his attentions on him. As imbued in Charles's advancing compositional language (e.g., *Psalm 67*), the veracity of his accounts about his father rings true,[100] although it is not formally recorded.[101] Still not yet universally acknowledged, many commentators continue to deny or otherwise belittle this critical factor in Ives's background. Swafford made some related observations that isolated various technical components in Ives's compositional style, of which three stand out:[102]

- *Melody*: Ives's wrote about his father's appreciation of local townsfolks' genuine expression as they sung in religious settings: the beauty of the natural, unaffected, unrestrained and heartfelt musicality being infinitely more communicative than merely the beauty only of the sound, which was an over-refinement at the expense of the music itself.[103] Ives would come to appreciate hearing music as if through his father's ears, finding its place within his own compositions, and characteristically emanating in the often strikingly rough-hewn melodic lines, and an almost raw musicality that speaks directly to it.

- *Harmony*: Charles recalled that his father, while not being averse to his son's 'experiments' on the piano, was, nevertheless, always insistent that he should be well-versed in the proper procedures of harmony, even as he disagreed with

---

[97] Swafford, *A Life With Music*, 48.

[98] Ibid.,, 442, n.2.

[99] Ibid., 51.

[100] Ives, *Memos*, 42–47.

[101] Swafford, *A Life With Music*, 88–98.

[102] Ibid., 88–98.

[103] Ives, *Memos*, 132.

much of the traditional premise from which it had evolved and been taught. Despite the lack of corroboration for Ives's attributions to George of many of his most extreme harmonic innovations,[104] one senses that, even allowing for the rosiest of recollections, Ives was touching upon more than a grain of truth.

- *Counterpoint*: Ives was thoroughly grounded in counterpoint during his years in Danbury. Despite recent musicological challenge, Swafford countered that Ives would have been thoroughly familiar with the common counter-melodies of the music of his father's bands from an early age, by default of his daily exposure to them.[105] Moreover, the surviving attempts in his exercises from these years—in Baroque-styled imitative fugal or canonic writing—also show that even the very young Charles was well aware of contrapuntal technique; far from major utterances, and usually incomplete, these simple exercises illustrate an exposure to it. Moreover, how likely is it that such a youngster—*any*—would have dabbled in such things *without* an awareness of what he was trying to emulate?

The record makes clear that George maintained a constant presence is his son's musical education, and continued to guide him, up until the time that Charles Ives left home for Hopkins Grammar School in New Haven in 1893—even up to the time of George's death in 1894. Furthermore, the youthful Ives was more artistically worldly and well-rounded than some have projected or assumed. George had taken his son to hear orchestra concerts by the New York Symphony Society on a number of occasions—it was an organization supported by no less an auspicious figure than Andrew Carnegie, and that played its concerts at the hall bearing his name. Ives had other opportunities to hear symphonic music, too, perhaps most noteworthy among them being his experience in Chicago at the World's Columbian Exposition in 1893.[106] His uncle, Lyman Brewster, had treated him to the trip, during which he heard the Chicago Symphony Orchestra.

More important, however, Ives first was exposed to Ragtime in multiple venues at the exposition, its syncopated rhythms striking a special chord in Ives's consciousness. If the orchestra in Chicago represented a step up in Ives's listening experience, it was probably the Ragtime performers who made a bigger impression. The idiom had just become a sensation in American society; Ives's exposure to it set the stage during his years in New Haven for encounters with the wild improvisations

---

[104] Ives, *Memos*, 140.

[105] Swafford, *A Life With Music*, 91.

[106] Feder, *My Father's Song*, 1–2

of an inspired ragtime pianist, George Felsberg, at Poli's Theater in New Haven.[107] In describing Felsberg's playing, with his characteristic infectious enthusiasm, Ives recalled that he could play and read a newspaper better than most pianists could play without one.[108]

Charles Ives: Youthful Virtuoso, Young Composer

By 1888, his reputation rapidly spreading as an organ prodigy, Charles Ives was regularly heard playing during church services, even sometimes substituting for his teacher, Ella Hollister. In 1889, Ives was fortunate to advance his organ studies with J.R. Hall, who was the organist at First Congregational Church in Danbury. Upon the appointment of Ella Hollister as the choir director at Second Congregation Church, the youthful Ives took up the position of organist there, too. The following year he would become organist at the Baptist Church of Danbury, a position he held until leaving home for New Haven in 1893.

Ives's studies with Hall were followed with tutoring by Alexander Gibson. Organist of First Congregational in Norwalk. Gibson was held in high regard well beyond his position locally, and under whom, in his capacity as a teacher in the increasingly prestigious Danbury School of Music, Ives would study advanced musical literature, from Bach organ works to other organ transcriptions of orchestral works by the masters.[109] William Osborne (formerly of Denison University) provided further detail of the organ literature that Ives played, citing many of the classics, as well as his favorite transcriptions. The length of the list and its technical and musical demands, is considerable, to say nothing of its breadth.[110] During this period of Ives's last year in Danbury, it must be assumed that Gibson's influence was second only to

---

[107] Sylvester Z. Poli, a highly successful theater magnate at the time, operated a chain of vaudeville venues, one of which was in New Haven.

[108] Ives, *Memos*, 56–57.

[109] Ibid., 49–50. This detail is more significant than might be supposed, because undoubtedly, some of Charles Ives's knowledge of the classical repertoire originated with Gibson. It is clear from what Swafford noted (Gibson tutored Ives "in the highest levels of the repertoire," *A Life with Music*, 64) that Ives already had a comprehensive knowledge of the classical literature well before he entered Yale and his studies with Parker—a crucial fact in understanding Ives's background. Regardless of the questioning in some recent scholarship, doubtless (from the surviving work in his hand), Ives also had been exposed to the music of Bach and other masters under his father, and surely, Hollister, too.

[110] William Osborne, "Preface" to *Charles E. Ives: Complete Organ Works* (King of Prussia, PA: critical edition, Theodore Presser Co., 2012).

George's. Perhaps Gibson is another figure to have been slighted in history; even *Ives* did not mention him in *Memos*.

The growing sophistication in Charles's compositions dating from this year, such as the *Benedictus in E* (1893) and the *Nine Canticle Phrases* (1894), both for unaccompanied chorus, even the *Canzonetta* (1893) for organ, surely speaks to Gibson's influence. George, thus, not only had given his son a solid musical foundation, but also had ensured that he had access to the very best teachers and opportunities available to him as he grew and developed; furthermore, it is clear that George was wholly cognizant of those situations in which his own knowledge or expertise was insufficient, or—judging by the episode with Hans Raasch—when a teacher did not measure up to his standards. No one should doubt that that the ever-watchful eye of George was steering every aspect of his son's musical education, and that, contrary to impressions so often painted of him, George was entirely qualified to know and assess his son's needs. As such, as Swafford assured us, George remained at the center of his son's universe in all matters relating to *theory*, 'conventional and otherwise.'[111]

Ives's daily piano practice routine was rigorous.[112] By his mid-teens, his growing command of the instrument pointed to a bright future. However, the challenges of making a decent living in music (even in major metropolitan areas), as demonstrated in his own household, likely damped his enthusiasm for it. His greater family might have discouraged it, too. [113] Ives's father, George, the only member of the family ever to try to make a full-time living in music, could hardly compete with the professional prominence of the greater family clan. Nevertheless, Danbury's young organ prodigy continued to develop, even as a singer, too. How does one reconcile Charles Ives's toils and energies for music against the practicalities staring him each day in the face? How many youngsters would have taken the same course having in mind only a hobby? It would surely limit participation in competing interests as a result. It appears, at this stage, Ives regarded music as a 'wait-and-see' prospect. He maintained, or resurrected that outlook even for a period after his Yale years, dreaming of finding his own path to success. The writer (albeit in times of infinitely better circumstances), knows of the lure of professional music making; it is very hard to accept that something so personally meaningful as 'just' a hobby.

---

[111] Swafford, *A Life with Music*, 43.

[112] Ibid., 51.

[113] Magee, *Charles Ives Reconsidered*, 55-56; also Frank R. Rossiter, *Charles Ives & His America*, 114.

Even in American high society, the organ, for many people, was the *only* source of instrumental music they might ever hear—during church services and recitals.[114] Its literature, required of virtually *all* organists of the day—notably Bach's fugues, toccatas and chorale preludes, and large quantities of transcribed standard classics— means that Ives could not have avoided a deep immersion in the grand European musical tradition *while still living in Danbury*. The assertion by J. Peter Burkholder, that, prior to his studies with Parker, Ives lacked a broad musical exposure, experiencing little beyond the assorted vernacular music of the day, is, thus, totally out of step with the facts.[115] He seemed to contradict that position, in surmising that, aside from his formal training, Charles had absorbed a good deal about compositional methodology from his efforts to imitate it during his early his years.[116] Magee claimed that, prior to Charles's attendance at Yale, "no single source" existed to show the youthful Ives following correct procedures of harmony and counterpoint. It seems she based that position on the relative few childhood exercises in George's copybook, and ignored the numerous early compositions that testify otherwise—among them, *Variations on 'America'* (1891–92), *Melody in F* (1893), and the pianistically well-written *Burlesque Harmonizations of 'London Bridge'* (1891).

The Innovator

Ives could not avoid the influence of a lengthy immersion in his father's world. The personification of the Civil War and town bandsman, George might have been the least conventional member of a prominent local family. Nevertheless, this mid-century New Englander still 'mirrored' the family's deep roots in the town's history and culture, as well as their socioreligious views that connected Unitarian-Transcendentalist philosophy to daily life. George's rebelliousness manifested itself in the choices he made in his career, even his thoughtful questioning of the musical status quo at the time,[117] though he never contemplated rejection of the prevailing social order in which he had been raised.

---

[114] Barbara Owen, liner notes, "Nineteenth-century American concert organ music," *Fugues, Fantasia And Variations*, New World Records 80280 (CD) 1994, Richard Morris, organ.

[115] Burkholder, *All Made of Tune*, 419.

[116] Ibid., "Ives and the European Tradition," 15.

[117] Carol K. Baron, "George Ives's Essay in Music Theory: An Introduction and Annotated Edition," *American Music*, Fall 1992, 239–88. The tonal ambiguities posed in Wagner's advanced musical language caused George to question the antiquated notational system of music, its rigid rules and self-limiting constrictions.

43

No less important in George's world, too, was his keen interest in the phenomenon of sound itself. The extra-musical sounds of nature, even the unpredictable, interested him as much as those in conventional music. Ives described George's dabblings in microtones: experiments with a slide cornet, tuned glasses, piano tuned in partials, and strings stretched over a clothes press.[118] The last two examples, in particular, are sufficiently unusual to be implausible as figments of Ives's imagination. George's fascination with acoustic phenomena extended, too, to sound effects in open spaces—such as the haunting reverberations of a cornet wafting across bodies of water, or the overtones of church bells—and probably were the initial trigger for Charles's *spatial* representations in music (such as in *The Unanswered Question*, *Universe Symphony*, or the *finale* of the Fourth Symphony). Closer to home, is it George we hear playing the flute over the water in *The Pond*? Can one doubt that the sounds of church bells wafting across greater Danbury are what we hear at the end of the Third Symphony, or perhaps, even, Concord, MA?

Conflicting musical entities, as if in the open air, appear in much of Ives's music. Perhaps nothing defines these phenomena better than what has routinely been presumed in one composition to be the clashing marching bands (that had so fascinated George) as they crossed each other's paths (in *Putnam's Camp*) around the town square. Again, never more apparent than in the *Scherzo* of the *Fourth Symphony*, Ives, nevertheless, did not describe anywhere representations of the phenomenon in either of these works! In fact, they are hard to quantify as such beyond a cursory assessment, despite the temptation to do so; old myths die hard (the subject of such representations will be dealt with in greater depth in Chapter 7). In *The Fourth of July*, however, the clashing of multiple separate performing groups is more obviously represented, even, too, in the raucous barn dance of *Washington's Birthday*.

Other likely allusions to George's awareness and connection to his sonic environment can be heard in the changing patter of footsteps and traffic below Ives's window in New York (*Scherzo: Over the Pavements*), the sounds coming from a casino in the distance inside Central Park (*Central Park in the Dark*), even in the last movement of the *Concord Sonata* with its sonic representations of the 'great outdoors' during Thoreau's two years at Walden Pond. One could argue that almost all of Ives's instrumental soundscapes were affected to varying degrees by such open-air phenomena, the imprint of George's world evident on his lifetime's work.

---

[118] Ives, *Memos*, 45.

Jan Swafford suggested that Ives's shared predilection for such programmatic elements was linked to George's penchant for the theatric;[119] George was a performer, after all. Common to all performers, he surely shared the fundamental drive to command attention (otherwise, appearing to the public to be concerned only with his 'art'). Looking to all avenues of expression and legitimacy in a provincial town, in which musicians, per se, seldom were granted much respect, even more, considered the celebrities they might have been in better circumstances, Ives—describing one such effort through the rosiest of spectacles only a devoted son might have—perhaps, what was George's greatest (and most theatric) stunt. With the debut of his 'Humanophone,'[120] Ives preferred to remember the occasion more as an example of his father's experimental bent, though, perhaps, it was in order to alleviate his father's subsequent humiliation. Nevertheless, the influence of this lowly, even comically absurd, 'experiment' can be seen throughout Ives's compositions in many of the angular, wide-ranging melodic lines he featured!

Ives's Transcendental roots

Swafford considered, too, that the soul of the *community* was manifested in Ives's choices of subject matter and instinctive use of quotations. The observation again points to the social awareness that was at the heart of the Ives family's 'secular-religious' heritage[121] that Baron had raised to correct the many inaccurate assertions about Ives's background in 2004.[122] Stressing the *inseparable* social and religious characteristics of the generally liberal Congregationalist-Unitarian philosophies, and, in turn, their obvious ties to Transcendentalism, it become immediately clear that the attitudes of Ives's family were long ingrained in him by observing the manner in which he had conducted his own life.[123] Swafford considered that Harmony Twichell (who became his wife), rather than introducing Ives to Transcendentalism, had been

---

[119] Swafford, *A Life with Music*, 93–94.

[120] Ives, *Memos*, 142.

[121] Richard Whightman Fox, "The Culture of Liberal Progressivism, 1875–1925," *Journal of Interdisciplinary History*, 23, 3 (Winter 1993): 645, n.6.

[122] Baron, "Efforts on Behalf of Democracy," 7–8.

[123] Swafford, *A Life With Music,* 12.

instrumental in *reawakening* him to the 'roots' of his upbringing.[124] Her role, thus was in encouraging Ives to remain guided by them.[125]

Transcendentalism, thus, hardly was something 'picked up' later, as Burkholder claimed, even in advance of the first major assault on the 'Ives Legend' by Maynard Solomon.[126] Such positioning casts Ives in a different light, which seems to have suited to the revised musicological projections of Ives. However, Ives's upbringing lies at the heart of his creativity—the very problem that American musicology cannot accept as a model for such a great creative force. Burkholder further dismissed the notion that Transcendental philosophy could have played a role in Ives's early musical work. How does one explain, however, the ethereal visions of *Psalm 67*, even the sense of eternity in *Psalm 100*, both of which seem wholly aligned with the Transcendentalists' philosophy of circular existence. These works emerged from Ives's early years in Danbury, and would become amplified in later works, such as *The Unanswered Question*, and Sonata No. 2 for piano, the *Concord*.

Swafford showed how Ives's roots also amplified the larger humanistic values handed down through generations of his family, and which lay behind many of his writings, as well as the subject matter of his compositions. Ives's staunch political philosophy from having witnessed firsthand the abuse of factory workers in his hometown[127] would be echoed in the way he conducted his life and business affairs.[128]

The use of borrowed tunes

The oft-stated point of view that Ives borrowed because he lacked the ability to create his own material is entirely inaccurate. The quotes almost never comprise an actual structural role in his music, his original melodies generally being more diffuse, pervasive and complex, as Baron demonstrated in her review of Burkholder's *All Made of Tunes*.[129] Criticisms that Ives borrowed tunes misunderstand his impulse to memorialize very personal associations, far from illuminating a weakness on his part.

---

[124] Swafford, *A Life With Music*, 226.

[125] Ibid., 258: "Ives grew up hearing Emerson's words through grandmother Sarah and his Uncle Joe, who knew the man personally."

[126] Burkholder, *The Ideas Behind the Music*, 5.

[127] Swafford, *A Life With Music*, 277

[128] Ibid., 210–12; 307–16.

[129] Carol K. Baron, review, *All Made of Tunes: Charles Ives and the Uses of Musical Borrowing*, J. Peter Burkholder, (new Haven, CT: Yale University Press, 1995), *Journal of the American Musicological Society*, 53, 2 (Summer, 2000): 437.

Firsthand glimpses of his own experiences, they put the listener directly into the scenes he was portraying—tying them, thus, as Swafford had remarked, to the larger community who cohabitated the best remembered scenes of Ives's life. Stuart Feder, ably summed up Ives's predilection:

> Ives had been known by many of in the family to improvise endlessly at the piano, carrying on a running conversation as if music and word blended in reminiscence and free association. The tunes would remind him of people and places and of the events and experiences of the past; and as he recalled them, the memories stimulated recall of still more tunes, which then emerged in the musical improvisation.[130]

In other words, the incorporation of these fragments into larger musical frameworks was second nature to him. Further supporting the notion that Ives did not need to borrow due to lack of creativity, Feder also noted that George Ives's own student assignments reveal little distinction as examples of 'sustained musical invention,' in contrast to his son's creative talents.[131] Unfortunately, the mischaracterizations of Ives's use of quotations have found a life of their own, apparently beginning with comments by Elliott Carter, whom Ives had mentored in the 1920s. The son of clients who became friends, ultimately, Carter (who had traveled to Europe to study with Nadia Boulanger) would return to the USA to find Ives's star in the ascent at a time he was struggling for recognition. He was a clearly uncomfortable with witnessing the 'hobbyist' composer—with all his inconsistencies of style, methods and work habits—rising to a level of international prominence to which, one can only surmise, *he* felt more deserving. Perhaps Carter considered that Ives had not made the necessary commitment to pursuing a professional status in the manner that virtually all serious-minded Americans had done before—and finishing their studies in Europe—even if doing so ensured their music would continue to be subservient to trans-Atlantic practices.

Over the years, Carter frequently made quite negative—even mean-spirited—remarks about Ives's music, which no amount of later remorse, backtracking, or, later in life, even the dedication to Ives of some of his works could erase. Whenever Carter had managed to clear the air, his old professional jealousy again resurfaced. Even as late as 1969, he expressed "disappointment" to Vivian Perlis (in the interview for her book, *Charles Ives Remembered*) that Ives, either could not, or was not prepared to,

---

[130] Feder, *My Father's Song*, 350.

[131] Ibid., 92.

invent his own melodic materials.[132] If, perhaps, attempting to elevate his own work at Ives's expense, surely, as a learned figure, he was well aware by this date (1969) of Ives's purpose in using of quoted materials, and cannot possibly not have been cognizant of some of Ives's own melodic material. As Philip Lambert repeatedly demonstrated in his book, *The Music of Charles Ives*, developments of systematic-based structures (certainly not quotes!) were at the root of many of Ives's advanced compositions.[133] Baron (the first scholar to use the term 'systematic' in relation to Ives's music) pointed out, too, in one example (the First Violin Sonata), the ways in which the musical quotes functioned peripherally to the systematically organized whole-tone themes and structure at its heart.[134]

Perhaps the most notable exception to the rule can be found in Ives's use of quotations in the Third Symphony, in which a few hymn tunes that actually do form the foundation of the music trigger endless chains of invention. Even here, though, the quotes appear just in fragments until the crux of the movements' structures are reached, so they do not constitute the bulk of the greater melodic invention, putting them more in line with Bach's chorale preludes. The Third Symphony is an atypical fork in the road, too; Ives never returned to the model he had perfected in one fell swoop—his own form of the ever-evolving through-composition vein of Bach and Wagner. It further demonstrates the characteristic of Ives's improvisations carried over into organized compositional structures that Feder noted.[135] This illusory element of continuous extemporization (coined by Burkholder, 'cumulative form')—would become, through more subtly applied ways, part of many more, perhaps even most, of Ives's mature extended compositions.

Carter's assessments were not met with universal accord, although the oft-stated sentiment still persists. Even as far back as 1979, a period when relatively little commentary about Ives's music existed, Christopher Ballantine was able to see clearly through the murky waters that Carter had stirred. He demonstrated the true function of the quotes, and how little bearing on the structure of the music they

---

[132] Perlis, *Charles Ives Remembered*, 145. The charge is, needless to say (?) incorrect (e.g., *The Greatest Man*; *Charlie Rutlage*; the 'Quasi-pentatonic' melody in the *Concord Sonata*; Ives's melodies do not resemble the quotes—generally being altogether more diffuse and angular. Besides, Ives's chief methodology involved little composition of "tunes," per se. As a conventional melodist, Ives's early songs reveal such a very large talent that the charge is clearly baseless.

[133] Lambert, *The Music of Charles Ives* (New Haven, CT: Yale University Press, 1997).

[134] Carol K. Baron, review, J. Peter Burkholder, *All Made of Tunes*: *Journal of the American Musicological Society*, 53, 2 (Summer, 2000): 439.

[135] *Op. Cit.*, n. 44.

played.[136] As it happens, European composers often had quoted the works of others during the nineteenth century.[137] William K. Kearns listed Mendelssöhn, Franck, Liszt, Gounod, Brahms, Wagner and Dvořák among those who had done so.[138] One does not have to look far to see it, too, in the works of Mahler, Tchaikovsky, Richard Strauss, and Schumann, to name just a few more. Even in America, the practice was widely known. Parker was no exception; among instances in which he had borrowed materials, the best known, perhaps, is the appearance of Mendelssöhn's *Wedding March* near the conclusion of *Hora Novissima*.

Kearns considered, however, when Parker made us of quotes it approached plagiarism, because their use seemed to bear no relationship to the context. This reservation does not seem unfair, because almost invariably, the practice, when legitimately utilized and common enough among composers of the time, involved a connection to the quoted materials—even those quoted by Ives. And certainly, no one seems to have looked unfavorably at borrowing such materials, even featuring elements from multiple periods in the same work (and in which Parker also excelled). Thus, one should never presume to conclude that quoting the work of others was due to a composer's lack of ability to create original material; the quotes—if not paying homage to the earlier figures who had guided them—have been long an accepted fact of life within the broad fellowship of musicians; the countless figures who indulged in it historically hardly were incapable of original melodic invention. As cultural attitudes have evolved over time, what might seem cavalier to modern minds likely reflects, too, a time in which copyright infringement had not yet occupied much ground between art and commerce.

Nicholas E. Tawa speculated that Ives's propensity to borrow musical quotes might have originated with awareness of the practice by the New England composers—perhaps, most notably, the 'Boston Six,' see Chapter 3.[139] The use of quotes in Ives's music, however, differs substantially from the practices of others, in the respects already discussed. More to the point, because Ives had featured quotes in his music almost from the start, and was more likely familiar with the standard classics long before he had much familiarity with the music of the 'Boston Six'—if, indeed, any—Tawa's speculation seems less than plausible. In a most general sense,

---

[136] Christopher Ballantine, "Charles Ives and the Meaning of Quotation in Music," *The Musical Quarterly*, 65, 2 (April 1979), 167-184.

[137] *Charles Ives and the Classical Tradition*, ed. Block & Burkholder (New Haven, CT: Yale University Press, 1996), 3, 14.

[138] Kearns, *Horatio Parker*, 241.

[139] Tawa, "Ives and the New England School," 70–71.

however, Tawa *was* able to demonstrate that Ives continued in the footsteps of the earlier composers of the New England school. The fact that popular and religious music played a prominent role in it cannot be denied; most notably, George F. Root and Lowell Mason contributed some of the most memorable melodies into the American tradition and culture. Ives, carrying many such melodies with him even into his last compositions, to some degree would see even his own melodic lines, their characteristic rhythmic and intervallic structures reflecting them. It seems entirely natural that domestic composers of the era would have been influenced by such notable sources, which were, at the time, the only truly American music.

However, outside obvious examples of quoted sources, such as in Ives's Second Symphony, it is problematic to align his particular penchant for quoting existing melodies with any of those of the composers in Tawa's argument.[140] The primary difference remaining is that Ives's quotes seldom are more than fleeting fragments of the totals. The Second Symphony's many quotes, even from major concert works, are very brief, even though a few vernacular elements, such as *Columbia, the Gem of the Ocean*, do sometimes appear complete. Soon after the turn of the twentieth century, however, quoting complete melodies would barely apply to Ives's music. If this matter has taken flight *beyond* merely demonstrating the influence of other sources upon his melodic contours, it is through failure to understand what Ives actually did.[141]

The experimenter?

Although, as J. Peter Burkholder demonstrated, Ives's music had ties to three long-existing musical 'traditions,' another he isolated, a fourth—what he termed the 'experimental'—became the mechanism by which they would be tied together.[142] The fourth element is what sets Ives's mature compositions apart from others, although 'experimental' is not necessarily the most appropriate term for what Ives did.

---

[140] Burkholder, *The Ideas Behind the Music*, 49.

[141] For example, see Burkholder, *All Made of Tunes*, 270; the assignment of the famous melody in the second movement of Tchaikovsky's Sixth Symphony ('Pathetique') as the source of the melody in Ives's song, *The Side Show* (No.32 in *114 Songs*) seems akin to an answer in search of a question. Other than the relationships of virtually any tonal source to another, it is hard to find any tune that does not resemble something else in some way. The melody that Tchaikovsky employed is little more than an ornamented scalic ascent over major sixth. Although Ives's tune also ascends—without ornamentation—it moves over a fourth before leaping up a third; beyond this point, to consider, as actualities, any further resemblances becomes entirely arbitrary; there are none.

[142] Burkholder, "Charles Ives and the Four Musical Traditions," in *Charles Ives and His World*, ed. Burkholder (Princeton: Princeton University Press, 1995), 3–31.

Although Ives explored many experimental ideas when involving fellow Yale undergraduates (those aforementioned 'stunts,' or 'party tricks'), it is misleading to assume that his major innovations originated as 'experiments.'[143] His early miniatures were built wholly on the applications of specific technical ideas; by the time he wrote them, any prior links to experimentation were no more than a seed that triggered something far larger, entirely cerebral and deliberate.

As a term, 'experimentation' implies that Ives did not know what he was doing—a mere musical dabbler, looking 'in the dark' for novel ideas and effects to try. Because, in reality, Ives's early so-called experimental works represent the expansions and structured formatting of basic initial ideas that *might* have developed from experimentation, his comments in *Memos* that some of these ideas—often hurriedly made in sketch form—were "hardly more than memos in notes" are self-effacing words for works that existed largely in their totality, if not in formal scoring.[144] Ives listed, specifically, some works that, although conceived originally in this manner, such as *The Cage*, and *In the Night*, had evolved far beyond 'mere' experimentation into truly systematic formulae.[145]

Despite George Ives's resistance to the application of unconventional techniques within actual works of music or performance,[146] he remained open, regardless, to musical and acoustic exploration; his own fascination with sounds of every conceivable description is well known.[147] It must be remembered, however, that these years preceded Ives's time at Yale—and his 'stunts' with friends—by *many* years, so his adventurism was nothing new. We can only imagine what might have emerged from Danbury had the alternate scenario played out. It is at this stage that Stuart Feder, post-mortem revisionist though he was, essentially dismissed the major tenets of the revisionist case, pointing out that Charles Ives really did come upon his ideas independently of other modernists, because he was 'not in a position' to be influenced by the avant-garde movements in Europe! He did not negate George's role

---

[143] Ives, *Memos*, 40–41.

[144] Ibid., 64.

[145] Burkholder, *The Ideas Behind the Music*, 49. The reader is referred to the writer's analysis of *The Cage* in his volume, *Charles Ives's Musical Universe*, 244–47.

[146] For example, see Ives, *Memos*, 115: "I don't think [Father] had the possibility of polytonality in composition in mind, as much as to encourage them and the mind to think for themselves and be more independent."

[147] Feder, *"My Father's Song,"* 93, 97.

either, because, in summing up, he conceded that George really had been Ives's most important teacher.[148]

Ives's European heritage, Transcendentalism and nationalism

There are other aspects of Ives's music that have been the subject of misunderstanding or misrepresentation, too. Implications that it was, perhaps, not as revolutionary as previously thought, reflect a failure to recognize that all music is inevitably tied in ways to what precedes it.[149] Indeed, the concept of renewal of existing matter lies at the heart of Transcendentalism. Emerson, the great Transcendental thinker, philosopher and author, considered that all means of expression existed from the beginning, and had merely been reused in other guises or orderings. To this end, this philosophy is infused in much of Ives's most advanced music; it means that, in an Emersonian universe, the mixing of different styles and techniques is of no consequence.

Eric Salzman argued, incorrectly, that Ives's music emerged as an entirely external phenomenon to the predominant culture of the West, although his assessment seemed refreshing among other dismissive assessments of Ives's contributions.[150] Where Salzman erred was in his train of thought: because American culture is essentially *an evolved continuation* of the same long-existent trans-Atlantic culture, Ives's music could *not* be detached from the music of the European masters. If it seems to defy its foundational roots, which are, in fact, quintessentially shared with all his predecessors, it is the many stylistic and technical innovations that make it sound so different. The unpredictability with which they are incorporated is the one aspect that differs from the European tradition. Although Ives's musical language still remains under the larger umbrella of Western culture, it could not have emerged from across the Atlantic. Similarly, Ives's Americanism, often confused with nationalism, is an authentic expression of it. Burkholder was entirely correct, therefore, in his assessment of Ives's supposed 'nationalism,'[151] his place in music, thus, far from an artistic anomaly, even more, an unlikely emergence of greatness rising out of

---

[148] Feder, *"My Father's Song,"* 116.

[149] *Charles Ives and the Classical Tradition*, ed. Geoffrey Block & J. Peter Burkholder (New Haven, CT: Yale University Press, 1996), 11.

[150] Eric Salzman, *Twentieth-Century Music: An Introduction*, ed. 3 (Englewood Cliffs, NJ: Prentice Hall, 1988), 134.

[151] *Charles Ives and the Classical Tradition*, ed. Block & Burkholder, 7.

obscurity that many earlier scholars proposed. Rather, *Ives's music was inevitable*, and among the most innovative in the entire history of music.

The Relentless Diminishing of George Ives and his Vital Role

One of the foremost issues in the redefinition of Ives has been the not-so-subtle shifting of strategic parts of his history to alternative, more musicologically acceptable, circumstances and influences. It has resulted in moving his educational background, and consequently, his music, ever more forward in time. Consequently, Ives's predictive innovations have become blurred into the broad overview of twentieth century musical progressiveness. The only reason it matters so greatly is that Ives's music has been made to appear more derivative than innovative, and Ives himself, less than credible as a person. The key to much of Ives's development, however, is George Ives.

One is faced with a modified image of a young Charles Ives arriving at Yale with barely any musical background at all, other than some casual immersion in hymns, band and popular music. The propagation of this image has become widespread. Furthermore, Ives's teacher at Yale, Horatio Parker, has been magnified, almost as Ives's equal as an innovator, even Ives's primary musical influence in this respect.[152] It has even been suggested that Parker might have introduced Ives to Transcendentalism.[153] So, no less surely than has George Ives's musical expertise been denied, than the formative role he played in Charles's entire background has been attributed to other figures—even more, almost exclusively credited to his academic years. Magee, who annunciated these sentiments most explicitly, claimed that Ives had gained little real musical education under his father's guidance, and consequently virtually everything substantive he would learn came from Parker.[154]

The writer has already commented on scholarship's distorted fantasy that great music is the province of academia, and often, even formal training.[155] Some of the greatest composers, far from eschewing the need for technique, even have possessed the level of creative intelligence and aptitude to school themselves, Brahms being one notable example. It is unfortunate that Ives has not been credited with the acknowledgment of possessing the same level of natural aptitude that countless great

---

[152] *Charles Ives and the Classical Tradition*, ed. Block & Burkholder, 12.

[153] Tawa, "Ives and the New England School," 54.

[154] *Charles Ives and the Classical Tradition*, ed. Block & Burkholder, 54, 57. See too, Magee, *Charles Ives Reconsidered*, 27–28, 48.

[155] Cooke, *Charles Ives and His Road to the Stars*, second ed., 51–52.

composers have similarly enjoyed—to reach astonishing heights without an academic or formal background. The refusal to acknowledge Ives's special circumstances further disallows something extraordinary in America that occurred as the direct result of an unorthodox training, such as countless other composers have received.

It is obvious that a large part of Ives's radicalism can be traced directly to his father's influence. One would never know it from much of the commentary, which has asserted that George Ives clung only to age-old musical ideas. Ignoring his own curiosity with sound—natural and manmade—many scholars choose to deny, or remain oblivious to George's advanced theoretical ideas (see later), not to mention Charlie's own tendency toward adventurism happening right under his own nose.[156] With Magee's demotion of George to *amateur* status, most notably upon her constant emphasis of the term to describe his musical activity—George, lowered further still by her projection that he only earned actual income from music *to finance his son's future college education*[157]—the scenario is exactly back-to-front. It was because George Ives realized late in 1890 that he could *not* make sufficient income from music to send his sons to college, that he abandoned his dream of carving out a living from it, going to work for his maternal uncle (Charles Merritt, for whom he held little affection, even, respect) as the bookkeeper at his hat factory.

Needless to say, most of George's music making did not fit the 'higher' societal image of art music, although it greatly appealed to Charles. Magee, again, while building her case that George was hardly a qualified musician, referenced the *types* of work George had to do, and upon which he had built his living, to diminish him.[158] To be fair, however, there can be no doubt that George, as a musician, would not have fitted a typical urban setting; however, it is precisely this aspect of his musical totality that makes him so interesting. Sadly, George thus dismissed, his idealism is reduced to addressing only the welfare of his family, his marginalization further reinforced by references to the numerous organizations from Danbury with which he was associated (being musically so apparently inconsequential) that they do not warrant mention by name.[159] Magee also debunked any suggestion that George might have had strong progressive leanings, commenting on *what* he did in order to make a living, rather than on *how* he envisaged better ways to proceed.[160] Feder guilty, too,

---

[156] Magee, *Charles Ives Reconsidered*, 6–37.

[157] Ibid., 37.

[158] Ibid,, 14–18.

[159] Ibid., 10.

[160] Ibid., *17*

of dismissive summation, reducing George's experimental bent to mere stunts and corny public-event contraptions (e.g., the 'Humanophone'), leaving an impression that George indeed *was* the "crank" that Ives believed some townspeople saw.[161] Ultimately, attacking Charles's portrayal of George as a visionary, instead, Feder rendered him a minor figure, whose memory and legacy was in need of 'rescuing' for posterity by his son. Seeming almost to undermine his larger case, he did, however, remark upon George's intensively studied and marked up handwritten lessons, and acknowledged, too, that George had let Charles work from them. Moreover, he also conceded that *Charles mastered the content*, because he seemed "reasonably prepared for advanced studies when he entered Yale," which totally contradicts the standard revised stance that Ives's level of musical education under his father was minimal.[162] Significantly, too, Feder wrote that, by the age of eleven, Charles's musical training under George included, in addition to harmony and counterpoint, studies in violin and cornet, sight reading, even *orchestration*. Feder also commented favorably on George's theoretical insights, which are components in Ives's early background that are far more significant than recently allowed.[163]

Growing up in a provincial town in Connecticut just after the Civil War, with few options for advancing his musical education then locally available, George had been fortunate to study with the organist and composer, Emile Gaebler, during his early years. By all accounts, Gaebler was a thorough musician and, as Feder described, as auspicious a teacher as one could have hoped to find in Danbury. George, later, was sent to New York to study music with Carl Foeppl, an émigré from Germany, of whom, unfortunately little has been documented. However, George's well-connected and well-heeled family would not have entrusted their son to a teacher coming with anything other than the highest recommendations, so it seems questionable to consider Foeppl's standing as less than at the top of his field. In view of the fact that George wished to pursue a livelihood far outside the societal norms of the day, it can only be assumed that his family would have done all in their power to help him succeed. Foeppl, therefore, must be taken seriously. Furthermore, because Foeppl would not have been likely to accept a less than adequately prepared student, it seems unreasonable, also, to underestimate George's musical education before this time.

If not possible, therefore, to discredit Foeppl, Magee, instead, dismissed the handwritten *lessons* George had taken from his studies with him in New York,

---

[161] Feder, *My Father's Song,"* 105–06.

[162] Ibid., 90.

[163] Ibid., 92.

terming them "copied" from an un-named, uninspired, text from twenty-five years earlier. The notes are, in fact, decidedly more colloquial and personal in style to have existed in any published volume. Feder, too, made the mistake of assuming the words were copied from an existing treatise. Below, transcribed directly off the page, just the opening sentences make it clear that what George wrote could not have been "copied" from any published Victorian text. Further disqualifying that theory, and, even, rendering them not remotely connected to any text of Foeppl, their casual fluidity hardly constitutes the words of a German immigrant likely still struggling with idiomatic and other linguistic issues. More particularly, no self-respecting editor would have allowed such 'off-the-cuff' prose into print:

> . . . are affected by combinations of sounds in which one or more notes appear that do not belong to the preceding key. These sounds may be harmonical notes as in the following examples. Or they may be passing notes, like the following. . . .

Actually, the words parallel the thoughtful, yet informal, writing style of one key surviving text—George's own teaching notes on music theory. The purpose for writing it might have been, as Carol Baron surmised, as one of several short teaching guides—otherwise unavailable and, perhaps in this instance, specifically for one person—Charles's friend at Yale, Garrison.[164] Certainly, by the early 1890s, George was confident in putting his ideas into writing. Ives, himself, remarked that he had "copies of some of his [George's] class talks"—likely, a direct reference to these pages.[165] The document's survival also serves to refute those individuals who maintain that George Ives had little musically substantive to share with his son.

Baron, as always, able to see where others have been blind, or deliberately obtuse, detailed the irrefutable evidence of an advanced, even predictive, musicianship, in George's ideas. He considered the existing musical notational system to be a compromise, which had evolved unevenly over centuries-past to accommodate the gradually expanding musical language—developed, by default, rather than for efficiency. George's essay is laid out in ways that make it clear he was well familiar with the state of music of the day, and the challenges that required solutions.

---

[164] Baron, "George Ives's Essay in Music Theory": 239–41. George Ives's lesson notes are preserved in The Charles Ives Papers at Yale University, MSS14.

[165] Ives, *Memos*, 45.

George's sophistication, hidden behind the easy-going, homespun manner of his essay, shows beyond any doubt his high level of musical awareness, especially the relationship of keys to tuning in the wake of Wagner's shifting chromaticism. George seemed to foretell things to come, as well as propose practical solutions; his understanding of the defining tones of keys, harmonic blends, as well as intervallic structure and spacing being keen.[166] Just as he recognized that 'tempered intonation' was in direct competition with 'just intonation,' George saw either as a compromise. Although the former solves the problems of tuning across multiple keys, as well as effectively blending tones within chords, it directly contradicts the natural aural instincts that create subtle differences of individually named pitches of any key. Thus, f# in G major is not the same pitch as g♭ in the key of E♭ minor, in which it appears slightly lower.

George's solution, therefore, did not rely wholly on accepted music theory, and included adjusting the notation by *listening*—unpredictable consequences requiring flexibility with the 'rules,' in which, for example, certain 'essential' tones might be omitted. He compared his approach to that of a painter, who develops the visual representations on the canvas by *looking* at the composites during the process of creating an artwork. These factors alone set him apart from the standard European 'guides' of music theory, offering a practical methodology for musical composition. Daring to stake his own ground by disagreeing in several respects with parts of the standard pedagogical texts—George offered alternatives, such as the equal treatment of all chromatic tones in numeric terms—unknowingly, thus, anticipating integer notation and a new era in music. It ought not to be surprising that his son incorporated some of these very tools in his own music (see Chapter 4). It is incumbent, too, upon us to accord greater weight to the veracity of Ives's words in relation to his father's musicianship and teaching. They will be found to be mutually supportive.

In this light, the now controversial letter from George Ives to Orrin Barnum comes to mind.[167] Charles, in paraphrasing a letter from George (famously lost) many years after the fact, in which he had discussed the need for music to experience growth and innovation, had unwittingly invited controversy. Carol Baron's worthy response (even) to John Kirkpatrick and others, who have posited and maintained that the 'letter' was largely the product of Charles's thought processes—rather than his father's—instead, however, points to its likely authenticity, *its content surely being outdated by the time Ives wrote of it, in full knowledge of the more recent*

---

[166] Baron, "George Ives's Essay in Music Theory": 238—88.

[167] Ives, *Memos*, 48.

advancements in music.[168] Moreover, Baron argued that the letter's larger perspective toward musical education in general contrasted with Ives's own usual commentary, in which his own experiences with Parker were usually imposed on everything—which is *not* the case here. Certain aspects of the letter seem to ring true with the tenor of George's essay, too, being fully in line with his questioning of the standard approach to musical tradition.

Excerpt from George Ives's study notes with Carl Foeppl

(Image courtesy of the Irving S. Gilmore Music Library, Yale University:
The Charles Ives Papers MSS14)

George Ives as a teacher

Ives, writing in *Memos*, emphasized that George's lessons had made their mark.[169] His understanding of harmony from George's perspective, versus relying on "the book," seems to be the clue—omitting critical tones, often the major or minor third

---

[168] Baron, "George Ives's Essay in Music Theory: 247–48. [ii] See, too, Baron, "At the Cutting Edge: Three American Theorists at The End of The Nineteenth Century," *International Journal of Musicology*, 2 (1993): 236–37, n.113.

[169] Ives, *Memos*, 42.

58

above the root—to the conjoining of chords in multiple keys. The ear was more likely to accept such polychords as being non-dissonant, because such strongly defining tones otherwise clashed by the interval of a semitone. In fact, polytonal combinations of this type often replicate extended chords of advanced harmony—and notably, jazz.[170]

Ives's recollections in *Memos* provide instances of his father's teaching and approach to theory that can be observed within his music. One must, of course, consider Ives's words objectively; recorded about four decades after the fact, as many observers have pointed out, likely, Ives was viewing his early years from an increasingly vague, or even glowing, vantage point. Nevertheless, to make the assumption, in the manner of Maynard Solomon,[171] that Ives was penning a largely fictional account of his life, or, more dismissively yet, that there is nothing of consequence in his recollections, is to miss the larger point. Much of what Ives discussed *is, indeed, reflected in his music*. Polytonal chords, for example, taken into the context of strictly monotonal compositions, can be made to function, too, within the dictates of conventional harmony. Well demonstrated in the Third Symphony, its harmony seems to echo polytonal compositions from the same time, most especially, the *Fugue in Four Keys on 'The Shining Shore'* (see Chapter 7). In fact, even most of Ives's more avant-garde works around this period dodge the specter of harmonic harshness by similar means.

Dissonance for its own sake?

In the years that followed, part of the complex maze of conflicting sonic layers in Ives's works also betrays his youthful sense that music had been made largely soft; in effect, it had become the domain of genteel society, something intended to be pleasant, sweet and soothing, its composers concerned with acceptance, and their music perceived as "nice," rather than expressing anything directly emanating from their deepest souls.[172]

At a time in which men made up most of the work force, the arts often existed within the domain of societies run by women of well-connected households. The stereotype was reinforced by the makeup of most musical organizations in America at the time, having been characteristically transferred into Danbury's society. As

---

[170] *Progressions* between polychords in Ives's work, however, remain entirely unconventional, being dictated solely by the judgment imparted by his ear.

[171] Maynard Solomon, "Charles Ives: Some Questions of Veracity," *Journal of the American Musicological Society*, 40, 3 (Autumn, 1987): 443–45.

[172] Ives, *Memos*, 130–31.

such, Ives perceived music typically as an emasculated art, despite the fact that men, and no less his own father, were the predominant creators and performers of music. Ives overlooked the fact that his own first teacher outside the home, Ella Hollister, was prominent among the society 'ladies' who organized musical activities in Danbury. For Ives, however, the term 'ladies' could have been applied to men *or* women, the social norm in the arts being at the focus of his contempt, rather than women, per se, whom Ives held in high regard.

To this end, Ives counterbalanced his intolerance of 'sissies' (a term that shows up with regularity in his writings), and any perception that he was less than masculine because of his pursuits in music, by building rugged soundscapes—and, even, too, in his youth, by his own participation in sports. Sports were seen by nineteenth century society as a masculine domain—primarily through the exploding passion for the new American pastime, baseball. However, in the author's opinion, Swafford's attribution of Ives's occasional 'profanity' and demonstratively 'manly' traits to the same source, were misplaced; Ives's crusty character was fundamental to his nature from the beginning, as witnessed by his youthful rebellious musical tendencies, as well as his sometimes cantankerous and quirky personality. Ives had inherited the very same characteristics from George.[173]

---

[173] Baron, "George Ives's Essay on Music Theory": 241. Baron found a direct correlation of personalities shared by father and son in 'the crustiness' she associated with New England.

Chapter 3

A World of Influences

Church Music, Camp Meetings, the 'Boston Six,'

Music Across the Ages, and Ragtime

*A*s the general dialog about Ives's musical background has devolved almost into a competition between George Ives and Horatio Parker—in recent years, at least—George has been the loser, while Parker has seen his star once again elevated in relation to the musical education of Charles Ives well beyond even what he might claim, in a complete reversal of 'The Legend.' Perhaps, however, it is possible for both figures to be on the winning end, as a result of what is demonstrable, or at least supportable, rather than just the product of agenda driven speculation or accusation. It will become increasingly evident, though, even during the times in which each of these figures was primarily responsible for guiding the young Ives through his musical training, that there were other powerful and parallel influences in play.

In relation to reacting to his surroundings, virtually everything Ives was exposed to would become part of his greater musical resource. Raised in a country, then, largely devoid of its own great art music figures, Ives was well aware of the national dependency upon immigrant populations to bring their culture of the old world with them. The inferiority felt by educated Americans for not having yet forged a worthy counterbalance to the arts in Europe was profound; in the mid-nineteenth century, not many Americans knew any music beyond the vernacular. In comparison, Ives's background was relatively sophisticated, having been exposed to Bach and contrapuntal literature from an early age, the piano music of the masters, vast quantities of organ literature, as well as organ transcriptions of orchestral works (for which it was well suited), vocal literature, even the symphonic music his father took him to hear in New York. However, his exposure to vernacular music was likely far broader than even its most ardent follower. Ives's long immersion in the hymns of church services and camp meetings, his extensive knowledge of organ literature, a lifelong exposure to countless band and dance tunes, Civil War and popular songs, and eventually, too, minstrel music and ragtime rendered Ives hardly musically naïve.

In practical terms, the organ surely was the young Ives's most significant source of music of the classics; the large volumes of repertoire he would have been required to learn and play weekly would have assured it. As the principal vehicle, too, through which most of the public would have been aware of any 'serious' music at all, it was perfectly positioned to assume the most prominent musical role in provincial towns and small cities. As such, by the mid-nineteenth century, a sizable 'crop' of organist-composers (including Dudley Buck, George Whitefield Chadwick, John Knowles Paine, George E. Whiting, and Whitney Eugene Thayer), had demonstrated that it was possible to build musical careers in America. Realizing that the incorporation of well-known tunes in large musical works was a means to find ready acceptance among less sophisticated audiences, these organ composers presented their works in church recitals—venues in which more of the public felt at ease—rather than 'high society' concert halls. As such, the larger churches in provincial towns were ideal settings—each with the added benefit of already having a built-in instrument. Successful musical formats popularized by these composer-performers included the tried-and-true showpieces: variations on well-known tunes, 'grand sonatas' and 'concert fantasias.' Works of the genre, typified by Buck's *Concert Variations on 'The Star-Spangled Banner,'* Op. 23 [1868], and *Grand Sonata in E Flat*, Op. 22 [1866]), Paine's *Concert Variations on the Austrian Hymn in F* [1860], and *Fantasie uber 'Ein' feste Burg,'* Op. 13 [c.1858–61]), and W. Eugene Thayer's *Variations on the Russian National Hymn*, Op. 12 [1875], found ready acclaim for these figures in venues outside the big cities.

Early in his composing career, despite his less than typical educational background under his musically inquisitive father, Charles Ives probably saw himself as another figure in the mold of his predecessors. Consequently, in 1891, as an organist and budding composer, Ives set about writing his own work of a genre already established by these figures. *Variations on 'America'* is a work that demonstrates not only the high level of writing skill he had attained, but also his virtuosic playing abilities, considered challenging even today. Regardless, the musical rebel already was in evidence with the inclusion of some polytonal interludes. Ives, thus, was revealed, even then, in the midst of conformity, as a musical radical—

direct evidence of George's experimental streak played out in his son's efforts. George, however, made his son take them out for its hoped-for publication, maintaining his view that such ideas had no place in actual works of music.[174] We must trust that Ives, however, replacing them into the variations some years later (they are penciled on the surviving manuscript), ensured they were accurate representations of the originals if more recent; as such, they are hardly wall flowers, their stark dissonance and brazen harshness making no allowance for genteel tastes of the day.

Daily life

The many festive occasions provided a means to alleviate the struggles of daily life, and grew from the culture of communal fellowship. Being, therefore, central to daily life in rural America, as a consequence, most of Ives's music contains at least an element of programmatic content centered on local customs—sometimes, much more than a minor part—even though he seldom 'spelled it out,' per se. These experiences are forged in distinctly personal ways, capturing the vivid dawn of the golden age in America, and Ives's determination that its people did not have to remain under Europe's shadow.

Ives's musical education in the years after leaving home in Danbury musical surely impacted his creativity and outlook. During his first year at Yale, outside his college classes, Ives took a series of private organ lessons with Dudley Buck during his freshman year, and later, it seems, from Harry Rowe Shelley. Lacking a true mentor in the wake of George Ives's untimely passing, Charles's hopes were dashed when he realized that Horatio Parker—unwilling to shed the somewhat aloof role of college authoritarian—was not able to act in that capacity. He found a sympathetic figure, at least, in John Cornelius Griggs, the choir director at Center Church on the Green in New Haven (where Ives would become organist), who acted in that capacity as much as he was able. Another, William Lyon Phelps, Ives's English professor, and whom Ives remembered with particular affection, was instrumental in guiding him through the classics of literature, a separate, but wholly related, part of his background.[175] Ives set many works from a wide variety of authors that likely reflect Phelps's influence. At the College Music Symposium of 1999, J. Peter Burkholder listed many poets—Shakespeare, John Milton, William Wordsworth, Walter Savage Landor, Lord Byron, Percy Bysshe Shelley, John Keats, Alfred Lord Tennyson, Robert Browning, Matthew Arnold, Robert Louis Stevenson, Rudyard Kipling,

---

[174] Ives, *Memos*, 38.

[175] It is curious that Phelps's great admiration of Parker's eloquence does not appear to have registered with Ives; perhaps, however, it did. See Kearns, *Horatio Parker*, 237.

Ralph Waldo Emerson, John Greenleaf Whittier, and Walt Whitman—among those whose works appear in his songs. Burkholder, too, suggested that Ives's works were inspired by literary figures, such as the *Robert Browning Overture* and the *Concord Sonata* (originally, which had its beginnings in works inspired by *Emerson, Hawthorne, The Alcotts* and *Thoreau*), likely a direct result of Ives's classes with Phelps.[176] Ives's college life is reflected in a number of compositions, some of which, regretfully, only exist now in fragments (e.g., *Take-Off No.7: Mike Donlin-Johnny Evers*, and *Take-Off No. 8: Willy Keeler at Bat*, although the surviving remnants of these examples have been joined one piece).[177] Works of this genre most often mentioned are *The Yale-Princeton Football Game* (1898–99), *Calcium Light Night* (1907), and the scherzo, *TSIAJ*, in the *Trio* (1904–11).

At Yale, however, Ives's teachers, though, were only part of the picture of great composer-unique character in the making; no doubt his devilish humor blossomed during his four years there. Surrounding himself with friends, Ives became a very popular figure at Yale, known for his good company and carefree spirits. Such attributes concealed his serious passions for music, which were not likely to be held in much regard by his contemporaries. Instead, Ives put his musical talents to work in light-hearted songs for social occasions on campus. Ives, however, with the exception of his musical studies and pursuits, was no more serious about his classes than his friends. The attitude apparently was all but mutually encouraged among students on campus, and Yale, being primarily a business oriented school, was not a place at which would-be composers went to study. It was only during Ives's years that the newly appointed dean of the School of Music, Horatio Parker, would embark on a decades-long agenda to build the music program to compete with the long established School of Music at Harvard. Thus, Yale was populated by the well-to-do, many of whom already had good connections for their future employment. Because most Yale undergraduates deliberately avoided academic excellence, low grades were considered a badge of honor. Social life on campus, especially attaining membership in one of the famous so-called 'secret societies,' was a higher priority. Ives was all too eager to share in the tradition, no doubt due, at least in part, to his desire to be accepted by his peers; in effect, they became his family. Ives would continue to find emotional shelter living in the New York 'digs' among the company of Yale graduates for ten years after he, himself, had graduated.

---

[176] J. Peter Burkholder, College Music Symposium, "Ives and Yale: The Enduring Influence of a College Experience," online, *Scholarship and Research*, 39, (October, 1999).

[177] Sinclair, *A Descriptive Catalogue of The Music of Charles Ives*, 151–52.

Ives's subsequent relocation to New York was accompanied by a brief tenure as organist and choirmaster at Old First Presbyterian Church, Bloomfield, New Jersey, a relatively short commute from Manhattan. Although he held the post from May 1, 1898 to May 1, 1900, details about his professional activities there are in short supply. Other than merely mentioning that Ives held the job in most texts, the Historical Society of Bloomfield, NJ, recorded just about all that is known:

> Old church calendars convey information that Ives led a song service the third Sunday of each month. There are several references to a 'Psalmist Hymnal,' which may have been made up of his own settings of the Bible. On November 5, 1898, the choir canticle was *The Light That Is Felt*. . . from a poem by Whittier. Another Ives vocal work, 'Country Celestial' [sic.] was sung by a tenor on July 31, 1899[178] . . . . When he played at 'Old First,' the organ works he used, according to programs, were written by Bach, Beethoven, Schubert, and Gounod, to name a few.

These comments, however, seem to pose more questions than answers, although they also offer some welcome clarifications; significantly, Ives's own accounts about the origins of his compositions is not only born out, but further reinforced. Was the "Psalmist Hymnal," perhaps, the collection of Psalm settings Ives had already written before (and, perhaps, even during) his years at Yale? Ives referred in *Memos* to "church anthems and to psalms, that Father let me work over—and some he tried in the choirs but had a hard time. The 150th Psalm was one—part of the 90th—and the 67th." In a later annotation Ives mentioned the "54th, and 24th also?"[179] With little else to link the title to, the prospect remains enticing, nevertheless, especially because nothing of record points to any other lost compositions that seem to fit this description. Does not, also, the date of the performance of *The Light That is Felt* contradict even Kirkpatrick, who considered that it belonged to 1899? The excerpt from *The Celestial Country* (presumably, No. 6, aria for Tenor) also offers a significant marker, and demonstrates that Ives had tried out segments prior to its full premiere in 1902; due to its placement late in the work, it seems to confirm the cantata was wholly complete just as Ives recorded on his work lists.

---

[178] Marguerite M. Elliott, "Charles Ives in Bloomfield: Organist at 'Old First.'" *The Town Crier*: Official Newsletter—The Historical Society of Bloomfield (Bloomfield, NJ) 1, 5 (January 1970), 2.

[179] Ives, *Memos*, 47.

Ives's New England Heritage: Church and Camp Meetings

Clearly, Ives was well familiar with the music of the more prominent domestic art music composers long before he attended Yale. These figures included, in particular, the populist organist-composer, Dudley Buck, whom Ives admired greatly. Buck's music was especially successful in introducing a higher level of music to unsophisticated (church) audiences than previously they would have encountered. Most, in nineteenth century rural America, would never have heard music other than in religious and festive settings—essentially only secular tunes and hymns. Buck's contributions typically feature within their thoroughly schooled foundation a hybrid of popular idioms and, notably, the incorporations of barbershop harmonies. The latter element, for which Buck is, perhaps, most often associated, cannot be overestimated, though his larger musical accomplishments reflect his carefully judged expertise, rather than any lack, thereof. If his music sounds dated today, it is only because musical awareness in America has grown so greatly in the last century-and-a-half, its presence at the forefront of new directions now long established.

The 'Boston Six,' on the other hand, wrote music intended for a higher level of audience sophistication, however. These composers, and who comprised the totality of the more formally-known 'Second New England School,' were cut from a different social cloth, and likely never attempted to reach Buck's audiences. The music of Horatio Parker, as one of the 'Six,' and as an organist (judging by the quantities written for organ music), probably was familiar to Ives even before studying with him at Yale. The other five figures rounding out the group, George Whitefield Chadwick, John Knowles Paine, Edward MacDowell, Amy Beach, and Arthur Foote, aside from their organ compositions, were variously responsible for composing symphonies, cantatas, and other large-scale compositions, as well as volumes of chamber music and songs.[180]

With the exception of Beach (who had been a major concert pianist), a critical part of the their shared common backgrounds was that they were all organists, meaning all had been exposed to much the same religious music as had the young Ives, including the works of Bach (religious music in its highest incarnation and common fare for organists), and large quantities of transcriptions of secular music of the European masters. Ives surely had many opportunities to hear the music by most of these composers, as carefully evaluated and noted by Nicholas E. Tawa.[181]

---

[180] Nicholas E. Tawa, "Ives and the New England School," in *Charles Ives and the Classical Tradition*, ed. Geoffrey Block & J. Peter Burkholder (New Haven, CT: Yale University Press, 1996), 62–63.

[181] Tawa, "Ives and the New England School," 57–58.

Of the 'Boston Six,' Chadwick, in particular, shared with Ives one attribute—holding an enthusiasm for utilizing the more uplifting elements of American vernacular music. Often pervading the musical character of his music, the sunny melodiousness is immediately striking, and perhaps the closest to establishing a national identity even before Ives's provocative music arrived upon the scene. Tawa noted, too, the strong influence of pentatonic elements in Ives's and Chadwick's work.[182] He did not appear to weigh, however, the likely influence of such characteristics found in Native American music, nor Ives's awareness of it, and which can be found in such works as his song, *The Indians*, of 1912. If Chadwick did not quote any particular vernacular melody, their intervals and simple harmonies—and echoed in the vernacular tunes of other cultures—might just explain, at least in part, the curious suggestion of Dvořák in his work.

If Ives's early-Yale and post-Yale works, even those of Chadwick, appear to reflect elements of Dvořák's melodic style, probably, however, it as much to do with those common vernacular roots shared with the other New England composers, rather than any attempt to subscribe to the latter's admonition that Americans model their music according to his dictates. In view of the fact that Chadwick's style substantially precedes Dvořák's 'American phase,' and indeed, there is little relationship between both Chadwick's and Ives's approach to orchestral writing, being far more intricate and varied than the more directly, even simply, conceived 'Americanism' of Dvořák. Clearly, any possible influence was the other way around.

However, the more direct influence of Antonin Dvořák, as one of the most prominent European composers, cannot be excluded either, as it makes sense that Chadwick might have deliberately modeled some of his writing style on the composers he admired. Dvořák's presence as Director of the National Conservatory of Music in New York City from 1892–95, at the height of his fame, further solidifies the argument, because he was clearly very popular in America. Moreover, it is hard to imagine anyone with serious aspirations in music who could not have been aware of him, nor the sound that is associated with two of his most important compositions written at the time: the *New World Symphony* (Symphony No.9, Op.95) and the *American String Quartet*, (Quartet No.12, Op.96). Both works were finished in 1893, and highly successful at the time (coinciding, too, with the composition of Horatio Parker's best known work, *Hora Novissima*, and Ives's admission to Hopkins Grammar School in New Haven). Dvořák, notably, had incorporated negro melodic elements in these works in order to impart an American character to the music; the

---

[182] Tawa, "Ives and the New England School," 70–71.

idea struck a discord with many Americans, Ives, among them, who considered any form of contrived nationalism to be wholly inauthentic, especially when advocated by a foreign national as a model for domestic figures to follow in their own music.[183] Artificial or not, the 'Americanism' of these works by a master composer is telling, nevertheless, sharing an idiomatic similarity heard clearly in Chadwick's music, and sometimes Parker's, too. Could the fact that both composers had received prizes from the National Conservatory under Dvořák's tenure (and influence) have played a role? (Parker also had taught there for a year before relocating to Boston in 1893.)

In Ives's case, other factors in the striking 'Americanism' of his music included his lack of opportunity to study in Europe.[184] As 'the thing to do,' most of his contemporaries and predecessors had done so, and likely, Ives felt a sense of inferiority on a social level among musicians. No doubt, it impacted his search for individually and originality. Byron R. Simms theorized that Ives's keen awareness of the perceived educational advantage of music studies abroad caused him to compose a group of 'German' songs; in some respects, therefore, they could have acted as compensation for what he might have been a lack of sophistication in others' eyes.[185] Although the long held position has been that Parker required him to write songs modeled on European standards as part of his course work, Simms concluded that both John Kirkpatrick and H. Wiley Hitchcock had been entirely incorrect in their assessments. Even in *Memos*, the brief outline of Parker's curriculum that Kirkpatrick included makes no mention of study via the process of imitating this variety of music.[186] Not only does the absence of reference to such requirements in Parker's course materials stand out,[187] but also the void of similar examples in the student works of other noted figures who attended Yale and taught by Parker!

The task, therefore, of composing the series of 'German' songs appears to have been entirely self-directed by Ives. The fact that he continued to write them *after* his time at Yale, however, further indicates that he considered them important to the outward perception he was thoroughly schooled in traditional composition. As a

---

[183] With George's disparagement of what he considered flawed and dated German methodology [see again, Chapter 1, Baron, discussion of "George Ives's Essay in Music Theory"], one can only imagine his son's reaction to Dvořák's own 'glib' imposition of American-inspired melodic structures upon an archaic German-centric methodology!

[184] Tawa, "Ives and the New England School," 68.

[185] Bryan R. Simms, "The German Apprenticeship of Charles Ives," *American Music*, 29, 2 (Summer, 2011): 139–67. In relation to his conclusion, see 156.

[186] Ives, *Memos*, 182–83.

[187] Horatio Parker Papers, Irving S. Gilmore Music Library, Yale University, Boxes 32–34.

consequence, too, perhaps, he retained an affection for the genre, and might have even thought he could improve upon it! Not coincidentally, other works by Ives in the European mold, including the first two symphonies, the cantata, *The Celestial Country*, and the First String Quartet, seem closely related to the genre, too. Notably, however, Ives ceased to compose 'German' songs after 1902, which was the year he "quit music." It was the year, also, that delineates the time in which Ives began to escalate and accelerate his more extreme ideas—despite experiencing a composing 'slump'—although, as the record throughout his time at Yale demonstrates, they had never been entirely put away.

As Ives moved ahead, his close ties to European models gradually faded from his works, too, even as he never completely detached himself from them—something since 'discovered,' and seeming oddly surprising. Perhaps most noticeable, too, was Ives's breaking from the frequent adherence by the 'Boston Six' to various types of substantive choral works—such as the cantata—that had become almost a default mode of musical expression in America at the time. This fashionable trend would retain a high profile with audiences in the New World until waning following World War I. After the "failure" of *The Celestial Country*, Ives would stand almost alone from that tradition, instead indulging in many modernistic works for unconventional groups of instruments, including symphonies, sonatas, and string quartets, all of which preserved something of the implied essence of those long established formats, if not the musical forms themselves. Concluding his observations, Simms also recognized that the dates newly assigned to Ives's songs are mostly too late in the timeline, which *does* concur with the writer's assessment of the new 're-dating' protocol, and consequently, one can presume, thus, in relation to the dates of all the works in Ives's entire catalog.[188]

With *From the Steeples and the Mountains*, in 1901, even the song, *The Children's Hour*—before Ives had made his final life-changing professional commitment that music remain an avocation, not a profession—he had already 'tested the waters' by charting new musical directions, leaving behind some of the restraints of traditional composing that had so shacked his predecessors to the dominant European musical giants. Ives would articulate later that such independent adventurism in music was prevented by well-honed tradition, even in the greatest *European* composers' work, as a result of their need for achieving the approval of their audiences, or else, face starvation from rejection.[189] Soon after, even in some of his relatively less progressive early works, such as *Thanksgiving* and the Third

---

[188] Simms, "The German Apprenticeship of Charles Ives": 165–66.

[189] Ives, *Memos*, 30.

Symphony (both essentially sketched in 1904), Ives would venture bravely into musical orbits that no audience of the time would have accepted. Nevertheless, something of the European methodology and stylistic demands, as seen in his 'German' songs, was carried forward even into these new musical avenues. The retained attributes can be seen in many later songs, most of them displaying the foundations of solidly laid traditional craftsmanship, from theoretical standpoints as well as for performers, despite the extreme modernity of their writing. In this respect, Ives seldom abandoned many of the traditional approaches to writing, including the long established qualities of proper voice leading and balance.

Ragtime

Ragtime—which found itself so powerfully received by Ives's rhythmic instincts that it was destined to weave into one of the dominant components of his compositional fabric—warrants a much larger place in the discussion than usually accorded it. Closely related to the earlier popular cakewalk idiom, by the 1890s, ragtime finally had become 'all the rage.' It seized Charles Ives's imagination during his Yale years in New Haven, as he recalled the effect that George Felsberg, the wild pianist at the local Poli's Theater, had made upon him, its metric bass line accenting strong beats, and off-beats carrying the harmonizing chords, usually, which are triads. The bass line ('stride'), the characteristically steady accompanying backdrop, thus—partly derived from the long established all-familiar march form—contrasts against the ragged ('ragged') contours and syncopations of the melodic lines above. It is hardly surprising that Ives would have identified with the magnetic impetus of the sound when he heard it.

Before Ragtime even existed as a term, Ives remarked upon the syncopated variants of hymn tunes that African-American congregants sang at camp meetings.[190] After the Civil War, an African-American boy whom George brought home with him was sufficiently captivated by the sound of George's band that often, he would sing along with it. However, George noted that the boy often would omit the fourth or seventh degrees of the scale in his versions of the melodies—tones that define the pentatonic scale—and, of which, Charles was well aware. Coincidentally, these tones are often missing in Ragtime tunes, too, although the seventh is frequently is 'replaced' by the sixth. Ives remarked, too, upon the typical shifting of rhythmic

---

[190] Ives, *Memos*, 53.

70

emphasis (from the first to the last beat of each bar) that he heard replicated many years later in a saloon in New York.[191]

Ives's exposure to the form might precede Gayle Sherwood Magee's account, however, in which she traced it, virtually in totality, to the Columbia Exposition of 1892 in Chicago.[192] It has been speculated that Ives might have heard Joplin at the exposition, because he, too, is known to have been in attendance there.[193] Although likely Ives did hear full-blown Ragtime for the first time there, in *Memos*, he traced some of its roots back even to "the old brass-band days," in which the musicians indulged in "swinging" and other forms of rhythmic displacement. He even quoted a fragment of a minstrel song (*I'm alivin' easy*) he had heard, also in 1892, in which its rhythm is decidedly 'ragged.' Ives considered that ragtime was a broad expansion of a number of similar trains of thought.[194] No less indicative of the evolution of ragtime, Ives also remembered hearing in Danbury some black-faced comedians in 1892 "ragging" their songs in the same rhythmic way, long ahead of its use in jazz.

Such defining rhythmic features connect, thus, the longer established minstrel music to the same formative roots, a type of popular music with which one can be sure Ives already was well familiar from an early age.[195] Because George had traveled on tour six times in as many years with a legitimate black minstrel group (Lou Fenn's Alabama Minstrels), it seems clear that the style would have been more than familiar to him. It is tempting to contemplate the strong possibility he had been exposed to Ragtime, too, especially in light of the fact that the term itself only would appear at the end of the nineteenth century. Likely, thus, it is conceivable that it was known only to his son, and not so surprising George had not remarked upon the idiom.

---

[191] Ives, *Memos*, 54.

[192] Magee, *Charles Ives Reconsidered*, 29.

[193] It is worth noting that Joplin, however, was not yet a big star, nor would he have been a featured performer in any capacity. He would have to wait until after 1899 when he became iconic for penning the *Maple Leaf Rag*.

[194] Ives, *Memos*, 56–7.

[195] Minstrel music does not have a particularly proud history. A racist entertainment format popular within white society prior to the Civil War, minstrel shows consisted of musical skits in which white performers in 'blackface; typically depicted African Americans in a bad light— slovenly, lazy, slow-witted, even clown like, foolish and simple. Although many black musicians performed in their own minstrel shows (which featured the authentic minstrel music that Ives knew and referenced), the predominant minstrel shows were staged by white people, who claimed to understand black musical culture. The degree to which their musical depictions were accurate remains highly questionable, although it is considered that the awareness of a different culture might have contributed to a future more balanced societal perspective.

The prominence of Ragtime within Ives's musical psyche cannot be understated; it shows up with remarkable regularity even in many of his most mature compositions. For the most part, however, one should not expect to find it occupying a larger share of the fabric than a portion, even when it survives as just a rhythmic skeleton of something far larger. In *Essays Before a Sonata*, Ives weighed in about its role, writing, "Someone is quoted as saying that 'ragtime is the true American music. . . . It is an idiom, perhaps a set or series of colloquialisms. . . . Ragtime has its possibilities. But it does not 'represent the American nation' any more than some fine old senators represent it."[196]

Louis Moreau Gottschalk (1829–69)

The precise mechanism by which Ragtime evolved, nevertheless, is hard to pinpoint, although surely it was the result of cross-pollination across multiple, often related genres. Pianist-composer Louis Moreau Gottschalk is generally considered to be the first to notate something of the characteristic rhythmic style that was emerging, soon to dominate the new popular idiom. Kirkpatrick discussed the development of the "syncopated style of . . . Gottschalk" into "the refined rags of Scott Joplin."[197] Gottschalk's elaborate virtuoso works cut a curious musical swath that was immensely popular in his day: a kind of Chopin and Liszt hybrid, often directly infusing old plantation tunes with Cuban syncopations and the traditional march 'stride' (bass tones on beats, diatonic triads on off-beats) into dazzling displays of technical and devil-may-care virtuosity. Gottschalk can lay claim legitimately to be the first composer to anticipate Ragtime, even, therefore, the composer who paved the road to jazz. Clearly he was a direct influence upon pianist George Felsberg, who, in turn, with his wild and 'phantasmogorical' Ragtime performances at Poli's Theater, had so profoundly influenced Ives during his Yale days.

Gottschalk, in merging 'popular' and 'art' music, ultimately led to the direct fusion of any of what were considered previously irreconcilable idioms—one of the hallmarks of American musical expression, however—perhaps, best exemplified in the twentieth century music of George Gershwin. The essence of Gottschalk's 'model' sometimes is echoed even in Ives's own work, Ives's own propensity to mix and match whatever suited his ideas being entirely typical. The striking absence, however, of references by either George or Charles Ives to Gottschalk is somewhat surprising, however. Surely, George, at very least, was well familiar with him.

---

[196] Charles E. Ives, *Essays Before a Sonata* (New York: Knickerbocker Press, 1921), 113–14.

[197] Ives, *Memos*, 39, n.1.

Regardless, the fact that any reference to Gottschalk is absent in all of Ives's commentaries is curious. If he not heard Gottschalk in concert somewhere, how could he have missed the quantities of printed sheet music by a personality, who, at the time of the Civil War, was an established icon, and America's best-known pianist-composer abroad? It seems no less strange that Ives would not have recognized the connections between Gottschalk's music and what he heard at the Columbian Exposition, or New Haven, even later in New York, because, most certainly, he was as musically aware as anyone during the entire rise and fall of Ragtime.[198]

One of the earliest—even, perhaps, the first—example of written music that is strongly suggestive of Ragtime appeared in Gottschalk's *La Gallina* of 1859. From the outset, its identifying stamps, and the characteristic features directly inherited from Cuban sources, appear in fast, syncopated shifts of the strong beats in the melodic line. The characteristic march 'stride' is present, too, although not at the same time, although, accompanying the 'stride' a form of syncopation is present (as would be typical in Ragtime), albeit slower, and less 'swung.' In a premonition of things to come, the Ragtime idiom seems *almost* formed; it is eerily close.

Almost as striking in its anticipation of Ragtime is Gottschalk's *Bamboula*. Written much earlier in his tragically short life, its frenetically feverish bravura is the product of a bout with typhoid he experienced during its composition in 1844–45. Directly quoting two Creole tunes, *Musieu Bainjo* and *Quan' patate la cuite*, the links to the future are less clear on the page, but immediately evident upon the most casual listening. The march-like 'stride' pacing appears in the lower line in near consistency throughout, and one can easily imagine an upper line 'ragged' rather than played with the straight rhythms on the page. However, the classic syncopated fast Ragtime rhythms do appear at times, such as at mm.54–55, so the die already was cast, even if not yet wholly coalesced.

Ives's Incorporations of Ragtime

Although Ives never wrote pure Ragtime in the commonly accepted sense of the term, his compositions were deeply affected by it; some even were wholly based upon it (e.g., *Four Ragtime Dances* [1899–1902]). Countless printed examples from Ragtime's ascent (containing for the purchaser most of the notes, if not the necessary interpretive finesse required to create Ragtime, itself) were produced in the 1890s. Its pronounced rhythmic character will be found infused even into many of Ives's most adventurously atonal explorations. Suddenly, the impact of expanding a simpler idea into astounding works of musical narrative immediately harks back to George

---

[198] Ives, *Memos*, 56–7.

Felsberg. Surely reflecting the impact of Ives's own listening experience, it can be nothing else. In Ives's works, the idiom often is intense, although, on the page, the notes might appear to work in defiance of it. Remarkably, no matter how extreme the complexity and modernism, Ives's incorporations of the idiom ring through precisely in line with its character. The result is achieved largely through his absorption of accented fast syncopations that shift forward the critical points of natural melodic rhythm—especially in what might have been, otherwise, merely heavy-footed, even-paced inflections.

Nevertheless, the regularly paced march-derived 'stride' that characterizes so much of the left hand notation in this style of piano writing is not necessarily more than partially present in Ives's Ragtime inspired compositions. Altogether too constricting, Ives was able to capture the heart of its easy 'stride' by larger rhythmic implications alone, making occasional use of strategically placed true 'stride' passages, too, only when the context demanded it. For instance, in segments in which the right hand writing features extremely complex rhythms, something resembling 'stride' is more likely to accompany it—although, however, seldom does it bear much resemblance to Ragtime's well-known metric pattern that leans toward on-beat bass tones, and off-beat triads.

Although likely to be found almost anywhere in Ives's output, unsurprisingly, Felsberg's influence, perhaps, is most apparent in Ives's piano music. With the rhythmic intricacies now stretched to a maximum, Ives's Ragtime inspired works surely leave little doubt who was the major influence in this part of his musical makeup. It seems further confirmed, because only after Ives's New Haven experiences do we see the incorporation of the idiom. Indeed, there is nothing for piano, whatsoever, in Parker's hand that bears any resemblance to the musical style of Ives's own pianistic writing, once he had encountered Felsberg. However, the diversity of compositional technique demonstrated along with Ives's incorporations of the idiom reflect countless other influences from the totality of his innate musicality, background, attitude and training.

Rhythmically, rhapsodic and free, Ives's piano writing possesses a wildly improvisatory element totally absent in Parker's more conservative, restrained—albeit, square—piano compositions. And because Parker was primarily an organist, whereas Ives was expert on both the piano *and* organ, such attributes would not necessarily be expected. However, at no time did Parker ever exhibit similar 'flights of the imagination' as found sometimes even in Ives's organ writing—long before he encountered Felsberg—such as in the noteworthy *Variations on 'America'* of 1891. It can only be assumed that the potential was the triggered years later at Poli's Theater.

It should not to be construed, however, that nothing of Parker's craftsmanly organization and studied musicality can be detected in Ives's keyboard writing, although Ives intimately knew popular genres long before he attended Yale. He continued to learn, nevertheless, the composers' craft for many years, and surely benefitted, in respect to artistic range, from Parker's music literature courses, too. In his classes, during the days before recorded music was available, Parker relished the role of performer in demonstrating the music of multitudes of composers, from which Ives, surely, drew further ideas of the possibilities for the instrument.

Ives's employment of vernacular materials and idioms in his work was entirely natural to him; he was situated ideally in semi-rural Post-Civil War America to be open to all that he heard, well-positioned to harbor no preconceived 'high-society' notions about what forms 'art' music should, or should not, take; Ives was free of the burden of societal affectation. Because no composer of his generation ever would have considered trying to meld 'lowly' elements of popular music with, and into, 'high' art, Ives's special circumstances point unambiguously to what enabled his unique and original creativity. It was a mode of expression that, wholly necessary to its relevance in the larger Western musical tradition, still remained firmly ensconced in it, in spite of 'shuffling' the components of its makeup.[199]

The Spell of the Ancients

J. Peter Burkholder identified the process of expansion of all composers' musical horizons by their absorption of what preceded them in "Ives and the Four Musical Traditions" (sub-heading, "The European Model"),[200] although he did not expand the timeline as far back as did Ann Besser Scott in her article, "Medieval and Renaissance Techniques in the Music of Charles Ives: Horatio at the Bridge?".[201] Examining innovations and techniques of other composers from the past that had played a role in influencing Ives's own ideas, Scott contemplated how Parker's music literature class might have introduced Ives to some of them. Ives's incorporations of them into his work, versus those of Parker himself, for whatever reason, point conspicuously to the mysterious workings of creative genius. Of course, to connect all music in Western culture to everything in its long history of development is eminently reasonable. Ives, as an American, was no less a part of it than any other figure,

---

[199] Ives, *Memos*, 53–54.

[200] J. Peter Burkholder, "Ives and the Four Musical Traditions," in *Charles Ives and his World*, (Princeton, NJ, Princeton University Press, 1996), 3–23.

[201] Ann Besser Scott, "Medieval and Renaissance Techniques in the Music of Charles Ives: Horatio at the Bridge?", *The Musical Quarterly*, 78, 3 (Autumn 1994): 448–78.

although Western art across the Atlantic was pre-destined by its very surroundings and circumstances to evolve in different ways. Ives was at the forefront of its evolution by way of his own eminently different surroundings and circumstances. It is entirely reasonable, too, to assume that Parker had played at least some part, no matter to what degree, in Ives's musical choices.

Scott's compelling, if circumstantial, case did not appear, however, to recognize that Ives's earlier background was no less likely to have included some exposure to music from far earlier times; notably, it featured some of the elements that typify his writing style long before his studies with Parker. In regard to works written during and after Ives's Yale studies, one can only conjecture the nature and circumstances of what led to the techniques he incorporated within them. Specifically, though, Scott noted the compounding of multiple musical components as many of his pieces reach their apex (Scott cited the concluding segment of the last movement of Ives's First String Quartet), as well as Ives's *early* incorporation of the technique (in the Second Symphony) that reflects a practice found in ancient motets.

Scott also noted similarities and parallels to *fauxbourdon* and *organum* appearing in Ives's new chord structures (in his use of quartal and quintal harmonies). In *Memos*, however, Ives credited his father with the idea of both chordal forms in relation to the intervals themselves, rather than their employment in parallel motion, such as the fauxbourdon-like harmonies of *Central Park in the Dark* (c.1906), and in which, another ancient technique appears: ostinato. Although determining the circumstances that actually influenced Ives's adoption of any pre-existing technique depends partly upon one's bias,[202] one only has to look to some of the music of Erik Satie (e.g., *Le Fils Des Étoiles* [c.1896]: Prelude de 1er Acte), to find virtually the same thing as in Ives's *Central Park in the Dark*, at least, in regard to fauxbourdon harmony in unconventional intervals. Scott cited Ives's utilizations of cantus firmus, too (e.g., the second movement of the Third Symphony featuring the hymn *Naomi* set as a cantus firmus against the primary material based on *There is a Fountain*), a technique found also in music as far back as the medieval period. Regardless, Ives's innovations surely reflect multiple inputs, which include both George Ives and Horatio Parker among them.

Proposing another potential link to ancient times is Ives's layering of *multiple* separate elements (a technique found readily in early music), Scott thought it might also have emanated from Ives's Yale years. One such usage occurs in the first movement of Ives's *Trio*, within a framework of 'successive composition,' in which four separate and independent lines ultimately combine as a whole. Ives's early usage

---

[202] Ives, *Memos*, 140.

of 'successive composition' also can be found in the *Three Harvest Home Chorales*, in which the second, 'Lord of the Harvest,' establishes three layers over the course of its duration, the third of which is set in two parts of varying intervallic makeup that finally fractures into four separate components at the initial climactic point. However, the technique use was far from unknown, and appears in music that might have been known to Ives long before he entered Yale. Wagner used the technique to great effect often, such as toward the conclusion of the Overture to *Die Meistersinger*. The fact, however, that Ives's father, George, was known to have been an avid admirer of Wagner's music also makes it equally possible that he had encountered successive composition early on.

Scott noted that the kinds of rapid and sometimes extreme shifts of melodic character (stylistic heterogeneity) often found in Ives's music can be found in many other musical formats, especially the madrigals of Gesualdo, in particular. If it cannot be denied that the principle long had existed in music—as had spatial entities, even microtones, too—what caused Ives to resurrect all these ideas and develop them in ways unique to him will, likely, never be known. The prospect, however, that it was a direct byproduct of having to find early comfort with less than familiar musical elements might be as likely a clue as any, having been instilled through George's penchant for assigning exercises that required the singing of melodies in one key while accompanying in another, not to mention his father's well-known musical curiosity and penchant for experimentation.[203]

Further examining Parker's course materials, and seeing the attention given to early music, Scott concluded that Ives gained significantly more from his time with Parker than he was prepared to acknowledge. The fact that Ives was reluctant to credit Parker as the most significant figure in his musical development is well known. But does that reality necessarily make Ives less than generous to Parker, or Scott's conclusions inevitable? In relation to early music and the musical education he had received from his George, Ives, himself, remarked that his father had admired the music of Monteverdi greatly.[204] Is it not therefore reasonable to presume that he had shared Monteverdi's music with his son? Although Monteverdi, as a sixteenth and seventeenth century composer, appeared at the tail end of the age of the motet, he was prolific in composing madrigals. *Ives's link, therefore to earlier musical forms and traditions surely remained strong, even as he sought to shift music to newer*

---

[203] Swafford, *A Life With Music*, 54.

[204] Tom C. Owens, *Selected Correspondence of Charles Ives* (Berkeley, CA: University of California Press, 2007), 70. Also, the files in the New York Public Library indicate there is an edition of music by Monteverdi that was donated by Charles Ives.

ground. As such, George could not have been oblivious to what had preceded Monteverdi, too, even if he knew little about it. Why would Ives have related—in a private correspondence, no less—George's affinity to this particular composer had it not had a basis in reality?

On another front, Scott demonstrated that the practice of borrowing can be traced as far back as, even, medieval times. And certainly, Burkholder's view that many of Ives's works are built upon a foundation of such sources, as referenced by Scott, still needs to be more closely examined. As a primary hypothesis that Ives's used quoted materials as a basis of much of his music, cannot be sustained, as previously detailed, their presence typically being anecdotal, not structural. In that borrowing can be found in the music of countless figures throughout the history of Western music, it is likely, therefore, that Ives had long encountered the practice. Having no reluctance to participate in it, vernacular tunes appear in his youthful compositions (e.g., *March No. 3, with 'My Old Kentucky Home'*), so Parker cannot be accorded the influence, by default, beyond reinforcement of Ives's general awareness of the practice. Perhaps more interesting is that—unlike the usage of existing melodies in other music—exactly what caused Ives to place borrowed melodies almost wholly independent of their musical surroundings is harder to determine.

In relation to the *stylistic* heterogeneity noted in Scott's article, and found—for instance, in sixteenth century practice, in which madrigals pitted startlingly different musical features against one another from phrase to phrase—in Ives's compositions, perhaps these ideas owed their roots, instead, to George Ives's humble 'Humanophone.'[205] With their potential of achieving more than just large leaps between pitches—e.g., different dynamics from note-to-note, rapidly changing rhythms—and, no less, the prospect for altering any musical parameter instantly, the 'Humanophone,' thus might have played a greater role than anyone has considered. And even though the practice stacking of separate entities in thirteenth century motets possibly could have been behind Ives's polyphony, the polyphonic nature of much organ music, perhaps, affected it far more directly, as a direct consequence of Ives's performing expertise and range of repertoire. Moreover, Ives's use of pentatonic intervals in his melodies surely was influenced mostly by his daily exposure to exposure to folk and popular tunes, even the religious music of the region—to say nothing his awareness of the serious compositions of 'local' composers, such as Chadwick, Paine, and perhaps, even Parker (!). All of these varieties of music would have instilled pentatonic melodic structure in Ives's psyche long before he attended

---

[205] Ives, *Memos*, 142.

78

Yale. It would seem that Parker's teaching of the classical links to folk music in traditional Scottish, Irish tunes—many of which had been imported and modified in the local idiom of New England—likely had little impact, because Ives had been no stranger to them from childhood.

Regardless, one must weigh all considerations in attempting to trace the vast amalgam of influences in Ives's music that suddenly emerged as something new. However, one must also accept that, even with the most diligent of searches, not all things can be known with the clear delineations that a forensic scientist might hope to be able to establish definitively. With many figures in recent scholarship relentlessly attempting to explain the unexplainable in Ives's music—perhaps, more than with that of any other composer—one must beware of over-indulging such efforts to quantify, in tangible terms, all that constitutes genius and originality. Some of the deepest workings of great creative minds never can be explained or properly understood.

The Timeline

Ives's music is hard to place in a neat order and to categorize into periods and styles; with its multiple methodologies unevenly applied, materials often redeveloped from other works over spans of many years, and sometimes confusing timelines of their evolution, the listener can be sure that a clear path to his compositional designs will remain always diffusely convoluted. As the countless twists and turns, junctions, reversals and sharp corners that characterize its makeup have allowed all manner of interpretations and agendas to slip by (often unchallenged), Ives's musical journey has been recounted according to many an individual's whim.

However, taking the original premise developed by Carol K. Baron,[206] the writer already has demonstrated that Ives's finished (or virtually so) compositions, indeed, can be accurately dated—in spite of the many irregularities—and, that his recollections of their place in the timeline are largely accurate. Ives's own work lists, having been scrutinized by John Kirkpatrick, are meticulously documented in his (Kirkpatrick's) catalogue, thus, appear to be accurate to within a couple of years, or so.[207] We might, however, attempt to list a number of hypothetical periods, in which some evolutionary steps can, indeed, be isolated:

---

[206] Baron, "Dating Charles Ives's Music: 20–56.

[207] Kirkpatrick, *A Temporary Mimeographed Catalog.*

- **1874–94**

  Commencing his studies at an early age under his father, (George Ives), Charles Ives received the most important parts of the foundation for all that he would do in music. His early compositions feature two distinct writing styles, actual attempts at creating substantive works, and those designed for festive, public events. Of the latter, largely traditional, such as *Holiday Quickstep* (1887), and *Canzonetta* (1893), both for organ (1892), *Postlude in F* for orchestra (1892), and several youthful marches (2–4) for orchestra (c.1892), these youthful excursions are straightforward to navigate. Of the former, works with a more serious purpose are more innovative and harmonically adventurous, often including ideas that George Ives encouraged or prescribed as exercises (even as he carefully monitored what would be presented to the public). These works are typified by their striking daring. Examples are *Variations on 'America'*; *Psalm 67* for chorus (c.1894); and *Nine Canticle Phrases* (1894).

- **1894–1898**

  Ives's Yale years under Horatio Parker were responsible for the necessary more disciplined organization to become a productive composer of large concert works. Although works, such as the First Symphony, First String Quartet and countless songs, poured forth in a largely traditional style (including the initial examples of the eighteen 'German' songs), Ives also was working independently on other, considerably less traditional, music, such as (the song), *The All-Enduring* (1896), (organ) *Postlude for Thanksgiving Service*, *Fugue in Four Greek Modes* (1897); and (orchestra), the *Fugue in Four Keys on 'The Shining Shore'* (1895). It has often been stated, incorrectly, that, only later after his student years, Ives turned to more radical styles.

- **1898–1902**

  These years marked a transition, in which Ives was completing or revising earlier, largely conventional, compositions from his Yale years, completing the last of the more traditional 'German' songs, while alternately exploring new ideas within 'take-offs' and other short innovative pieces, as a well as integrating the old with the new, or expanding other sketches and ideas into actual works of music. His innovations during these years occupy largely harmonic considerations, and the reorganizations of tones into lines independent of key, some even featuring actual tone rows. The Second Symphony (1902) and *The Celestial Country* (1898–1901) represent the most traditionally based; *From the Steeples and the Mountains* (1901) is a surprisingly cutting-edge work, boldly embracing multiple innovations, including integer-based melodic organization and development.

- **1903–08**

  Aside from some large works from the period that (only) partially cross the line into latent modernism, such as *Thanksgiving* and the Third Symphony, both essentially from 1904, this period marks the confident emergence of new innovations incorporated within large musical structures, and a transition between traditional and modern. It is the period of emergence and development of rhythmic innovation (versus the earlier harmonic innovations), continued and altogether new cyclical manifestations, all manner of intricately 'coded' designs, even early dodecaphony and serialism. The seeds of many later works were sown during these years, too, often appearing substantially expanded within multiple compositions. Examples typifying the period can be found in chamber orchestra works, such as *The Unanswered Question*, and *Central Park in the Dark* (both c.1906), both of which demonstrate rhythmic, dodecaphonic and harmonic innovation. Coded tonal organization and serial rhythmic design can be found, too, in the song, *In the Cage* (1906); the *Three Page Sonata* (1905) is characterized by its complex systematic structure. The discarded and lost *Emerson Overture* (aka *Emerson Concerto*), which became the basis for the first movement of the later *Concord Sonata* (pub. 1920), probably dates from as early as 1905, according to John Kirkpatrick.[208] The score, reconstructed by David G. Porter for its premiere in 1998, is remarkable for the early incorporations and advanced developments of most of Ives's harmonic and harmonic innovations.

- **1909–17**

  As Ives's most productive period, it saw the larger and mature integration of all of his innovations within the totality of his greatest masterpieces, including the Fourth Symphony (1916); First Piano Sonata (c.1914, per Ives); *Putnam's Camp* (1912); *Second Orchestral Set* (first version c.1915); the *Concord Sonata* (first version c.1915, pub. 1920); most of Section A, *Universe Symphony* (1916); even the final realizations of earlier sketched short pieces and 'take-offs,' such as the *First Set for Chamber Orchestra* (1913); *Scherzo: Over the Pavements* (1914); *The Gong on the Hook and Ladder* (1911); and many highly individualistic songs, sonatas, quartets, etc.

---

[208] Vivian Perlis, *Charles Ives Remembered* (New Haven, CT: Yale University Press, 1974), 215.

- **1918–34**

  Representing the culmination of Ives's most productive years, with some major works emanating from his pen. Ives also wrote additional songs (and organized over a substantial collection of them from across his output into *114 Songs* [1921]), polished the *Concord Sonata* for publication (1922), totally rewrote the *Scherzo* (c.1923) in the Fourth Symphony from materials he had used previously in the discarded *Hawthorne Concerto*, adapted a version of mostly the same music for piano with *The Celestial Railroad* (pub. 1925), took up sketching the *Universe Symphony* again in an unsuccessful effort to complete it (c.1923), and wrote his four *Emerson Transcriptions*, as he reconsidered additional materials from his defunct *Emerson Concerto* that he would utilize in the first movement of the *Concord Sonata* for its second edition. Other works, such as the *Third Orchestral Set* (c.1921) were begun, though only partially completed—the composer's exhaustion becoming clear in its regressive, almost rôte, language. Ives also regrouped many small-scale early works and orchestrations of songs into a total of ten sets for chamber orchestra, some appearing in more than one.

- **1935–54**

  The final period of Ives's life; the work that he undertook during his period is commonly misrepresented. It is most typically stated that Ives spent these years revising his earlier works. Although, undoubtedly he worked obsessively on the *Concord Sonata* and made changes to it for the second edition (1947), restoring materials excised from the first, as Kyle Gann has demonstrated, representations that the revisions to the sonata were more than slight are gross exaggerations of the reality. Mostly, the revisions, such as they are, do not substantially change the music. Beyond Ives's frenzied efforts to leave his mighty sonata in a form closest to his aspirations for it, one is hard pressed to find much that Ives worked on with such zeal, and frequently, even, *at all* in his later years; in this respect, his revisions to *The Unanswered Question* (1906) stand out prominently, even though they do not change the music in any substantive manner.[209]

---

[209] The subtle changes Ives made to *The Unanswered Question* actually resulted in greater consonance, as demonstrated by Carol K. Baron, in "Dating Charles Ives's Music: Facts and Fictions": 26–30, not dissonance, as has been claimed. Other work included the completion of the score of *Thanksgiving* in 1932–33, in which a few subtle changes to the sketch were made, mostly in respect to the placement in the texture of the two primary hymn quotes at the end of the piece. Ives also updated the song, *He Is There!*, into *They are* There! for chorus and orchestra in 1941, and changed the final ending and chord (the famous "blat") of his Second Symphony in 1951 for the first performance. Most of Ives's late efforts, however, limited as they as they would be, were organizational, rather than creative.

82

The new Ives Legend

As the writer demonstrated previously in 2015 (in *Charles Ives's Musical Universe*), the timeline does influence the historical perspective and one's conclusions. Near irrefutable facts reveal a portrait of the composer far closer to the projections of the so-called 'Ives Legend' than much scholarship has allowed in recent years.[210] Ives's work and attainments have been undermined more by limitations of vision and misdirected energies than efforts to deal with the reality, which, ultimately, cannot assert control of something that is far bigger than itself. Great music never has, and never will been, defined by specific methodologies and musicology any more than can nature be controlled and understood by the dictates of man's will, nor the need to believe he has command of it.

---

[210] Antony Cooke, *Charles Ives's Musical Universe* (W. Conshohocken, NJ: Infinity, 2015), 515–67.

Chapter 4
George and Horatio

George Ives

Horatio Parker

c. 1892
{{PD Art}}

c. 1916
(PD-US)

        *T*he two figures at the epicenter of Ives's musically formative years were polar opposites. The fame of one, his distinguished formal role, even social prominence (Horatio Parker), seemingly eclipsing the other (George Ives), whose formative role in Charles Ives's musical background has been diminished in recent scholarship. Both figures played a massive role in Ives's musical evolution. Both merit a closer examination.

George Ives's Danbury World

George Ives's son, Charles, often accused of exaggeration in recent scholarship, always strongly emphasized his father's role in his musical education. Some scant exercises from early childhood preserved in George Ives's copybook have been used to discredit the significance of his teaching, but Charles's grounding in harmony and counterpoint can be demonstrated via a number of early compositions that confirm the validity of his words. Both technical disciplines appear to have been well established long before entering Yale, just as stated in *Memos*: "Father had kept me on Bach and taught me harmony and counterpoint from when I was a child until I went to college."[211]

To discount recollections as specific as these is a presumption of possessing such unique insights that written words by the "accused" can be altered to suit a narrative for which there is no evidence. Moreover, to propose that Ives, a spiritual person who lived according his family's high ethical values, of the kind of dishonesty required to record such falsehoods about his own father requires that we suspend our instincts, as well as what can be demonstrated.[212] Regardless, the tacit and circuitous upholding of Maynard Solomon's argument—despite its lack of acceptance in Ives scholarship—has meant that just the *act* of challenging Ives's words has allowed the accusation to stand.[213] To support the more universally accepted values of 'presumption of innocence,' there is a mountain of evidence.

George's training was undoubtedly unconventional, though appears to have been sound. As Ives famously recalled, "Father used to say, 'If you know how to write a fugue the right way, *well*, then I'm willing to have you try the wrong way— *well*. But you've got to know what [you're doing] and why you're doing it.'"[214] According to Charles, George would tolerate only a certain amount of a "boy's fooling," though remained adamant that his son should learn to do things properly before breaking the rules. The youthful Ives benefitted, too, from his father's open mindedness, which connected *all* sound to music, strongly questioning the status quo, and, according to the surviving evidence,[215] encouraged discovery, though he only

---

[211] Ives, *Memos*, 49.

[212] Carol K. Baron, "Efforts on Behalf of Democracy": 6–43.

[213] Solomon, "Some Questions of Veracity": 443–70.

[214] Ives, *Memos*, 47.

[215] Evidence that must include his lesson notes of c.1894: Carol K. Baron, "George Ives's Essay on Music Theory: An Introduction and Annotated Edition," *American Music* (Fall, 1992): 239–88.

permitted accepted methodology in works of actual music.[216] Whatever his shortcomings (mostly, the ability to teach large-scale composition), Parker would address them at Yale. George Ives's copybook comes up with regularity in almost every musicological commentary about Charles's background. In recent times, it has been used mostly against him, not only for the examples of music so carefully copied into its pages (as if they represented the *totality* of George's knowledge), but also for the exploratory fragments in Charles's hand. The latter appear in what would, otherwise, have been blank pages, and have been improperly projected to represent the *totality* of Charles's education with George. Quite aside from what materials once surely existed outside the copybook,[217] Magee's assessment that none followed "the standard rules of harmony or counterpoint" would not be fair even *if* Ives's early musical dabbling had represented the totality of his education.[218] Magee failed to cite the real evidence of the youthful Charles's actual compositions, other than to condemn *Holiday Quickstep* (which *does* follow protocol, nevertheless).[219]

What Magee chose to omit from her assessment were the examples of finished compositions from Ives's years prior to attending Yale—which disprove her claims because, clearly the standard rules of harmony and counterpoint were, indeed, followed. Examples of such complete compositions are *Communion Service* (1893), *Crossing the Bar* (c.1891), both works for *SATB* chorus, and *Gloria in Excelsis* (c.1892), for unison chorus and organ. Consequentially, despite attempts to decry George's professional expertise and teaching skills, the results of his influence upon his son, clearly, are in no short supply, despite all insistence to the contrary; the fact that the young Charles even *attempted* such challenging ideas in his father's copybook tends to point to conventional skills long practiced—these fragments surely were not *actual exercises prescribed by George*.

The misconstruing of Ives's musical education and development has extended, too, to other commentary. Laurence Wallach, for example, though generally supportive of Ives, suggested that the motivic element, so strong in Ives's music, was due to his studies of fugues with Horatio Parker.[220] If he meant to imply, too, that

---

[216] This point contradicts the popular notion that George was behind all of Ives's more 'shocking' early compositions.

[217] James B. Sinclair, *A Descriptive Catalogue of the Music of Charles Ives* (New Haven, CT: Yale University Press, 1999), 558–60; 561–62.

[218] Magee, *Charles Ives Reconsidered*, 28.

[219] Ibid., 19–21.

[220] Laurence Wallach, "The New England Education of Charles Ives," Ph.D. diss., Columbia University, 1973: 271–72.

Ives had *not* studied fugues with his father, clearly, Wallach must have discounted Ives's early efforts, because fugal-styled imitative, motivic counterpoint had been part of his background years long before he encountered Parker. Among Ives's surviving exercises is a sixteen-bar example—the 'Counterpoint Exercise in A' of 1891, which shows the young Ives comfortably engaged in traditional counterpoint. Another—a relatively difficult challenge for the young Ives to undertake in 1892— is the fragment of the *Burlesque Canon in C* at the unison. Initially, in three parts, before expanding to what might have been at least four—it provides some indication of Ives's sophistication, and that he *did* have a grounding in advanced counterpoint.

A 'Burlesque Canon' six-bar fragment at the unison

[Geo. Ives's copybook, p.87]
Image courtesy of the Irving S. Gilmore Music Library,
Yale University: The Charles Ives Papers MSS14

Another example, a mere six-bars of a polytonal four-part canon at the sixth is from late in Ives's Danbury years: 1893. As such, it can be assumed to reflect, perhaps, too, some of the influence of Gibson's teaching, and Ives's increasing sophistication (see overleaf). Stuart Feder, to his credit, tried to treat the matter objectively, seeming to realize that the blank pages Charles had "filled" with unconventional 'exercises' of his own making (and uncorrected by George), demonstrating their differences, *and* mutual dependence.[221] Philip Lambert pointed out that many of these early examples show elements of systematic innovation, and the clear cooperation, even collaboration, between father and son[222] (see page 92).

---

[221] Feder, *'My Father's Song,'* 92.

[222] Philip Lambert, *The Music of Charles Ives* (New Haven, CT: Yale University Press, 1997) 15–22.

A "Burlesque Canon," in four-parts, entering in four keys at the major 6th.

[Geo. Ives's copybook, pp.163]
Images courtesy of the Irving S. Gilmore Music Library, Yale University:
The Charles Ives Papers

John Kirkpatrick, in summarizing what exists of Charles's studies, remarked, however, when comparing the materials under Parker's teaching against those that have survived from Ives's Danbury years, they reveal a more stringently applied scholarship than do those scant few fragments. Although one would not have expected less of the rigorously stringent Parker, die-hard refusals by those critics who fail to accept that Ives's musical background was substantial, however, completely ignore the evidence. The quantities of finished, and partly finished, pieces from the period convincingly demonstrate Ives's theory-based proficiency, and stand as testimony to George's teaching.

Ives's imminent priority is yet more evident, however, in numerous early choral works, although the accuracy of their dates has been challenged by the comment—"summer of 1894" that Ives assigned to many of them—namely, *Psalms 24, 54, 67, 90 & 150*. Recalling that George had tried out these works with his choir, it seems certain that Charles Ives was a veteran of musical exploration long before he entered college.[223] It has been theorized that Ives's intended implication was to place the compositions within George Ives's lifetime in order to establish their predictive priority. Again, Ives has been positioned as dishonest, and in view of the fact that the writer has demonstrated that the dates of most of Ives's works (no less than those known to have been written at particular times) are verifiable to within a year or two, the accusation is less than charitable. The implication enables continued acceptance, of course, Maynard Solomon's contention that Ives had falsified the dates of his compositions.

Efforts made by others to place the psalms at the *end* of Ives's Yale years are far less supportable even than the period to which Ives assigned them. The near uniform style of all of these particular settings is greatly at odds with those psalm settings known definitively to have been made just two or three years later in New Haven. Sinclair remarked, of each of these works, that because Ives was in New Haven in the fall of 1894, he would "not have had time to go to work with his father on [these pieces]."[224] However, Ives surely was in Danbury during the summer, so his whereabouts in the *fall* seems hardly relevant. However, should we accept that no less than five psalm settings emanated from exactly the same period? The answer to the dilemma, however, seems due to conflating the date of the *fair* copies and those of the actual creation of these works.[225] The prospect looms too, that, collectively, these various psalms were indeed among the collective "Psalmist Hymnal" of Ives's Bloomfield, NJ, recollections (see again Chapter 1).

Ives referenced in *Memos* something that sounds very like the moving 'wedge' structures that Lambert had discussed,[226] as well as chordal structures built from stacked thirds, or other extensions of the common triad.[227] Should it, therefore, be a surprise to find in George's copybook, examples of both, in this instance, lying discretely on the same page (see overleaf). Later, Ives directly credited his father with the very idea for these intervallic structures, not to mention alternating (odd/even)

---

[223] Ives, *Memos*, 47.

[224] James. B. Sinclair, *A Descriptive Catalog of the Music of Charles Ives* (New Haven, CT: Yale University Press, 1999), 264–76.

[225] Carol K. Baron, "Dating Charles Ives's Music: Facts and Fictions," *Perspectives of New Music* (Winter issue, 1990): 20–56

[226] Lambert, *The Music of Charles Ives*, 20-21.

[227] Ives, *Memos*, 43. Kirkpatrick, in his footnote [1] listed examples of these same chords that made their way into later compositions.

meters, different divisions of the octave, and the greater acceptance of dissonance.[228] Casting George as the originator seems increasingly plausible—his known penchant for the unconventional clear even in his own (1894?) lesson notes.

Polytonal chord stacking in wedges

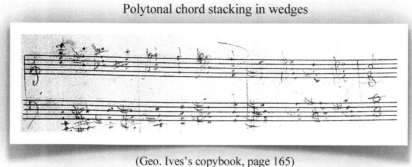

(Geo. Ives's copybook, page 165)
Image courtesy of the Irving S. Gilmore Music Library, Yale University:
The Charles Ives Papers MSS14

In forming a systematically-coded chord of ever-smaller intervals, from the bass up, Ives's unconventional leanings are further confirmed, even from his earliest years. Starting with a low 'c', then a major seventh, the youthful Ives constructed a chord of ever diminishing intervals, a semitone less with each added tone above the root (see overleaf). Such demonstrations of harmonic curiosity and systematic thinking points to George's openness, acceptance, and even, perhaps, their very instigation.

Although Burkholder recognized that Ives incorporated earlier "experimental" innovations into his advanced compositions, he was apparently unaware of the systematic methodology often lying deep within them. Hardly superficial and merely tacked onto the structure, the significance of Ives's systematic organization is that it extends to the deepest levels of his most advanced and creative processes, and cannot be overestimated.[229] These particular important examples, for whatever reason, have been omitted without comment in Sinclair's supposedly complete catalogue, the loss being all the more significant because they demonstrate something of Ives's early leanings in the application of serialism to harmony. They are real evidence of Charles's musical background and direct connection to George's unconventional thinking, or, at least, his open-mindedness toward innovation and experimentation. It

---

[228] Ives, *Memos*, 140.

[229] J. Peter Burkholder, "Charles Ives and the Four Musical Traditions," in *Charles Ives and his World*, ed. Burkholder (Princeton, NJ: Princeton University Press, 1996), 3–34.

Ch. 4   George and Horatio

is equally clear that the extension of this type of thinking led directly to Ives's increasing musical adventurism. This particular type of structure was to reappear as late as the 1920s in the highly coded fabric of the *Universe Symphony*.

Ives's Systematic Chord

(Geo. Ives's copybook, page 165)
Image courtesy of the Irving S. Gilmore Music Library,
Yale University: The Charles Ives Papers MSS14

Ives's efforts at "making chords a boy's way,"[230] also touch upon his early exercises with other types of related systematic musical organization that led to differently structured (e.g., quartal and quintal) chords in compositions, such as *Central Park in the Dark* (c.1906).[231] Remarking, however, only upon the stacking of thirds, clearly the larger concept already was in place. Ives also mentioned youthful attempts at polytonality with his early psalm settings: "two or three keys were tried out, or at least thrown together. Father let me do it, if I knew them well enough to play without looking at the notes on the paper."

Ives's development of polytonality also appears linked directly to the piano exercises his father prescribed, which involved playing a melody in one key while accompanying in another.[232] Ives's brief comments depict it as something of a game,

---

[230] Ives, *Memos*, 47.

[231] *George Ives's Copybook*, 165; referenced in John Kirkpatrick, *A Temporary Mimeographed Catalogue of the Music Manuscripts and Related Materials of Charles Ives*, (1969), 219 7C1, 220 C10.

[232] Ives, *Memos*, 46.

"a way of playing off-beats on the nearest black notes (as in *The Arkansas Traveler*), singing the air, right-hand chords in G, left-hand bass in G, and off-beats *pp* in Gb, etc." Relating the anecdote as late as 1931–32, why would he have felt any particular need to fabricate the tale? Ives seems to have taken to polytonal counterpoint early, regardless, his comfort level with it seeming quite natural to him in a number of early works, even as he never openly connected his father's exercise to such things, though his claims about his father's perspicacity seem supported by the surviving fragments of polytonal fugal and canonic attempts. Such examples of unconventional harmonic structure appearing *in his father's own copybook* tend to suggest that such matters were discussed, even, perhaps, that George was the source.

The specter of a woefully unprepared Ives entering Yale, as has been often portrayed in recent times, contradicts the surviving evidence that he was probably far better prepared than most entering music freshman. The evidence of his technical sophistication includes, too, the existence of his father's own teaching document, which reveals a musical thinker far more insightful than would be expected of a nineteenth century bandsman. Baron noted and detailed his solutions—at the time, not yet contemplated by the leading European theorists.[233] George realized that true modulations had been confused with the often-ambiguous transient chromatic motion within larger overall tonalities; either that, or he was attempting to quantify the ambiguous tonalities trending in music at the time. As such, he advocated a new system *that treated all twelve chromatic tones equally*, considering it had become a necessity. Predictively, George had Ives raised the prospect of integer notation, naming the individual and equal divisions of the octave *1–12* (rather than *0–11*)! Eventually, of course, Schoenberg's dodecaphony would bring about the abandonment of tonality altogether—the most extreme of all possible solutions to the challenge.[234]

Of course, no less a figure than J.S. Bach, in composing the preludes and fugues of *The Well-Tempered Clavier*, BWV 846–893, effectively, built a case for the adoption of some form of a tempered tuning system—if not precisely fitting the precision in modern times of 'equally-tempered' tuning—especially in relation to the non-sustaining tones of stringed keyboard instruments. As Baron discussed, it cannot be reliably determined exactly what forms of pitch tempering entered common practice in Bach's wake, because true equal temperament, as known today, was not universally adopted until late in the nineteenth century.[235] Bach, nevertheless,

---

[233] See again n. 5: Baron, "George Ives's Essay on Music Theory.'

[234] Ibid., 249–52.

[235] Baron, "At the Cutting Edge: Three American Theorists": 244.

avoided the issue of finding a new method of notation and theory, and demonstrated the effectiveness of some form of adjusted pitch, so that keyboard instruments could transition through multiple keys without the severe intonation problems of natural tuning. Though not attempting to replace the existing clumsy notation system, George did raise the prospect, and criticized its orientation for being centered on C major. Throughout the centuries after Bach, there is little to suggest that anyone seriously entertained the idea of a new notational system before George, somehow, came up with the idea! And, there is no possibility that the document is not his own.

Additionally, George's essay makes note of the important role of the *ear*. Outside purely theoretical guidelines, George recommended that the student test harmonies at the keyboard, while taking care to evaluate and understand what was heard *in the air*. In this respect, he explained in detail how several factors natural overtones, specific placements of tones in chords, and even more, the defining role of thirds, and how this interval affects the perceived outcome. Illustrating his remark by pointing out that a dominant seventh chord does not always require its inclusion above the root, because, "by adding the 7th to the 5th, we gain a third and that is enough for any chord." The thinking is no less remarkable than the date at which George put the words on the page.

George, thus, demonstrated in the most practical terms that the ear ultimately must dictate all musical functions, a simple principle that transfers readily to countless other applications. Because the foundation of all conventional harmony is built of combinations of two qualities of the third (spaced three and four semitones apart, respectively), and the quality of any particular chord is determined by the specific order of these thirds comprising it, George, effectively, had laid the groundwork for some of the polytonal efforts (comprising two tonalities that could be blended as one) that his son would try in the 1890s, such as in *Psalm 67*. In this particular work, by maintaining over most of its duration a larger sense of tonality within single momentary, yet undefined keys, he steadfastly avoided the clash of the defining thirds a semitone apart—saving such dissonances for specific dramatic points in the setting of the text. Also remembering his father's admonitions of the effect that the specific register of any tone relative to another has upon consonance, Ives generally avoided low-placed thirds (also sounding harsh) accordingly.[236]

---

[236] The low placement of the third was avoided since early times, in which the sound of such intervals in the male voices always featured in religious settings was heard as harsh, even dissonant.

David Eiseman[237] made a similar observation; however, like George himself, it has suffered, too, from revisionist interpretation that George's essay was hardly more than a practical guide, with nothing else to distinguish it.[238] Taking, out of context, single sentences or paragraphs of the article, Eiseman *appears* not to comprehend the totality of George's thinking and observations.[239] However, Eiseman's recognition that George realized that all things in music theory would be better served by its practitioners taking into account *the way applied principles sound*—that music could not be constrained by the rigidity of mere rules that place "theoretical" considerations above the "natural"—reveals the true meaning of his words.[240]

The sentiment seems to be projected another way by George's attitude toward performance, his well-known advice to Charles about the rough singing of a local stonemason speaking volumes, "Don't pay too much attention to the sounds . . . you may miss the music."[241] In other words, one has to learn to listen *for what is not quantified. Or quantifiable.* George's understanding of the role of higher overtones within harmony, notably in his rejection of the prevailing wisdom of the time that sevenths in dominant harmony acted as a dissonance—rather than the foundation of a new third, extended still further into harmonic considerations.[242] His emphasis on the practical effect of choices in notation is striking, too, noting that not all things appear standardized in theoretical texts. Although George Ives left little behind as tangible testimony of his forward vision—the lack of broader-based evidence being all too conveniently used to discredit him—this one surviving document stands in the way. A treasure trove of ideas expressed succinctly in the perceptive manner of a wise practitioner, George had annunciated, in his own terms, some of the very ideas and principles that Charles incorporated later in his innovations and compositions.

Regardless, George's essay has not met with universal recognition of its advanced thinking by everyone in the musicological community. Magee, for example, blithely dismissed it, declaring that it was neither innovative, nor

---

[237] David Eiseman, "George Ives As Theorist: Some Unpublished Documents," *Perspectives of New Music*, 14, 1 (Autumn–Winter, 1975): 142–47.

[238] Gayle Sherwood Magee, Charles Ives: *A Research and Information Guide* (New York: Routledge Music Biographies, 2002), "General Music Studies": 3, n.169.

[239] Eiseman, "George Ives As Theorist: 142.

[240] Ibid.: (142).

[241] Ives, *Memos*, 132.

[242] Baron, "George Ives's Essay": 248–49, and represented in George's words, 256–63.

experimental; worse, she proclaimed that George was *behind* the times.[243] To grant George more credit, however, would have undermined her larger case that Charles Ives had not received much substantive musical training during his formative years in Danbury. Jan Swafford, in remarking that George had not undergone any change over twenty years, no doubt was referring to the band music he played.[244] Surely his words were not intended to indict George's thoughtful and insightful approach in relation to his own vision of the future of music. It seems to me more likely Swafford was referring to George's shrinking professional opportunities, which had rendered his musical presentations tired and stale, while his thought processes continued to advance.

Along the same lines, Magee's comments that younger musicians had moved onto more up-to-date music making seem valid, but hardly grounds for an indictment of George's thinking. If George's most visible work as a working musician consisted of the same repertoire of tried-and-true band tunes, it was commentary of his increasingly depressing lot in Danbury's musical life. Ingrained in his psyche over the course of his life, virtually automatic at this stage, he would have felt little incentive to expand his repertoire; likely, he could not rebuild his repertoire at this late stage, *nor would his existing audiences have embraced it*. George's innovative ideas about music theory, however, represent a diametrically opposite universe to his approach to making a living. Baron noted that George's thinking about harmonic progressions and chords, no less predictively, seemed to foreshadow the evolution of tonality in the twentieth century, especially in respect to chromatic transitions rather than true modulations. His ideas, penned in the early 1890s, represent a lifetime of involvement in music. Stretching back comfortably to years encompassing Wagner's mature work (and forward to the musical aftermath to which they respond), they are, truly, at "the cutting edge," as Baron had realized.[245]

Feder, initially, took a positive stance on George's notes, clearly able to see that it was not a mere pedantic regurgitation of existing pedagogy. Struck by its "fresh" approach, surely, Feder seemed to grasp George's unique outlook, his astute sonic awareness and the interaction of pitches.[246] Regrettably, Feder missed the visionary aspects altogether, concluding that George only offered an original presentation of traditional materials! In regard to the constant obsession to compare George's role

---

[243] Magee, *Charles Ives Reconsidered*, 17 & 184, n.18.

[244] Swafford, *A Life With Music*, 66.

[245] Baron, "George Ives's Essay in Music Theory": 252–53. See again n. 168, part ii.

[246] Feder, *"My Father's Song,"* 93.

with that of Parker, it should be obvious that they cannot be so equated. In a straight match-up, Parker, whose breadth of knowledge as a professional composer and distinguished university educator is clear. Parker, however, lacked George's insights, intuition, and curious streak. So, specifically what did Charles Ives gain from Parker?

Yale: Parker, and The Second New England School

Books published about Charles Ives only a few years ago usually pay Horatio Parker short shrift, in regard to his own auspicious background and place in American music. Today, most recent texts credit Parker for a larger musical influence on his young student than is supportable. But Parker's 'star' has fallen precipitously as a prominent composer, due in part to the faint praise ushered from the less-than-enthusiastic appraisals of his now far more famous student. William C. Rorick, who had made that assessment, also aptly remarked that Ives's words had "shrouded" the image of Parker held by modern audiences.[247] Did Ives's less-than-rapturous summations of Parker, therefore, despite always being softened by some positive affirmation, play the largest role in clouding the way history sees him?

Horatio Parker was born in 1863, his birthday falling between those of Charles and George Ives. However, Parker was much closer to Charles Ives in age, being just thirty-one years old when Ives entered Yale. The misleading impression from the mere eleven-year age separation becomes dramatically highlighted by the yawning gap between Ives's and Parker's music. Seemingly out of the blue (though not in actuality, as the writer will show), Ives, the long awaited, if not yet recognized 'Great American Composer' would redirect music in his country toward wholly unchartered territories, against the crosswinds of long-established traditional indoctrination. It is all the more remarkable that he navigated those unchartered expanses with such confidence, and over such a short period of time.

Today, Parker is looked upon by the few people who know his name as a minor composer of forgettable talent, who lived and worked during a time when American music had no worthy identity of its own. The reality, however, speaks partly of an ill-deserved injustice, because Parker *was* a notable talent in his own right. Nevertheless, despite possessing more than a degree of musical originality, he lacked the kind of true creative genius that advances cultural norms into a new age, his work being often somewhat interchangeable with others. Roger Sessions, a distinguished composer, and also a student of Parker, unintentionally damned his teacher with faint praise. After having listed Parker's great skills and musicality, Sessions remarked that he

---

[247] William C. Rorick, "The Horatio Parker Archives in the Yale University Library," review, *Fontes Artis Musicale*, 26, 4 (October–December 1979): 298.

"lacked originality," a fatal flaw to lay upon any composer, if ever there were one.[248] However, such perceptions are not responsible for the changing fashions in American music that ultimately doomed Parker's relevance in the concert hall. Beginning in the years after World War I, the well-loved cantata format (such as Parker was best-known for) slowly lost favor with audiences. Certainly, it was a stunning reversal of fate; at the turn of the century, Parker was the iconic figure, and Ives the unknown. Ives's perspective about Parker was not likely shared by most people at the time, and no other student of Parker is known for having been so lukewarm toward the distinguished composer and educator. Ives, however, was unlike any of Parker's students; a latent musical original, Ives's creativity, intelligence and musical gifts were matched by no one in America in his day. In comparison, almost anyone would have appeared (to Ives) as overly beholden to tradition and "the German Rule."[249] There can be no doubt that Parker is better known for Ives's catch phrase than any of his music, with the possible exception of *Hora Novissima*.

It becomes clearer, of course, why George Ives was so pivotal in his son's music, though there is nothing to suggest that even he had any awareness his son was destined to be the figure that would shake up music in America, and for whom the country had so patiently waited. Nevertheless, if we reverse Ives's and Parker's positions, it is noteworthy just how insignificant *Ives* appears to have been in Parker's eyes; the lack of reference to him, even in 1942, at the time that his daughter, Isabel Parker Semler, assembled her biographical work, *Horatio Parker: A Memoir for his Grandchildren Compiled from Letters and Papers*, is striking.[250] At the date of publication, Ives already was a celebrated composer in rapid ascent (in the wake of the *Concord Sonata*, famously described by Lawrence Gilman in his 1939 review as "the greatest music by an American"),[251] and surely, by then, the most prominent among any of Parker's former students. It is as disappointing as it is surprising and revealing, especially when numerous other composers and students feature in it so conspicuously. We can take it as indicative of Ives's likely repudiation of the type of composer described by Parker's former student and friend, David Stanley Smith, when he wrote in 1930 (of Parker), "with pretense or shams of any kind he had no patience, and he was quick to detect them in some of the modern fads of polyharmony

---

[248] Kearns, *Horatio Parker*, 233.

[249] Ives, *Memos*, 49.

[250] Isabel Parker Semler, *Horatio Parker: A Memoir for his Grandchildren compiled from Letters and Papers* (New York: G.P. Putnam's Sons, 1942).

[251] Lawrence Gilman, review, Charles Ives, Sonata No.2 , "*The Concord*," *New York Herald Tribune*, Jan. 20. 1939.

and polycacophony."[252] The reference to such matters seems to imply many a shared conversation about even Ives himself. Even in 1942, with his 'star' in the ascent, Ives *still* was not about to be accorded recognition by the musical establishment of his day for his efforts in such "fads."

From his teens, Parker, as a student of **George Whitefield Chadwick** between 1880–82, would be thoroughly educated in the German late-Romantic school of music. At the time, would-be American composers studied abroad with leading musical pedagogues, and Chadwick, one of the 'Boston Six,'[253] was no exception, and like most American composers of the period, had spent extended time abroad. Studying with Carl Reinecke and Salomon Jadassohn in Leipzig, and later, Josef Rheinberger in Munich, upon returning home, he became well known in American musical circles, his work encompassing many genres, from symphonies to string quartets, large works for chorus, even opera. Elements of his New England cultural surroundings were reflected in his music—melodically, at very least, having a spirit sometimes reminiscent of Dvořák—for reasons likely more to do (than anything else) with the common roots of many imported folk melodies, further evolved in the folk music of America. Chadwick, perhaps the most 'American' sounding composer to date, nevertheless, failed to chart a course that escaped the larger trans-Atlantic shadows at its heart. After Parker became Chadwick's student, he would earn his unbounded admiration over the years.[254] Parker, usually considered a thoroughly conventional figure, paradoxically, often found himself at loggerheads with Chadwick—surprisingly, displaying more than a few traits of Ivesian rebel spirit; however, it is matter of the relative use of term.[255] Although such rebelliousness increasingly characterized the arts at a time when Western culture was rushing headlong to reject Romanticism, at this time, America, even the world, still was not ready.

Chadwick ensured Parker would experience more of the same strict pedagogical rigors he had dealt with personally by sending him to study with no less a dogmatic taskmaster than Rheinberger—a teacher whom Chadwick, himself, had derided as

---

[252] David Stanley Smith, "A Study of Horatio Parker," *The Musical Quarterly*, XVI, 2 (April 1, 1930): 153–63.

[253] Gilbert Chase, *America's Music: From the Pilgrims to the Present* (Chicago: University of Illinois Press, 1992).

[254] "George Whitefield Chadwick," in *History of American Music*, vol. 4, ed. W.L. Hubbard, of the series, *The American Encyclopedia and History of Music* (New York: Irving Squire, 1908–10), 4–7.

[255] Burkholder, "Ives and the European Tradition," in *Charles Ives and the Classical Tradition*, 12. See, too, Kearns, *Horatio Parker*, 239–40.

"conservative, almost to the point of pedantry"! Chadwick surely considered Rheinberger's disciplined methodology to be in his rebellious student's best interests.[256] David Stanley Smith, in his study of Parker, thought that the "stern rule" of Rheinberger tamed Parker's rebellious spirit.[257] If Parker's experience with Chadwick and his subsequent training in Germany did not quash that spirit entirely, he became equally strict and dogmatic in his teaching style! However, Parker, despite becoming a staunch musical disciplinarian himself, never did fully relinquish his rebellious tendencies. His success with largely traditional methods did not assuage his dissatisfaction with the compromise he had let govern his work, causing him to spend many of his later years indulging his more adventurous style, often to the detriment of his success. Parker's radicalism, however, was largely confined by novel, truly creative and adventurous harmony at times, rather than by any of the twentieth century trends just awakening.

Once under Rheinberger's spell, however, the appeasement of the whims of late American nineteenth century audiences seems evident in Parker's output of eminently listenable music of the largely traditional vein. Chadwick remarked on the effect it had on him: "Parker saw the fine series of organ sonatas by Rheinberger unfold, as the master would bring in new manuscripts. His love for these perfect and varied compositions was based not only on his healthy admiration of a good job, but on a sentiment not unlike the devotion that gripped the students of César Franck."[258] Only when one examines the works of Rheinberger through the lens of time, however, does one realize the degree to which Chadwick's words disconnect with the reality. Rheinberger might have been a fine teacher, but as a composer, his works are sorely lacking—even the best among them dull, plodding, uninspiring, and creatively stunted to modern ears. The unexpected was exchanged for the predictable, formula for anything truly inventive or memorable. In the circumstances, it is no small wonder that his American students usually ventured no further, although the music of Chadwick and Parker is altogether more artistic and interesting than their German taskmaster left behind, Chadwick's works, especially, still able to reach audiences today.

Quite aside from the obvious largely Euro-centric language of his music, Parker's reputation as an advocate of disciplined, if not necessarily inspired, craftsmanship is well illustrated in relation to his use of traditional counterpoint. The

---

[256] George Whitefield Chadwick, *Horatio Parker; 1863–1919* (Yale University Press, 1921), 9.

[257] Smith, "A Study of Horatio Parker," 154–55.

[258] Semler, *Horatio Parker*, 60–61.

more progressive of Parker's most ambitious projects, the opera, *Mona*, was a critical failure; defined by "pervading chromaticism, vacillating tonality, and angular melody" (a summation by William K. Kearns), likely no one today would find it as hard to accept as did Parker's audiences, who, as his followers, expected the type of music they had come to associate with him.[259] Though comparisons of Parker's rebelliousness with that of Ives are instructive, they understate the nature and degree of all that separated them—but also what might have brought them together as kindred spirits.[260] In turn-of-the-century America, the expected continued subservience to the long dominant European model is hard to appreciate today, only a little over a century removed from the time; the arts in America today are defined by progressivism. If Parker made an effort toward it with *Mona*, a more innovative and original composition from a different mold—it remains, nevertheless, shackled to the ties of a musical foundation long-established by his trans-Atlantic predecessors.[261] Altogether more chromatic, less harmonically traditional and formally proportioned than before, this work was perhaps best aligned with the extreme post-Romanticism of Richard Strauss, whose music, to Parker, remained a benchmark of modernism. Figures, such as Stravinsky, and even more, Schoenberg, of course, were off limits.

His reputation as reactionary and inflexible is not wholly deserved, however; within the decade following Ives's departure from Yale, Parker had embarked on two ambitious, more modernistic, short tone poems for orchestra: *A Northern Ballad* (1899) and *Vathek* (1903). The first featured a shift in orientation toward more Anglo-Celtic idioms—a far cry from his Germanic musical roots—though even more, from readily identifiable American influences! *A Northern Ballad*, a vigorous, immediately attractive and rhythmically arresting work, at times, tapped into similar language as both Delius and Grieg. Thematically, nevertheless, the melodic roots still hark back to the folk influences of his New England heritage. The second work, *Vathek*, in full Gothic grandeur, characterizes Parker's later, harmonically more diffuse (and less accepted) style. Patterned to a degree on Richard Strauss's tone poem model (continuing the evolution of Wagner's diffuse tonal techniques), Parker wished to be known for music other than those of the then-fashionable cantata mold. Clearly, by this time, he *had* developed greater expertise in pure symphonic orchestration, but it was too late in the timeline to have influenced Ives.

---

[259] William K. Kearns, *Horatio Parker* (Metuchen, NJ: The Scarecrow Press, Inc., 1990), 240.

[260] Burkholder, "Ives and the European Tradition," 12.

[261] Ibid., 147–48.

Parker's own thoughts on music are particularly interesting, in that they appear, superficially at least, to parallel Ives's own. Capturing the contempt Parker held for the well-worn diatonic melodic forms so popular among unsophisticated listeners, he summed it up almost as would have his famous student—"If we give people weak music they will accept it and love it. Likewise will they accept strong music, and love it infinitely better in the end, for they also can respect it . . . I want you to consider our Hymnal in this respect. . . the minor ones of our great-grandfathers, like "Windsor," a splendid type [,] will flourish long after the last vanilla-flavored tune has vanished."[262] However, what Parker considered "strong" hardly compares with anything Ives might have considered to be in that vein, so despite the boldness and conception of Parker's best work, it never crosses into anything approaching truly revolutionary musical territory. Music historian, Alan H. Levy, understood well the situation for domestic composers, having seen clearly that anyone with serious aspirations in America had to 'tow the line' of what was acceptable to audiences, or face the virtual certainty of "committing professional suicide."[263]

In relation to Parker's rebellious element, judged by modern standards, there is nothing written by him that demonstrates what could be considered particularly radical or especially progressive, a concession even Kearns made.[264] Again, it illustrates the dilemma of all full-time professional musicians, who remain always dependent upon the critical acceptance of audiences. Those who pursue music according to their own terms, freed from the threat of rejection, know well the risks of consequent starvation, even that their music might never be heard at all. Although critics of the 'Boston Six' accused them of social indifference, an intellectual elite too busy enjoying their privilege to connect with the outside world: composers who were dependent on music for a living found it necessary to stay within the bounds of readily accessible music that their audiences demanded.

Ives, however, would learn to suppress his latent radicalism, at least during his Yale years; Parker, like most good teachers attempting to instill solid principles, was not open even to the slightest tweaking of the 'rules.' Ives's grades in Parker's courses were another matter, however. Was he under-recognized by his esteemed professor, however—or, with his provincial background—was he never accorded the serious recognition he deserved? The lack of comment is especially noticeable, because so many of Parker's other students were much lauded by him in later years.

---

[262] Semler, *Horatio Parker*, 74–75.

[263] Alan S. levy, *Musical Nationalism: American Composers' Search for Identity* (Westport, CT: Greenwood Press, 1983), 6.

[264] Ibid., 239.

Even after Ives had composed much of his First Symphony, a masterful work by any standards, and very much in the musical vein of the times, Parker, *still* did not acknowledge the accomplishment and potential of his precocious student. Regardless, even if Ives's compliance with Parker's strict directives had been reluctantly conceded, the results ought to have been an obvious indicator to Parker of a formidable talent, the mature skills demonstrated within them surely typical of few composers of his age.

Reading Parker's daughter's biography of her father, one cannot escape a sense of entitlement, and yet-to-be-earned social rewards and associations in which Parker indulged, even as a student, which tend to confirm that he aspired to become part of the social elite. When he traveled to Germany to continue his studies, before beginning his studies in earnest and living on borrowed funds from his two benefactors—"the Carters" or a "Mr. Burr"[265]—Parker spent some months traveling around Europe sightseeing and enjoying life in the taverns, while almost demanding that further funds be sent to maintain his financial solvency. A subtly defensive posture is apparent, however, as the more Parker's homebound letters emphasize his frugality, the protestations mask the very lack of demonstrating it.[266] Parker's humble circumstances, indeed, comparing quite well to those of his future student, Charles Ives, stand in stark contrast to the lifestyle to which apparently he felt entitled.

One again has the same impression of Parker by his ready embrace of English society (one that Americans generally perceived as highly sophisticated), following his initial invitation in 1899 to perform *Hora Novissima*, and the many subsequent trips to England that followed. Parker relished his acceptance in the upper crust of such an enlightened and 'civilized' society. In diametrical contrast, Ives eschewed the comfort of composing the type of music that was likely to find easy acceptance by the high society concert-going elite. However, *did* the erudite, well-spoken, socially and culturally elite (nay, even, *elitist*), refined and educated, trans-Atlantic-studied-and-polished Yale professor harbor an element of snobbery towards the 'provincial' youngster, who, in spite of attempting to emulate his professor, probably only reminded him more of the person he had worked so hard to eradicate? Likely there is more than a grain of truth to it. Ives had steadfastly clung to the influences of his provincial culture, musical background, and fiercely independent spirit. If Ives had been looking for a fatherly role model in George's wake, Parker came up woefully short.[267] There is a revealing tale, too, involving, George Chadwick

---

[265] Semler, *Horatio Parker*, 43.

[266] Ibid., 47–58.

[267] Semler, *Horatio Parker*, 94.

(Parker's teacher), who visited Ives's composition class at Yale during Ives's senior year. Parker criticized one of Ives's songs (*In Summer Fields*, 1897) for its frequent modulations; Chadwick remarked, much to Ives's delight, that it was "as good a song" as Parker could have written.[268]

William Lyons Phelps, who had impressed Ives greatly in his studies of American literature, remarked upon Parker's perfectly annunciated speech, "without one shade of affectation or pedantry,"[269] and also noted Parker's demeanor, even his "beautiful, *cultivated* [author's emphasis] accent. "To people who did not know him well he sometimes seemed cold and aloof. To ignoramuses who attempted to discuss music with him he was annihilating . . . He was severe with the orchestra at rehearsals." Parker had become Rheinberger, at least in the manner he dealt with his students. As a man of impeccable orderliness, both in his public persona as well as his work habits, Parker always remained acutely aware of his dependency on music for a living, always ensuring that his work was properly represented. He never would have allowed himself to be perceived as anything less than the epitome of professionalism; consequently, his materials always present an extremely workmanly approach.

For some years, Ives apparently took what he observed to heart, his own fair copies during these years being virtually as neat and ordered as Parker's. It took many years of isolation for his better-known muddled sketches and scores to emerge, however, although decidedly beautiful fair copies of a number of works still emanated late in the century's second decade, as Baron remarked.[270] As the years passed, Ives, despite consistently providing copyists with, at least, *clear* fair copies, concerned himself less with the esthetics of his penmanship, although his finished works typically are quite legible. His sketches were more likely to suffer from disorder—which from Ives's standpoint were fully workable (*he* knew, after all, the intent, his uncanny ability to compartmentalize things in his own mind well-known)—though difficulties will be encountered by anyone else trying to determine the correct path to finish an incomplete work. Because of the tangled and disordered array of manuscript pages of Ives's work habits, suffering, too, from chaotically disorganized storage in his West Redding barn, the disarray caused John Kirkpatrick to spend years sorting and assembling the vast collection of materials to render them usable—an almost inconceivably lengthy and tedious proposition. No professional composer would

---

[268] Ives, *Memos*, 183–84.

[269] Kearns, *Horatio Parker*, 237.

[270] Carol K. Baron, "Dating Charles Ives's Music: Facts and Fictions," *Perspectives of New Music*, 28, 1 (Winter, 1990), 40.

proceed in this manner. Ives's status as a composer marching to his own drum is clear in this regard. However, part of the problem is that by the time he ceased composing, he had little expectation of performance for most of his music, and even less energy to correct the problem.

Postlude, from *Three Compositions for Organ*,

Horatio Parker (1896)

Excerpted third page of the manuscript (fair copy) {PD}

Ironically, the strict constraints that Parker imposed on Ives (and his fellow students) were not tempered by his own struggle against conformity; instead, they further alienated him from registering any empathy for similar spirits. Kirkpatrick had noted that Ives's counterpoint exercises under Parker were more "exigent" than those he wrote under the guidance of his more relaxed father. George Ives had been a free spirit, too, having pursued music in unlikely circumstances, and not nearly the hard-nosed disciplinarian Ives encountered in Parker, whose reserved aloofness ensured their relationship would remain somewhat restrained, even strained at times, over Ives's entire four years Ives at Yale. However, despite Ives's criticisms of Parker, he held him in considerable esteem, regardless. We can assume, therefore, that they were, at least, cordial to each other.

It was a strange contradiction. Secure in his prominent societal perch, Parker still maintained something of his old breakaway *inner* identity, contrary to the (post-Romantic) compositional language of his later music. Regardless, Parker must have considered New England to be the center of the arts in America, and sought to undo its dependence upon the powerhouse abroad. His attitude was not unfounded, because the reality was that much of the country's culture, character and spirit, emerged from his region of the country. Regardless, in spite of Parker's own ultimate dissatisfaction with the tried-and-true writing style for which history has tagged him and his contemporaries, at no time would he, nor anyone else, have had the slightest notion of what was needed to allow them to accomplish their aspiration. Little did Parker, too, suspect that the very person to fit that description was already present, right under his nose, and that his under-recognized student was playing a direct role in becoming the composer of which so many had dreamed.

Kearns remarked upon Parker's less-than-positive opinion of the rigors of his German training, even its music, and especially his criticism of the constraints of fugal counterpoint, despite his noted excellence as a practitioner of the form.[271] (Such an attitude harked back to his student days with Chadwick, showing that his rebelliousness never was really extinguished, even after years of immersion in traditionally practiced dogma.) The observation is notable, because Parker not only mastered the German musical tradition as a student, but featured fugal forms *in the compositions* most important to him—even in the face of his claim that as his German training had acted more as a refinement of his skills than a foundation. Instead, Parker stated that French musical culture was the "most conducive to composition."[272] Anything identifiable in Parker's writing as typically French existed, perhaps, only

---

[271] Ibid., 9.

[272] Ibid., 9.

in his imagination, rather than the distinct musical features reflecting the impressionist leanings of the leading avant-garde French musical exponents of the day. French composers, such as Fauré, Franck, perhaps, even Satie, and, later, Debussy and Ravel, and with whom, presumably, Parker identified, shared little with his musical language or style. German origins, however, seem evident in virtually all the music of the early American composers. Their music exudes, nevertheless, the spirit of their time and place, replete with its quaint anachronisms, awkwardness and weaknesses, born out of an unfulfilled desire—and, especially yet, the methodology—to create something of their own.

Hardly less remarkable is that Parker, for all his refined demeanor and sophistication (and suppressed radical instincts), often wrote in a style that reflects the sweet sentimentality and overly decorative idiom of Victorian parlor music, such as the delightful, if, ultimately superficial, *Suite* for piano trio, Op.3. It seems especially contradictory for one well known for his contempt of the "sickly sentimental hymn tune," a summation of his attitude regarding the state of popular hymnody of the day, and surely a 'swipe' at the appeal of evangelical Protestantism to the less musically sophisticated, educationally—and, dare we say—'lower' classes.[273] Indeed, William Kearns considered that Parker, himself, was unable to entirely escape the very idiom he so despised in his *own* hymn settings![274]

On the other hand, Kearns offered that Parker's songs, as contributions to the American art song form, if not overly abundant, were of a high order, and *not* typically sentimental—perhaps, a kinder assessment than warranted in absolute, rather than relative, terms. Parker's songs, nevertheless, often *were* the product of some of his more creative and original visions. In relation to the large volume of near-forgotten works of the genre, late Victorian songs have not aged well, however. Even those by Parker, presumably, which would have provided a model for Ives to emulate in own his songs from the period, nevertheless, also reflect the familiar saccharine Victorian taste. Ives openly disdained many of his own such efforts—publishing them, nevertheless—in *114 Songs* of 1921, complete with a disclaimer! The same characteristic melodramatic and florid style is evident, too, even in Ives's *The Celestial Country*. It was precisely the idea, of course, because Ives was trying to emulate Parker's road to success.

To portray Parker dismissively does not take into account his attempts to find avenues to assert at least as much originality and daring as his audiences would allow, nonetheless. In most instances when he did so, he was met with rejection and failure.

---

[273] Kearns, *Horatio Parker*, 202–05.

[274] Ibid., 204.

American audiences had spoken, and their message was loud and clear. If Parker's music remains eminently listenable, his failure to find long term acceptance is due more to being a prisoner of his circumstances than it is to a lack of basic aptitude (Kearns cited his operas and [later] choral works in this respect).[275] Still, it is necessary to recognize that Parker's beacon, considerable as it was, nevertheless, was not bright enough to shine a light that would illuminate new musical roads in America, however, and certainly as long as he depended upon music for his livelihood.

Succinctly, Kearns had encapsulated what separated Ives from the previous generations of American composers. Parker had traded his modest background, not unlike that of his precious student, to become a product and captive, nevertheless, of the 'establishment' and its genteel society's arts culture. At the time, Ives's world was mundane in comparison, but more practical in its ability to survive each day in a microcosm of authentic emerging American culture. Ives's cultural heritage, emerging from a part of the country that most city-dwellers would have considered the hinterlands, reflected American society *outside* urban centers. Even more, it outlined the contrast with the artistic trappings that had both rewarded Parker and stifled his instincts—in effect, a deal with a somewhat benevolent devil.

Criticizing the staid attitude within the arts in America at the time, Kearns listed its emerging domestic voices, such as composer, Aaron Copland (1900–90), author, philosopher and poet, George Santayana (1863–1952), and also Edward Robinson, critic for *The American Mercury*—all of whom had virtually demanded that domestic practitioners of the arts should expand their professional work to reflect social concerns of the day.[276] Regardless, the difficult circumstances of America's professional composers precluded the development of a truly national identity, by default. Their primary obligation was to their audiences. Kearns remarked upon what these figures' far-distant dream of the definitive 'Great American Composer.'[277] Indeed, as Kearns pointed out, neither Parker nor his contemporaries viewed themselves as that person, but considered their role was to enable that figure to emerge.[278]

---

[275] Kearns, *Horatio Parker*, 232.

[276] Ibid., 233–34.

[277] Ibid., 235.

[278] Ibid., 235.

Parker's Influence on Ives

Ives first encountered Parker at the height of his newfound fame, following the rapturous reception of *Hora Novissima* at its premier, the main work for which Parker is remembered today. The performance took place in 1893, during Ives's year at Hopkins Grammar School; attending Yale in the fall of 1894 coincided with Parker's appointment as Battell Professor of theory and music. Parker, at only thirty-one years old, no doubt, was too engaged in newfound public adulation to pay much attention to an almost pathologically shy freshman from Danbury. Nonetheless, it was Horatio Parker, a young composer hailed as a genius on the cusp of a high profile career, who would set a career model to which Ives inwardly aspired.[279]

It is indisputable that, Ives's studies with Parker resulted in his transformation from a composer of short pieces, albeit some of them quite extraordinary and forward looking, into a composer of large musical essays in well-established formats: sonatas, symphonies, string quartets, etc. The impetus behind it would have encompassed at least the following factors: (i), Ives's existing awareness of such music (ii), Parker's renowned lecture demonstrations of a wide breadth of music literature in his weekly history of music class (iii), Parker's disciplined tuition and Ives's need to produce substantive works for his classwork (iv), competition with fellow classmates (v), the effect of working with an accomplished and recognized composer, and being exposed to his works, both in sheet music and performance. Regardless, it should be noted, Parker's output was dominated by choral music, with very few models of stand-alone orchestration at the time Ives was at Yale; this aspect is usually overlooked in assessments of Parker's direct influence on Ives, despite Chadwick's assessment of Parker's "genius for tone-painting with the orchestra,"[280] though "strange that he should have composed for the orchestra alone."[281] In a striking instance of praise seeming to be accorded Parker's orchestral writing, Amy Beach remarked on how impressed she was with the orchestral segments of the 1915 opera, *Fairyland*, but one soon comes to realize that she was referring more to its melodies and harmony than to anything else. [282]

---

[279] Smith, "A Study of Horatio Parker": 157. Parker's star ultimately would not sustain itself even throughout his relatively short life, and his long line of choral works, ultimately, would find neglect in his homeland, but became increasingly performed in England, a land, which, at the time, was literally packed with choral societies.

[280] George Whitfield Chadwick, *Horatio Parker, 1863–1920* (New Haven, CT: Yale University Press, 1921), 15.

[281] Ibid., 22.

[282] Kearns, *Horatio Parker*, 172.

In a direct comparison, Ives's orchestration seems infinitely more subtle and integrated than Parker's, whose writing is strikingly monolithic and chordal—typically featuring linear blocks of contrasting instrumental choirs. In this respect, Parker's primary instrument, the organ, is always present in his creative thoughts, whereas, one always senses in Ives's orchestration an infinitely keener awareness and sensitivity toward the many unique sonic footprints of varying instrumental combinations. Because Ives's background in Romantic symphonic literature was likely well established before he set foot in New Haven, much of the material Parker covered in his music history and literature classes was not new to him; indeed, much of it apparently was outdated. A careful inspection of Parker's course reveals much about the music Ives was exposed to, and offers more than a tangible clue about what Ives knew, and when he knew it.[283] Of all the subjects that Parker taught—harmony, counterpoint, history of music, strict composition, instrumentation, free composition, and practical music (whatever that might have entailed)—only one, the history of music, was concerned with musical literature.[284] Significantly, it extended *only up to the time of Beethoven.*

So how did Ives become endowed so quickly with the kind of facile and mature mastery of orchestration necessary to compose his remarkable First Symphony? Not venturing beyond the end of the Classical age and the beginning of the Romantic, it suggests that Ives must have arrived at Yale with a substantial background in symphonic music of the day. There seems to be no other explanation for the command of orchestration and substance so convincingly on display in his first large-scale symphonic excursion—in no way what one might expect of a 'student' work! Moreover, Ives's orchestral music reveals no obvious link to Parker's—unlike the vocally-oriented *The Celestial Country*, which shows its ties readily to Parker's *Hora Novissima.* It should not be assumed, therefore, that Parker was responsible for providing the major part of Ives's command of the orchestral medium, even though surely he must have contributed to it.

During Ives's Yale years, most of Parker's symphonic and chamber works were youthful excursions from an entirely different time, long before he became a celebrated composer. Largely written more than a decade earlier, while he was still studying abroad with Josef Rheinberger, as student works, they were not compositions upon which Parker's reputation rested. Similarly, they were *least* likely to have been among those works that Parker would have referenced in his teaching. It is clear that Ives could not have become a master composer and orchestrator in a

---

[283] Ives, *Memos*, 182–83.

[284] Ibid., John Kirkpatrick editorial, Appendix (6), 181–84.

semester or two, especially had he really been the naive son of an amateur, small town musician of revisionist projections.

Parker, however, differed with most musical academics at the time, believing that the training of composers was infinitely more important than the study of music history, or other purely non-applied musical studies. As a practical musician, first and foremost, Parker was highly critical of academic music curricula that over-stressed peripheral studies, such as music history, musical esthetics, acoustics, even as he mastered the curriculum himself, becoming notable for the lecture demonstrations at the heart of his academic reputation. Ives was fortuitous to encounter a professor with such an attitude (even if he failed to recognize it), coming just in time at what had always been, first and foremost, a school for business professionals. Part of Parker's graduation requirements included the composition of at least one fully-scored symphonic movement. Because Ives only audited Parker's weekly music history class[285] for his first two years at Yale, any formal tuition in composition and orchestration with Parker would have taken place over just the next two years. The situation is indicative that Ives's early immersion in the works of the masters surely was already quite advanced. On top of anything he had been taught, as a busy working organist, he would have played many transcriptions of symphonic masterworks and developed the ability to analyze them.

Ives's Road to the Stars more closely examined

Although Ives's output covers approximately a thirty-five-year period, his major years of development, however, cover a much shorter span—essentially from his mid-teens up to just beyond the new century's first decade. Consequently, works from within those years will be the most indicative of Ives's musical evolution, and the effects of external influences upon him. Most valuable for our purposes will be:

- Musical examples surviving from the earliest years during which Ives was being taught primarily by George Ives and other teachers in Danbury, and representing largely conventional writing.

- Examples that demonstrate Ives's early and increasingly radical innovations.

- Examples from Ives's explosively innovative in the new century's first decade.

- Examples of Ives's maturing compositional language.

---

[285] Ives, *Memos*, 26–27.

Because Ives never revealed much about his methods, other than some of the most general commentary in *Memos*, stubborn refusals by others to look at the whole picture have obscured the man, his music, values, culture, history and insights—even more, the ways in which his music functions, interacts, and came about in the most musicologically unexpected of circumstances. The following chapters are intended to aid in finding at least some answers to the workings of Ives's creativity.

Chapter 5

Works that Reflect Ives's Early Influences

hile living in Danbury, Charles Ives had been remarkably active as a composer during his teens; a few of his compositions already anticipated the future. These youthful excursions were written under George's watchful eye, and sometimes, his guidance, too. Immediately noticeable is the large proportion of church related works from the period, so clearly, music for the concert hall was not yet on Ives's mind. As a busy organist, Ives was constantly immersed in religious music, so it is hardly surprising that he wrote mostly for his instrument and/or choir at this stage of his life. After he left his New York church position in 1902, during the rest of his life, he wrote virtually nothing for organ solo, the instrument, apparently having been a means to an end. The predominance of music featuring chorus among his early compositions speaks loudly, too, to his opportunities to hear these pieces performed by his father's choir; it also points to the central role that the church played in the lives of Ives's family members. With the prominent absence of Ives's religious and cultural background in much recent scholarship, suddenly the reality of growing up in as the son of a slightly wayward member of a prominent family in a largely rural area, with strong roots in its societal order is clear. How many teenagers, otherwise, would have written so much material for church services? How many would already have been guided by such a serious philosophical outlook on life?[286] A representative group of such works appears overleaf:

---

[286] I draw the reader's attention again to Baron's article, "Efforts on Behalf of Democracy," 2004.

Selected Early Choral Compositions

Psalm 42 (1887)
Easter Anthem (1890)
Crossing the Bar (1890)
Communion Service (1893)
Nine Canticle Phrases (1894)
Psalm 67 (1894)

More indicative of Ives's training than the few pages of youthful exercises are his actual compositions—at least nineteen religious choral works date from the years before entering Yale (although he ventured, "20–25" in his somewhat confusing and hurriedly made initial works list scrawled on the back of a company calendar). Among the manuscripts that have survived, not all are complete, and it cannot be assumed that Ives finished all of them. However, even of the eight surviving that are incomplete, only three consist of merely a few bars; the other five incomplete works are fairly extended, in spite of lacking defined endings. Several of the remaining ten are quite substantial in scale; dating from 1887 through 1894, one must look carefully between the lines, however. Sinclair's catalogue[287] features the revised dates, presumably as reassigned by Magee; they do not hold up under scrutiny, however, due to the conspicuous lack of corroboration, aside from virtually conclusive handwriting evidence. Magee cast aside Ives's own recollections, work lists and dates, facilitating the 'new' dates of his compositions to later years.

Consequently, what Ives had accomplished as a youngster is diminished, if not effectively removed from the record. The natural inference, of course, is that Parker was all but fully responsible for all of Ives's musical training. Musically, most of these early choral works are consistently constructed according to traditional methods, although Ives, apparently with his father's blessing, was not averse to occasionally throwing caution to the wind. Correspondingly, some unlikely inclusions further color the traditional harmonic language already evident under George's guidance.

Psalm 42 demonstrates that Ives, at about thirteen years of age—and certainly long prior to his exposure to Alexander Gibson at the Danbury School of Music— already was with composing within the traditional musical formats of church practice, at ease, and wholly familiar, with it, too. He did acknowledge having received his father's help in writing it, although Kirkpatrick concluded that none of this youthful

---

[287] Sinclair, *A Descriptive Catalogue of the Music of Charles Ives* (New Haven, CT: Yale University Press, 1999).

60-bar work predates 1890;[288] Sinclair put it at 1892,[289] thus, contradicting Ives's inscription that places it in 1887 (having crossed out both 1886 and 1888). No matter, however, even the later date points no less to Ives's level of accomplishment in his early years, and the latest among them (1892) still predates Ives's departure from Danbury for Hopkins Grammar School in New Haven. Regardless, Kirkpatrick's observation is valuable, because it hints at the path that Carol Baron later (1990) followed in devising her forensic system for dating Ives's manuscripts.[290] Whatever date one accepts in this instance does not alter what it demonstrates in respect to the music itself, or what it illustrates. The youthful Ives is revealed as a highly artistic musician of keen melodic and harmonic gifts, the essence of the same unmistakable, late-Victorian voice heard later in *The Celestial Country*, already substantially formed.

Easter Anthem, from 1890, as it has survived, is not a complete work, though it consists of eighty-nine bars written for chorus accompanied by organ. Its style, again, wholly representative of the era, contains few surprises from a technical standpoint, although its conventionally oriented four-part chordal scoring is surprisingly noble in its implications of religious countenance to have emanated from a composer so young.

Crossing the Bar, for mixed chorus, again reflects its time period through the late-Victorian harmonization, now less than staid, at its core. Another work that has had its date of composition subject to being shifted forward in time, in Sinclair's catalogue, an attempt to assign an earlier date to its first performance ("possibly" 1890) than to its of its composition ("possibly" 1894) stretches all credible scholarship. Convincingly moving through transient keys and musical contrasts, the occasional chromaticism in the harmonies brings Buck's work to mind (Magee referenced its "quaint Victorian-style harmonies," seeming to discredit her hypothesis that Ives had few technical skills prior to studying with Parker).[291]

---

[288] Ives, *Memos*, 147, & n2. and further that a performance of a work with the alternate title, *As Pants the Heart*, under an apparent pseudonym, is documented to have taken place in 1891.

[289] Sinclair (*A Descriptive Catalogue of the Works of Charles Ives*, [New Have, CT: Yale University Press, 1999], 149.

[290] Carol K. Baron, "Dating Charles Ives's Music: Facts and Fictions," *Perspectives of New Music* (Winter issue, 1990): 20–56. Baron demonstrated that very visible changes in Ives's handwriting—evident even over short periods across his entire creative years—offered real insights into the dates of his compositions, rather than blandly accepting the arbitrarily determined new dates of revisionist projections.

[291] Magee, *Charles Ives Reconsidered*, 49, 28.

Communion Service, for mixed chorus, like the *Nine Canticle Phrases* (below), again, has been arbitrarily re-dated by both Sinclair in his catalogue to 1893 (who, later in his commentary acknowledged that the premiere took place in 1890!), and Magee (the incomplete 92 bars of its dissonant *Credo*)—to 1894.[292] It does, in fact, belong to the earliest date, Ives having scrupulously notated that his father had copied and sung the work at the Episcopal Church in Danbury in November 1890. Oddly, the surviving manuscript is not in Ives's hand, and appears to be George's. Although largely set in traditional (mostly) four-part harmony, Ives threw in just enough oddities to sign his own stamp—such as the almost bizarre g# in the third bar of the opening *Kyrie*, not to mention the equally strident parallel fifths in the third bar of the *Sanctus*. Hardly demonstrations of poor tuition, these quirks are typical of the composer's style and the types of irregularities that have been used to illustrate the charge that he was not schooled in any significant way in theory and harmony prior to entering Yale.

Nine Canticle Phrases, for mixed chorus, is a set of hymn-like phrases Ives penned for use in the morning prayer service of St. Thomas's Episcopal Church in New Haven. The specificity of their use has prevented tampering with the work's date (1894), and the assignment to later times of their simple, but creative manipulations of otherwise traditional methodology. Although characterized by mostly four-part chordal writing, Ives wrote to his father about the approach he had taken in harmonizing the melodies, which were built on Gregorian tones. With this observation alone, it should be clear that Ives already was well educated in musical forms through the ages, his familiarity with the Gregorian psalm tones being an especially unusual testament to his early technical prowess. Ives described how he did it, with "diminished chords in the same key, or go to a 1st. and a # remove." The diminished chords are not hard to locate, demonstrated by the opening of his setting for *Canticle ix*, for instance. The musical effect is remarkably modern and otherworldly, especially having come from the hand of a 'provincial' youth from Danbury, CT.

Psalm 67, of all the mixed choral works listed in this segment, stands apart as the only one that is truly modern in outlook in its totality. Described by Swafford as "cosmic barbershop," the little masterwork thoroughly lives up to the image.[293] All the others stay mostly close to the traditions of conventional progressions and four-part writing. Here, in a complete contrast and break with the past, what can only be described as a stunningly original otherworld musical vision, virtually cosmic in

---

[292] Magee, *Charles Ives Reconsidered*, 56.

[293] Swafford, *A Life With Music*, 81

116

scope, is an especially telling utterance from a composer so young. Indeed, the other psalm settings often grouped with it—*24*, *54*, *90* and *150* (Ives had mentioned in *Memos* that his father's choir had 'tried' and struggled with at least the first two, and possibly the others as well—seem to have emanated from a place of the same sonic aura.)[294] Because of the connections Ives made with these undated works to his father, they are usually assigned—quoting from Sinclair's catalogue—to "possibly in summer of 1894" and, consequently, the dates of all five works made vulnerable to skepticism. Notably, *Psalm 67*, arbitrarily post-dated in Sinclair's catalogue to 1898, has routinely been utilized to place its *composition* at the end of the decade, rather than prior to George's death.[295] What is not usually brought up is that the only surviving manuscript of the work is the *fair copy* only, not the materials of its actual composition, as Carol Baron raised in her disagreements with the new dating protocol in general.[296] The most important aspect of the work, however, is missing in these revisionist reassignments—its almost clairvoyantly predictive musicality—that certainly did *not* come from Parker! Magee, also, still missing no opportunity to underline her projection of George Ives as an amateur, suggested that the harmonies might have emerged as a result of his non-professional, bent—in other words, it was beginner's luck—to explain great artistic originality, thus, as belonging more fittingly to the domain of the lowest musical class to which she could assign it!

In all, these early works warrant careful perusal; they are more valuable in all that they represent than commonly allowed. In fact, the more adventurous among them serve to dismantle the major arguments used to deny Ives his place as, according to no less a figure than Igor Stravinsky, "The Great Anticipator."[297]

---

[294] Ives, *Memos*, 47.

[295] Solomon, "A Question of Veracity": 460; Solomon took a mailing address written on the sketch, and stating the incorrect dates that Ives had used it (1899–1900)—it should have been 1889–1900—placed it accordingly. Magee assigned it to the period 1898–1902, based on uncorroborated findings connected primarily to the paper on which it was written; Magee, "Questions and Veracities: Reassessing the Chronology of Ives's Chord Works," *The Musical Quarterly*, 78, 3 (Autumn 1994): 441.

[296] Baron, review, *Journal of the American Musicological Society*, 53, 2, Summer, 2000, 442, footnote 10: J. Peter Burkholder, *All Made of Tunes: Charles Ives and the Uses of Musical Borrowing*, (New Haven , CT: Yale University Press, 1995).

[297] Igor Stravinsky, *Expositions and Developments* (Berkeley, CA: University of California, 1959), 98. Despite the well-known iconic standing of Stravinsky's quote, the source is remarkably hard to find, many commentators and scholars routinely (and surprisingly) failing to cite its source, although readily raising it; e.g., Andrew Buchman, "Ives and Stravinsky," in *Charles Ives and the Classical Tradition*, ed. Geoffrey Block & J. Peter Burkholder (New Haven, CT: Yale University Press, 1996), 147; Richard Taruskin thought it no more than a "standing joke at the time" (presumably due to its likeness to the monicker given to Abraham

Ch. 5 Works that Reflect Ives's Early Influences

Organic Compositions

Variations on 'America' (1892)
Canzonetta in F (1893–94)

At the time Charles Ives left home for Hopkins Grammar School to cram for the entrance exams at Yale, none of his finished pieces could be considered broad musical excursions—in the manner, say, of extended works in sonata form, for example. Consequently, it has been all too easy to dismiss them as inconsequential. If he did nothing else, Horatio Parker was about to have either a direct, or catalytic, effect on the young composer that resulted in the composition of large works framed in substantial, if traditional, formats. There is nothing to substantiate that such models were unknown to Ives previously; the circumstantial evidence would seem to make it clear (e.g., as experienced firsthand in the many organ transcriptions of major works of music all organists were expected to know) that Ives was well familiar with all the traditional formats. Regardless, it is enlightening to look at the two complete larger-scale works that Ives produced prior to the period usually associated with his most significant and substantive output.

Variations on 'America,' for organ, Charles Ives's youthful masterpiece, is a testament to his accomplished musicianship. Discussed and analyzed in detail within the writer's *Charles Ives's Musical Universe*,[298] its relevance in relation to Ives's recollections about George Ives's teaching cannot to be overlooked. Magee, however, instead of according George the deserved credit for steering his son through the composition of this intricate work—and, consequently, having to acknowledging the pivotal role he played in his son's training—tried to *disassociate* father and son by claiming that Ives had deliberately separated himself from George by choosing a patriotic tune, rather than one played by George's 'amateur' bands. However, George's bands played many such tunes, among which *America*, surely, was one. Magee offered no explanation for how such a sophisticated work had emanated from

---

Lincoln, "The Great Emancipator"), apparently unaware of its origin, in his *Music in the Early Twentieth Century: The Oxford History of Western Music*, "Containing Multitudes [Transcendentalism, II]," (Oxford, UK: Oxford University Press, 2010), 263; or Bayan Northcutt, "The Double Life of Charles Ives" *The Independent*, 12 January, 1996, merely quotes the label, as if everyone knows its origin. Harold C. Schonberg got it right however, in *The Lives of the Great Composers* (New York: W.W. Norton and Co, 1997), 556, but failed to provide the whereabouts in Stravinsky's writings it can be found. Just because Stravinsky's book is out of print at this time should not render its contents unknown or not properly identified.

[298] Cooke, *Charles Ives's Musical Universe*, 31–36.

a composer whose early training she had made to appear so inadequate.[299] The date of composition of Ives's *Variations* almost certainly was 1891; two documented performances appear to confirm it, even though it was listed under a different name. The first is a violin and organ version, the title only slightly spurious: *National Airs for Violin and Organ, arr. with Pedal IV Variations.* It seems, however, to be the same piece, if not an earlier version. The second performance (entitled *Variations on a National Hymn*) took place in Brewster, NY on 1892 February 17, again, not long after Ives completed it.[300] In light of the lack of evidence of the existence of any other work(s), all three appear to be one and the same.

Famously one of the works in which George Ives's resistance to more radical ideas appeared in actual performed works, for once, it was not Parker standing in the way of modernism—it was George! It is why the two stridently polytonal interludes the were disallowed in the only surviving version in George's hand, though they are penciled on his fair copy that was prepared for possible publication, and sent to Ashmall, the publisher, in 1892.[301] George recognized that Ives's listeners would not be ready for such an abrasive aural assault; it was returned, nevertheless, unpublished in 1894, but should settle, once and for all, any question about its date. Ives remarked that his father had allowed him to try the interludes in the Brewster concert, despite his thoughts on the matter. It is an odd contradiction: even as George, experimenter and proponent of truly modern ideas, required Charles to embrace multiple tonalities in exercise assignments (to develop the senses), he could not embrace it in actual musical composition.[302] *Variations on 'America'* also reveals something about George's expertise, both as a musician and teacher, because as Feder pointed out, its frequently imaginative and innovative writing is clear evidence of George's guidance, *because his corrections appear over the manuscript.* Remarking on the level of expertise Ives had reached by the time he had reached his mid-to-late teens, Feder even compared its chromaticism to the music of Cesar Franck.[303]

Canzonetta in F (c.1893–94), though less substantive than *Variations on 'America'*, demonstrates again the high level of sophistication the young Charles Ives

---

[299] Magee, *Charles Ives Reconsidered*, 26.

[300] See Sinclair, *A Descriptive Catalogue*, 248. Remarks reproduced in a letter drafted by Ives in answer to issues raised by E. Power Biggs about the *Variations* provide a window into Ives's keen and self-deprecating sense of humor.

[301] Ives, *Memos*, 38.

[302] Charles Ives, *Memos*, 88, 115.

[303] Feder, *"My Father's Song,"* 114.

already had attained before attending Yale. So named from the inherited song-like qualities of what originally were Italian madrigal-like compositions, 'canzonettas' were popular format at the time, appearing among the works of a number of his celebrated predecessors, such as William Dawson Armstrong (1868–1936) and Arthur Foote (1853–1937), even Horatio Parker, and George Chadwick. The link to it in America, however, likely is mostly through Chadwick's lineage, whose teacher, Josef Rheinberger, also utilized the format and presumably handed it down to his students.

Ives's *Canzonetta*, though, in character, denoting something even lighter in substance than most madrigals, reveals a remarkable propensity for building upon motifs, with extremely confident flexibility managing chromatic modulations; conspicuously again, it dates to the years prior to Ives's exposure to Parker. By this time, Ives's musical training included not only what his father had taught him (which included hearing major symphonic works in New York concerts), but also organ studies with Ella Hollister, and advanced studies with Alexander Gibson at the Danbury School of Music. To take the revised view that Ives would not have been thoroughly familiar with many works of the standard literature while still living at home seems to ignore the obvious, especially his broader experience, as an organist, having wide access to the classics. The technical acumen of Ives's pre-college days could not be more apparent.

Beginning innocently enough, initially, the *Canzonetta's* simple harmonies firmly adhere to the tonic key, F, with only one brief, chromatically altered shift through G in the first eight-bar segment—and falling back immediately. The next eight-bar segment completes the first section, still in simple diatonic fashion. It is not until the next, middle section, that some moments of more noteworthy harmonies occur. In m.15, a C# diminished seventh chord and a memorable two-bar figure—the tones of which, otherwise, would have suggested E minor—is interjected by the right hand with a chromatically ascending motif (almost implying the 'fate motif' from Beethoven's *Fifth Symphony* that is found in many of Ives's compositions), before being answered by an evolution of the figure.

Followed by another interjection of that ascending motif at T6, the music begins to shift toward the ultimate tonality of the section (E)—a surprising tonal destination compared to the outset, which began a semitone higher. Subsequently inverting the chromatic motif, and placing it as a single melodic line, Ives added an eighth-note to its beginning. After repeating it at T9, and continuing the bass motion in an implied, though not literal, sequence from m.6, the accompaniment matches a descending scale to the motif, joined in parallel sixths during these transpositions. Furthering the purpose toward a gradual confirmation of E, eighth-note movement in the right hand

120

adds the seventh to make Em7. In the next bar (m.27), a B triad in the left hand shifts to a clear implication of the dominant from in the middle of the next bar, with the inclusion of the seventh (in which the harmony outlines F#°, though it implies B7). With a new figure above (in m.28) the shift into E major is completed, though not yet confirmed. The new figure, extended by the initial two-bar figure in m.31, is harmonized again by B7. Still transient, moving through major chords E, G and C, the final confirmation of E (via G#°7) in the left hand, and a change of key signature to E in m.34, the shift is complete.

In the next segment it can be seen that Ives's movement of transitional harmonic roots allow progressions to feel wholly natural without a single dominant chord:

$$I-VII-I-IV-II-II\emptyset 7-VII-7-Vm-II-\#IV°-7$$

Melodically, Ives developed the last three notes of the second figure that was introduced in m.28 (also again interjecting the motif that resembles the 'fate motif'), as the section concludes on an unexpected C7 fermata, and a return to the opening materials and conclusion stepping back up to the original tonic key of F.

Can the *Canzonetta* be considered experimental in any way, even likely, perhaps, as just a little hard on Victorian ears? The question, of course, cannot necessarily be answered. Would George Ives have approved such novel ideas more readily than he would have approved the interludes in *Variations on 'America'*? If we should conclude that George's stance meant that *no* musical adventurism in concert works was to appear under his watch, we only have to examine *Variations* to realize that George was far from strict in this regard. For all his posturing, clearly, he was trying to ensure that Charles did nothing without full rationale, and perhaps he was not quite so opposed to radicalism in actual compositions, after all.

Once at Yale, there can be no doubt that, for all Ives gained, the music he wrote for Parker represented a step backwards, creatively; although he never put his adventurist ideas aside, it would take a number of years once again before Ives confidently 'broke the rules,' and consistently threw caution to the wind with the visionary works that exploded onto the scene from 1906 on. Regardless, even in later years, one cannot escape the telling residue of Ives's time with Parker, even after the flowering of his many years with his father had been translated into substantial works of music. Critical to this discussion, *none of those attributes could have emanated from Parker*. Ives already had revealed their origins.

Instrumental Compositions

Holiday Quickstep, **picc, cornet, pf., vlns. (1887)**
March No. 3, with 'My Old Kentucky Home,' **small orch. (c.1892)**
Variations on 'Jerusalem the Golden,' **band (1889?)**

     Holiday Quickstep, Ives's youthful little work, often cited as a watershed in his development, no less often finds its significance dismissed. Magee, for example, criticizing its melodic qualities, harmonies and musical direction, indirectly, also marginalized George, who guided his son in writing it (again tagging him with the term, "amateur.").[304] Swafford's appraisal, however, could not have been more different, recognizing that a thirteen-year-old had convincingly absorbed the music of his father's parade bands.[305] Even such clear and convincing demonstrations of Ives's technical and musical ability prior to 1894 do not dampen continued projections that *only under Parker's guidance* would Ives finally receive the education in harmony, counterpoint, orchestration and composition that he so 'desperately' needed.[306] The argument will only abate with time and the continued exposure of the evidence itself.

     March No. 3, with 'My Old Kentucky Home,' for concert band, and among the more delightful creations for the youthful composer, likely dates from his waning days in Danbury, some time in 1892. It is possible that Ives wrote it after he had left home in 1893, although everything about its style and manner points to his Danbury years, the quaint traditions of New England (and his father's bands) ringing through each of its 121 bars. Beginning with a short introduction, the march begins in F Major in a jaunty 6/8 meter. This, the primary theme, is presented with the full ensemble, and concludes with a short 'codetta' in unison octaves; repeated with reduced ensemble, the unison codetta brings the segment to a quick conclusion, immediately followed by a gentle contrasting episode, and a solo trumpet taking the lead over woodwinds. The episode leads directly and seamlessly into an upbeat *My Old Kentucky Home*, led by the trombones and divided into a three-part segment that is complete in itself, before being followed by a second episode in three distinct short chromatic segments, which serves to bring the march back to the opening primary theme. Played now once only, the primary theme comes to a rapid ending, truly characteristic of the form. The plan for the march is straightforward, its two themes—

---

[304] Magee, *Charles Ives Reconsidered*, 20–21.

[305] Swafford, *A Life With Music*, 51.

[306] Magee, *Charles Ives Reconsidered*, 48.

that by Ives and *My Old Kentucky Home*—are indicative of Ives's thorough immersion in George's bands and the idiom:

[Intro] [Primary theme (2x)]   ["My Old Kentucky Home"   ]
    I—(**A**i–bi–**A**ii–bii)—**B**i-ii-iii-iv–(**C**i–cii–ciii–civ)—(**D**i-dii)-(ciii-civ)
                [episode]
                                          [Primary theme]
(a-aii-b-bii)–(c-cii)–(d-dii)-(f-g-h-i-j-k-l—)–(**A**-bi-**A**ii–bii)–
  [Climbing Bridge   ]
                                    [Primary theme—end]
(a-aii-b-bii)–(c-cii)–(d-dii)-(f-g-h-i-j-k-l—)–(**A**-bi-**A**ii–bii) **|**
  [Climbing Bridge   ]

Variations on 'Jerusalem the Golden,' again in F, consists of just 78 bars, apparently for band (the only surviving short score does not work well as a keyboard or organ piece), and another delightful relic of Ives's early life, it appears to be one and the same piece he described in his 1929 'Conductor's Note' to accompany the *Scherzo* of his Fourth Symphony. Here, Ives described an early 'spatial' work: an unusual arrangement of the band in the town square, in which the primary group was surrounded by two or three smaller antiphonal groups in unusual acoustic locations that weaved in and out of the texture through the variations. The theme—the well-known hymn—begins the piece in chorale style with understated brass, and concludes with one of the antiphonal groups (woodwinds) joining in with arpeggiated eighth-notes and a brief, partly chromatic bridge that leads back to a variation: the melody in full scoring, with the moving eighths interspersed at key points in the phrase. A short chromatic episodal bridge follows, gently scored for woodwinds that ends with a strong perfect cadence by the whole band, and then the first true variation in the minor. Featuring solo trumpet, the variation is notable for its operatic style, clearly pointing to the work of Giuseppe Verdi (and to the young Ives's obvious familiarity with his music). This variation is followed by an even more full setting of the main melody, eventually accompanied by a 'walking' bass line as it rises progressively to a grand cadence, and soft final 'amen' cadence.

Songs

At Yale, Ives became increasingly prolific as a songwriter, expanding the format while he worked out his creative ideas. Aided by the piano and his voice, and frequently carried into his compositions, most of his early efforts, thus, had started purely as songs, written within the standard 'parlor' genre of the day. Although he

Ch. 5 Works that Reflect Ives's Early Influences

did not consider this type of work worthy of inclusion in *114 Songs*—he *did* include some of them, nevertheless—tagging these examples as having "little or no musical value." People, thus, would know what to avoid![307]

Slow March **(1888) [#114]**
A Song—for Anything **[song version] (1892) [#89]**
At Parting **(1889)**
Friendship **(1892)**
Canon **(1893) [#111]**

Slow March clearly was *not* the product of passion for dissonance; indeed, what it contains lies at the very heart of Ives's down-to-earth authenticity that, for open-minded listeners, it is the real channel to appreciating his music. Simple reflections of daily life, portrayed without pretension, paint Ives's personal experience with an unfiltered directness that put the listener into his world. Such immediacy, so instinctive in the young—retained in Ives's consciousness—was carried over into his mature music, albeit increasingly refined.

The song also reflects his close-knit family. H. Wiley Hitchcock documented that several members had contributed the words: both parents, his uncle Lyman Brewster, and his paternal grandmother.[308] The fourteen-year-old Ives's naive little eulogy is to a deceased and loved pet; we hear the same tears of loss that so poignantly mark "From Hanover Square North, at the End of a Tragic Day. . . ." that conclude the *Second Orchestral Set* (1915) almost thirty years later; the same tears shed for the loss of Danbury townspeople's family members in *Decoration Day* (1913); Ives's own losses (his father and unborn child) in the Third Symphony (1904, rev.1909–11), in which his fading innocence is captured again—before ultimately being shattered by approaching war, serious illness, and political disillusionment. Even late in Ives's composing timeline, these emotions, still virtually intact from childhood, can be encountered in the touching sentiments Ives felt toward his own father in the song, *The Greatest Man* (1921).

Musically, *Slow March*, at first hearing seeming to be a most basic setting, hints of the fluent harmonic sophistication that is to come as the song proceeds. The first half is wholly conventional—never venturing far from the simple somberness

---

[307] Charles Ives, *114 Songs* (New York, Knickerbocker Press, 1921), Appendix.

[308] H. Wiley Hitchcock, *Critical Commentaries for Charles Ives: 129 Songs* (Middleton, WS: American Musicological Society, 2004), 1.

reflected in the funereal setting. Nevertheless, a few, but entirely telling, poignant strains of angst reveal Ives's truly creative talent: toward the end of the third system, the dominant chord appears in the minor, resolving to the similarly transformed tonic; a half-diminished treatment of the subdominant in the last system adds a further tinge of regret, before the major is reaffirmed—quoting from Handel's *Saul*: 'Dead March,' as it does so—to allow a final sense of 'Amen' again (and characteristically) with a plagal, rather than a perfect, cadence.

At Parting dates from Ives's childhood, and the song in which an unresolved dissonance had so displeased Parker; its refinement and sophistication is remarkable for a fifteen-year-old. Although the song's easy sentimentality was precisely what Ives would later shun, the natural musicality and authenticity of emotion coming from one so young is striking. The freedom with which in its brief middle section moves (which acts more like a bridge) from the primary key (G major), to traverse through remarkably remote key centers and subtle harmonic shadings, is again testament to the expertise he had acquired long before attending Yale. Such direct evidence of his abilities are diametrically opposite to Magee's almost callous dismissal—based, presumably, on the short excursions in George's copybook. The vocal range is also noteworthy, incrementally traversing low to high registers across subphrases, ultimately reaching the major seventh of the key and up to the tonic (the 'Romantic semitone') that creates the yearning associated with the subject of the song.

Another song from Ives's Danville days is *Friendship*, from 1892. At eighteen years of age, he no doubt was beginning to reflect on his approaching circumstances that would take him away from home and all the people with whom he had grown up. Aside from the now-well-practiced language of the song, Ives had already learned to stamp a unique identity on each—in this case, it is the opening phrase of each verse. Here, he manipulated the emotional connection through neighbor-tones and harmonies, which provide the mood right from the outset, the primary line weaving through a line of adjacent pitches:

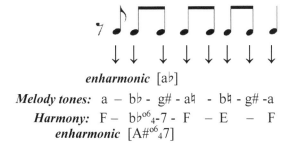

enharmonic [a♭]

Melody tones: a — b♭ - g# - a♮ - b♮ - g# -a

Harmony: F — b♭♭$^{o6}_4$-7 - F — E — F

enharmonic [A#$^{o6}_4$7]

Ch. 5 Works that Reflect Ives's Early Influences

It is this small part of the song that provides the memorable 'hook,' the part by which we remember it. Indeed, the characteristic is notable in virtually all of Ives's songs from the period, showing his substantial understanding of the medium, and his remarkable sophistication. The other noticeable trait is that the young Ives is very much the melodist, which ought to end any further disparagement concerning his use of quotes and his ability to write his own tunes.

Ives included *A Song—for Anything* in *114 Songs* as an example of how a song should *not* be written (and even more never performed!). It does have some redeeming features, nevertheless, which, again, are indicative of Ives's technical sophistication. The highly amusing, typically 'Ivesian,' anecdote attached to this sheet music reveals, too, a greater cultural sophistication among his well-respected extended family than that of the contemporary general populace. Nevertheless, if the song lacks the degree of artistic refinement that Ives would come to demand of himself, along with its adherence to pedantic broken chord alternations in the right hand over a predictable bass, it demonstrates a certain notable harmonic agility.

Specifically, in m.4. Ives shifts between tonic and dominant seventh harmony via a diminished seventh, which does much to establish the late-Victorian melodramatic flavor of the setting. The third bar of the second system heeds George Ives's admonition to listen to the effect of a chord, rather than be bound by stringent rules (the *sound* of what is committed to the page being allowed to overrule the theoretical)—in this instance, the third of the half-diminished seventh VI chord being left out in the accompaniment. Present in the vocal line, its absence in the accompaniment is not missed, even were the voice absent. Approaching the conclusion, Ives set up a stream of chromaticism through one segment, wholly fitting of the idiom, while decidedly demonstrating his technical sophistication:

mm.15.   **16.**   **17.**   **18. 19.**

II - III7 - VIIø7 | I7 - IV - VI7 | ♭VII-II7(M)-I-V7 | I - | I - ||

Canon was written, apparently, in 1893; some confusion exists about the date, however, because in *114 Songs*, Ives listed it as 1894. Sinclair listed it as "adapted in 1894 from material composed in Jan.1893," so, at least, it cannot be credited to studies with Parker. Regardless, it stands in testimony to Ives's fluent command of harmony and counterpoint, his unique creativity, and the easy flexibility with which he uses the medium. In just thirty-five bars, Ives revealed more about his genius than in practically any other work from his Pre-Yale days, and also succinct refutation to the stubborn refusals by some to grant Ives his due.

Set as a true two-part canon at the octave, with a few notable exceptions in the strictest application of the form (the substitution of a# in the piano part in m.12; the short piano interlude in the canonic movement between mm.24–25; the substitution of c#–a for d–b in the piano at the end of mm.28/mm.29; the cessation of the canon itself in m.33; and the brief resumption of canonic interplay in compressed form [now just two beats apart] in the last two bars.) In mm.3–7, the absence of the harmonic third, both in the tonic and dominant harmony, again harks back to George Ives's teaching (notably his lesson notes), in regard to the *sound* versus the theoretical. Revealing that Ives already knew much about composing for the genre before entering Yale, a striking resemblance of settings may be observed in Ives's song and Parker's *Morning* (1893), never more clearly in display than such in bars as mm.29–31.

The stridency of the cross relationship between the bass line and the voice from m.11 to m.12 is only amplified by the dominant harmony in m.12 that assumes the *major* seventh form. (A minor seventh drop in the bass line in m.11 is echoed from m.14–15 by its ascent across the same interval.) Passing through various chromatically altered chords (relative to the tonic: E), the harmony, overall, occupies the dominant harmony throughout mm.12–19. By m.21, the harmony shifts from Em7 to D7, with an unexpected resolution to B (rather than B7), which, in turns, leads back to E major. A small melodic alteration at the ends of m.28 and m.29 between both canonic voices accommodates the sudden dominant seventh quality accorded the tonic. Passing through its resolution to A major, and a diminished sharpened from of the harmony, the canonic motion ceases as the song concludes with a classic IV-V-I cadence and a brief, compressed recommencement of canonic interplay. Again, for anyone to assert that Ives lacked an advanced technical background prior to attending Yale, illustrates, either, a woeful lack of expertise, or a willful denial of the truth.

Ch. 5 Works that Reflect Ives's Early Influences

Chapter 6
Works From Ives's Yale Years

$\mathcal{T}$he copious numbers of substantive works written while Ives was a student at Yale offers a real opportunity to evaluate what he gained during these years. Their representation is sufficient to allow a more serious consideration than perhaps has been given in the past to determine what seeds from earlier years blossomed as a result of scholastic necessity, stimulus, and growing maturity. Bearing in mind the skills Ives already possessed from his earlier years, clearly demonstrated in the previous chapters of this book, it is entirely reasonable to suppose, among the music of Ives's Yale years we should find:

(1) Purely academic excursions for Parker's class, and
(2) Compositions Ives undertook as requirements in creative composition.

Perhaps there is no better place to start than with strict examples of a traditional format in works that stand alone (in this instance, fugue), and as incorporated into larger compositions, (fugato applications), under less rigorously applied constraints.

A Tale of Four Fugues

by Ives:

Fugue in C Minor **(1898)**
First String Quartet, **first movement [fugato] (1896)**

by Parker:

Fugue in C Minor, **from** *Four Compositions for the Organ*, **Op. 36, No. 3 (1893)**
"Pars Mea, Rex Meus," [fugato] No.4, from *Hora Novissima* **(1893)**

Ives always maintained that his father had raised him on the music of Bach, and taught him well in harmony and counterpoint. He complained, too, at Yale, that he had felt stifled because Parker covered again much the same ground, even using the same textbooks. Ives's remark on his father's insistence on knowing how to excel in traditional fugal writing before attempting to break the rules is, of course, well known.[309] Thus, unless one is predisposed not to take Ives at his word, it is entirely reasonable to suppose that many examples of imitative counterpoint, other than the short experiments from early childhood in his father's copybook, existed at one time; furthermore, that Ives began his time at Yale with more than a casual acquaintance with all forms of baroque music also via his years as a church organist.

Parker, with the strictest of approaches to the art of musical composition always in mind, taught traditional counterpoint, along with harmony, form, and orchestration. Having stated that "the best way to appreciate music is to make it,"[310] it is not surprising, therefore, that Parker's students would have been required to demonstrate excellence in all forms of musical composition, and would have made every effort to please their teacher by emulating his style and technique. Fugues were among his class assignments; representing the highest form of traditional polyphony, Parker's mastery of it was widely recognized in his time.

A couple of Ives's student fugues for organ have survived from his Yale years, and are quite instructive in revealing what he learned for his teacher. Of them, the *Fugue in C* minor almost seems to mirror one by Parker: the *Fugue, Op. 36, No. 3*, also in C minor and dating from 1893. Both are entirely traditional, academically pure in approach, with no apparent attempt to stake any allegiance to personal style. Ives's resentment of having to indulge his teacher with this type of exercise was reflected in his comment on the copy of another surviving example, in E flat major, from his time with Parker: "A stupid fugue on a stupid subject." Both of Ives's fugues confirm Parker's thorough attitude in relation to being able to demonstrate 'proper' contrapuntal practice, the adoption of the half-note as the prime rhythmic unit in his fugue (not to mention Ives's) underlining it.

Of the two organ fugues under discussion in this section, Ives's fugue likely dates to his junior year, its possible direct influence by Parker's fugue seeming, thus, quite plausible. Because pure fugues by Parker that appear in the strictest format are not plentiful, such as this example, it seems quite realistic as well to posit that this particular work—published within a group, *Four Compositions for Organ*—was perhaps one that Parker used as a model in his classes. Ives's fugue is not only in the

---

[309] Ives, *Memos*, 47–49.

[310] Smith, "A Study of Horatio Parker," 158.

same key, but also shows remarkably similar traits, despite the obvious differences between them. One departure from one to the other is that Parker's is a double fugue. Nevertheless, on the page, the two pieces look almost as if they could join onto each other, their identical registers, fundamental pacing, and adherence to diatonic, motivic, rhythmic elements, appearing virtually matched, even as Ives's is in 4/2, and Parker's in 6/4. Both beginning in the pedals, their ascending figures easily could belong to each other, their respective subjects occupying four bars. Neither features a true countersubject, although Ives's does briefly establish one through the first two-and-a-half subject entries, before abandoning it for free counterpoint. Episodic material is drawn from the same material in Ives's fugue. In Parker's fugue, such material is taken from near the opening of the first subject, as well as being redeveloped in diminution into a rhythmic, cyclical feature that defines his *second* fugal subject. They are wholly conventional in the tonic/dominant appearances of their four initial fugal entries.

A shared feature of both examples is the use of short diatonic sequences. A long established technique, it is also the root of all cyclical applications, such as the innovative cycles that Ives would pioneer. Returning to them with regularity as a device in his early radical compositions, and throughout his output, it is easy to see where the idea might have come from, although having long been a church organist, Ives *surely* was thoroughly familiar with the form already. Diminution, rather than augmentation, also is common to both fugues, although Parker took a four-note fragment from the *end* of the first subject as his second subject, to reappear in diminution in eighth-notes (with few exceptions, eighth-notes do not appear in Ives's fugue). The figure Parker utilized is common throughout Western music—a 'turn'—consisting of neighbor tones above and below the fundamental, and is found in Ives's fugue, too; the first tone, tied to a whole-note at the *end* of his little-used countersubject, and variously placed thereafter in free counterpoint, is common, thus, to both. This detail alone seems to strongly suggest that Ives was influenced by Parker.[311]

There remain some differences, however. Ives took the opening tones of his subject and used them extensively in diminution, inverted, and in slight variation, through the course of his fugue, and also included a stretto, missing in Parker's, although both fugues approach their respective conclusions with sustained chords in the manuals and even-paced motion in the pedals. In Parker's, the motion is built from his second subject; in Ives's, from the three-note, quarter-note scalic figure that appears at the end of his countersubject that is used with regularity throughout his

---

[311] See Appendix II, n.2.

fugue, and also in inversion. In many ways, the little figure resembles the primary four-note figure that defines Parker's second theme! Despite the differences that separate the two respective traditional fugues, their character and execution seem in close proximity.

The (double) fugato movement that begins Ives's **First String Quartet**, was written at Yale in 1896—again with the same half-note rhythmic unit. Despite being largely traditional in style, if not quite, in model, it reveals much about the latent musical genius behind it. Originally an organ fugue, Ives surely considered it of sufficient merit to rework and position it as the first movement in his string quartet, even going to some lengths to deny its earlier identity by removing it from his final version of the string quartet and applying it to his Fourth Symphony.[312] A good example of fugato writing within one of Parker's compositions can be compared with Ives's work. For chorus, his esteemed Yale professor positioned it within a larger original segment of his iconic cantata, **Hora Novissima, No.4, 'Pars Mea, Rex Meus.'** Although the entire work will be examined later, this isolated segment warrants an examination in the context of the present discussion. These two examples of fugato writing found in these respective larger concert works offer different clues, however, to the purely creative and independent artistic decisions made by each. As such, they act as another indicator of the degree of creative influence Parker exerted upon his student. It must be said, however, in conclusion, that of the two, it is Parker's that fares less well in the comparison, Ives's being more fluid, and more interesting harmonically.

Ives was able to throw convention aside sufficiently to produce a piece of music that, despite adhering to many of the tenets of conventionality (nothing less would have passed Parker's muster), does so, nevertheless, with such an undisguised lack of uniformity that the music no longer sounds in any way generic. It resonates, in fact, entirely as a composition by Ives. Posing as a double fugue, the movement never fits the form at all, being, in totality, no more than fugal in nature. From virtually the outset, Ives's original treatment of the materials suggests a countersubject upon the second (dominant) entrance of the subject (quoting the hymn, *Missionary Hymn*), which is entirely subverted by its *absence* against the next (tonic) entrance, and further still by its *reappearance* in the next entrance in the dominant key—though more than a bar earlier than its expected position—forming, instead, the upper line of

---

[312] Ives considered the movement integral to his much later Fourth Symphony, and recorded that it was composed in 1916, rather than acknowledge its Yale-years origin. Regardless, although he extracted it from the string quartet, his wishes to see the quartet considered complete without its inclusion is seldom respected, the movement having found its way back into the official published edition.

a one-bar bridge to the next statement of the subject! As a result, the subject is offset relatively by this amount in its counter-play. Ives's second subject (the hymn, *Coronation*) does not feature a countersubject at all, placing, instead, variants of the *first* subject against it in free counterpoint, while never following the expected I-V-I-V series of entrances. Indeed, most respective suggestions of the second subject occur in the same voice (first violin), more often appearing as a vaguely implied chain of sequences than fugal entries, despite the impression of conventionality given.

Parker's fugato segment in *Hora Novissima* (starting within movement *No.4*, after the largely homophonic introductory segment) is no less revealing. However, it is by the *lack* of departure from the very same regimens, which constrained his more academically oriented organ fugue, that sets it apart from Ives's quartet movement. Eminently solid and workmanlike, as would be expected, nevertheless, its reliance on tradition ensures that it does not break the boundaries established by generations of previous composers, nor even, the standard formatting of his organ fugue. Parker's fugato, also having no countersubject, states the subject (unlike Ives's), in conventional fashion (I-V-I-V). After a short episode, it appears again in the relative minor (C), all four voices appearing in the expected sequence, though a short episode bridges two bars between the second and third statements. A further episode begins and ends with chains of diatonic descending stepwise sequences, and a mid-section based on the first four notes of the subject in diminution in the bass, and ascending scales in thirds in the tenors and sopranos. Further statements of the subject are accompanied by imitative statements of the same scale figure, in yet further diminution, leading and accompanying two more statements of the subject and a brief stretto built on its first three notes. From this point, the music returns to its largely homophonic texture. It is only with the scalic figure that Parker, perhaps, allowed his more creative side to enter the texture, though no one should doubt Parker's mastery of the format as is demonstrated in this example, and for which he was justly revered.

It is instructive to note that both quoted examples begin with a figure that is shared via inversion; in this respect, Ives demonstrated his affinity for such connections that are found throughout his music, not to mention his unique approach to writing this simulation of a double fugue. Both subjects feature, too, the same neighbor-note figure found in the other previous examples, a figure that appears extensively in Ives's episodic writing of this example. Including, too, the recognizable and obvious quote from Bach's own *Toccata and Fugue in D Minor* (Dorian), BWV538, not only is Ives's propensity for musical quotations striking and further demonstrated, but also the breadth of his musical knowledge and ease in departing from the expected norms. The movement continues in approximate simulation of a fugue, though it is never constrained by any particular rule. There is even a stretto, so one might be forgiven for thinking the music has traversed a conventional outline. Needless, to say, the additional quoted material, its handling, and the eventual (1916) expansion of the original fugue into the third movement of Ives's Fourth Symphony, deserves more than the casual comment of this stylistic comparison. A detailed analysis may be found in the writer's *Charles Ives's Musical Universe* (West Conshohocken, PA: Infinity, 2015), 400–10.

Regardless of the conventional essence of both works, it is Ives's that breaks away to reveal something decidedly more interesting and personal, almost in spite of its self-imposed shackles. Likely, the influence of George, too, is reflected in Ives's fugato.

Verdict: Ives's abilities in traditional counterpoint likely were refined by Parker through his rigorously austere approach. In freer creative applications, however, Ives emerges as the true original creator, his greater individuality, in this instance within an old format makes it more his own. Overall, Parker's influence, though present, in respect of the type of writing shown here, ought not to be overstated.

A Tale of Four Symphonies

> **by Ives: First Symphony**
> **by Dvořák: Ninth Symphony (*'From The New World'*)**
> **by Chadwick: Second Symphony**
> **by Parker: First Symphony in C Major**

It would have been all too convenient to have been able to link both the first symphonies of Ives and Parker, both works emerging from their respective student years. The lack of a ready comparison also reveals, however, Ives's vast potential, and Parker's apparent lack of it—even more, any sense that he was sufficiently aware of the prevailing idiom of the day to have absorbed it. At the time Parker wrote his *First Symphony*, it is clear that he was little more than talented imitator of a long established format. Any hope for discovering the opposite vanishes at once upon examining the score. Kearns remarked that it lacked originality, and emulated a pre-Romantic model "no later than early Beethoven."[313] The observation, perhaps, points to the reason that Parker went *no further than Beethoven* in the music literature classes that Ives had attended.[314] Although, Parker might have expanded the course

---

[313] Kearns, *Horatio Parker*, 208.

[314] Ives, *Memos*, 182.

134

in later years, Ives's exposure to him was at the start of Parker's tenure at Yale, his reputation resting most securely upon his choral and vocal works, and an absence of notable orchestral work.[315]

Regardless, the propagation of fictitious accounts of the music that Ives studied with Parker have traveled far beyond the actual descriptions of the syllabus in Parker's classes. In the Critical Edition of the symphony, for instance, James B. Sinclair implied, if not precisely enunciated, that *under Parker*, Ives studied Schubert, Brahms, Tchaikovsky and Dvořák, "among others," yet there is no documentation to the writer's knowledge that supports the contention.[316] At the time Ives encountered him, with the singular exception of his Overture for Orchestra: *Count Robert of Paris*, Op.24 (1890), Parker was yet to pen a significant orchestral work. Any other purely symphonic compositions reach back to his own student days. Even so, the overture, nevertheless, does not equate with some of the more significant orchestral writings yet to come from Parker, especially the growing sophistication of the composer in his writing for the medium.[317]

Parker's symphony, however, falls in line with the work of a reasonably proficient, if not particularly innovative, composition student, considering the enterprise of undertaking a work of its scale. In stark comparison, Ives's first excursion into the symphonic medium, as a work that presumably was fully formed, if not, *perhaps*, entirely finished before he left Yale, is masterful in its conception, execution and maturity. It is far beyond anything that an objective listener might anticipate in a 'student work.' For Parker not to have openly recognized the enormous talent he had under his wing also could help to explain the mixed feelings Ives always felt towards his esteemed Yale professor—the regard in which he held him, effectively, countered by his protests of Parker's rigidity. It might also do much to answer Magee's assertion that Ives did not accord Parker the gratitude to which she felt he was entitled.[318]

Ives's symphony has provided endless controversy, not only in attempts to place it outside Ives's years at Yale, but also by its theorized links to other works of the genre, popular melodies, and most of all, to Dvořák's Ninth Symphony (*The New*

---

[315] Cantatas and other similar large-scale works, such as oratorios that involved chorus and/or soloists were highly fashionable during the era, and widely embraced by his senior American contemporaries, such as George Chadwick and Dudley Buck.

[316] Charles E. Ives, First Symphony (New York: Peermusic, 1999), Preface by James B. Sinclair, iv.

[317] Review, *New York Times*, 11 December,1890, 4.

[318] Gayle Sherwood Magee, *Charles Ives Reconsidered*, 48.

World).[319] Compounded by expressions by some of the 'certainty' that the *New World Symphony* was 'known' to Ives,[320] the 'Dvořákian' connection, real or imagined, unfortunately, has stuck; references to it appear with regularity in books, articles and program notes. Audiences, however, often must be left puzzled, because, in truth, there is little about it that sounds like anything Dvořák wrote.

Ives has been criticized, too, for making changes to his symphony, even, too, for possibly having *completed* it (despite his many annotations in the materials to the contrary) over four years after graduation. Ives can be partly blamed for inviting revisionism upon his symphony, having listed numerous dates of the various manuscript components of all four movements. They range from as early (impossibly?) as 1895, up until 1902—one notation emphasizing that the first movement was <u>not</u> part of his thesis—thus, contradicting the commonly accepted view that this definitive part of the work was written for his Yale graduation![321] The latest date, 1902, is, however, more puzzling. Likely, it is a reference to some revisions Ives made prior to having the symphony copied, which might not have taken place until as late as 1908. It does seem reasonable, however, to assign the majority of the symphony to Ives's years with Parker, and mostly to the later dates, with only some revisions and emendations undertaken prior to the making of the ink copyist's score. Because Ives had numerous disagreements with Parker about many aspects of the symphony, it is entirely realistic to propose that, later, he might have wished to revisit and 'repair' parts of it. It is wholly unrealistic, however, to consider that the symphony was anything less than fully conceived during Ives's Yale years, *and* had been completed in substantive form at the time.

Conforming to the current climate of Ives scholarship, however, the completion, and even much of the symphony's main composition, has been shifted forward gratuitously by four years—to Ives's post-Yale years—conveniently in line with Ives's own reference to 1902.[322] As a work that represented a musical language Ives was in the process of abandoning, if, indeed, he did later undertake changes to the work, *surely*, they were for little more than its fine-tuning for posterity. Making later revisions and refinements is far from a particularly unusual practice among composers. As extended a timeline as any exists in relation to Brahms's own first symphony, for which the composer, himself, cited a twenty-year plus timeline for

---

[319] For example, see Sinclair, *A Descriptive Catalogue*, 4.

[320] Burkholder, *All Made of Tunes*, 89–102; *Charles Ives: The Ideas Behind the Music*, ed. Block & Burkholder, 22–27.

[321] Magee, *Charles Ives Reconsidered*, 60.

[322] Ibid., 60.

136

finalizing the version known today. Mahler similarly returned to his first symphony; completing it in 1888, he revised in 1893, and again in 1896, still tinkering with it into his final years. Bruckner, similarly, revised his own first symphony repeatedly, the various versions coming into being after the first (1866), followed by revisions in 1868, 1877, 1884, and 1891; comparable examples can be found in near endless supply, and yet, one does not encounter any comment that any such revision was, in any way, improper to for their creators to undertake—except in the case of Charles Ives, who has been unceremoniously positioned on the losing end of moral scrutiny.

Returning to the premise that Ives not only had heard the *New World Symphony* at the time he wrote and also modeled his own symphony on it, having denied both—to believe the premise demands one concur with Maynard Solomon's charge that Ives was dishonest. It is a duplicitous path that revisionists, tacitly, have managed to travel, consecutively feigning fundamental disagreement with Solomon's premise. Ives, of course, even as late as 1944, steadfastly continued to deny that he had heard the symphony, even at the time he had written his *Second* Symphony.[323] To this writer, at very least, Dvořák's and Ives's respective works do *not* sound sufficiently similar that one would be likely to confuse them. Thus, had Ives been attempting to emulate, or 'outdo' Dvořák, as Burkholder proposed,[324] one could argue that he ought to have been able to do so *better*.

Aside from sharing the same late-Romantic language, neither composer treads the same ground from a musical/technical standpoint. Ives's symphony is, in fact, more complexly structured, more detailed, intimate and intricate, its orchestration considerably more varied, its potential, remarkably, better understood; on the page, these differences are immediately striking—in actual sound, no less so—the more uniformly textured blocks of sound in the *New World Symphony* (much like Parker's own later orchestration!) showing little resemblance to the subtleties of Ives's more fleeting sonic imagery. His work does not appear to have been *modeled* on the other—even less, *paraphrased* in any particular way—other than by incorporating features one might expect to encounter within the standard symphonic literature of the day.

The power of suggestion never should be underestimated. To further support his conjecture that Ives was conversant with Dvořák's symphony, Burkholder remarked that a piano reduction of the symphony was found among his possessions,

---

[323] Charles Ives, letter to Elliott Carter, October 20, 1944, the Charles Ives Papers, MSS14, Yale University.

[324] Burkholder, *Ives and the Classical Tradition*, 23.

and that Ives had marked it up.[325] The piano score that Burkholder referenced, however (by Paul Juon), was published by N. Simrock in 1906. Clearly, it did not influence Ives's composition; furthermore, it reveals nothing about the date that Ives procured it, even though the casual reader, regardless of Burkholder's intention, would be likely to conclude that, in some way, the piano reduction is the 'smoking gun' that catches Ives in a lie. Although Ives's letter to Carter is regularly misconstrued (Ives did not deny that he had ever heard the symphony), his copy of the sheet music is irrelevant. It proves nothing, except that Ives did familiarize himself with the symphony at some time during his life. Although nothing precludes the possibility that Ives had seen Dvořák's score or, had even heard a performance of the symphony during his Yale years, nevertheless, there is no evidence to support it. His reluctance, however, to acknowledge any common elements (the only example truly worthy of the comparison is the theme of each respective slow movement), *accidental or not*, merely demonstrates the same impishly rugged 'Yankee' spirit for which Ives is known.[326] The overly contrived 'discoveries' of shared features in the respective works have sustained common perceptions of supposed fact.

As a typical late Romantic work, a large part of it was written in the idiom of the time, so it is not surprising that the symphony should fit the mold, and that, even, certain aspects might remind one of other contemporary works. Although Ives's symphony *does* carry distinctive elements of other composers' voices, Ives's own, nevertheless, is unmistakable, already. The writer's view is that even if a few of the supposed modellings, perhaps, even a couple of quoted paraphrases, are valid, Ives, after all, had been raised within the existing tradition of quoting other composer's works. There has long been a widely held misperception that he was alone in this respect. Part of Parker's teaching required Ives to emulate the styles of existing music, as evidenced in Ives's student fugues, for example. Parker, himself, was no stranger to quoting existing works, too. Kearns commented at length upon this propensity, which he considered inexplicable, because of the lack of creative context to which Parker applied them. Consequently, he considered that the artistic standing of his music might have been compromised. That critique, however, might be applied equally to many other works of the time, in which context—even quotes from other stylistic periods—is no more likely to be especially relevant. Being entirely part of the cultural esthetic of the time, it seems no one cared about such incongruities.[327]

---

[325] Burkholder, *All Made of Tunes*, 89.

[326] John Kirkpatrick, "Preface" to the score, *Charles Ives:* Symphony no. 4 (Associated Music Publishers, Inc., 1965), viii. Kirkpatrick termed Ives's reticence to reveal everything, his "New England sense of privacy."

[327] Kearns, *Horatio Parker*, 241.

Indeed, only in recent years has purism and authentic performance practice become an issue at all. One must ask whether the practice, therefore, in Parker's hands really has reduced his music to a chameleon-like pastiche, any more than it has to that of anyone else. In comparison, Ives, though, once free of the shackles of conformity, is revealed in his twentieth century compositions as an original, by the *manner* in which he quoted other materials.

As the practice of quotation in Ives's hands set him apart from the pack, it renders his music unmistakable and wholly new (there was never a truer manifestation of the spirit of renewal in Emerson Transcendentalism). By using brief fragments of tunes—on top of the main fabric of the music to recall events, places and emotions—their function is entirely different, the incorporations existing mostly *in a separate layer on top of the main structure of the music*, and representing one of, if not the most, misunderstood aspects of Ives's music.

The Language of Ives's symphony

Ives's symphony, in conforming to the symphonic model of the day—in America, at any rate—is typified, perhaps, best by the works of George Chadwick, not only in its immediate sound, but more through its constantly varying intricacies of orchestral texture. For all their New England charm and freshness, however, in comparison with Ives's symphony, Chadwick's symphonies speak in less substantive, more sentimental and infinitely triter terms. Moreover, they suffer often from a lack distinctive primary material. While claiming the same fresh spirit that speaks through Chadwick, almost paradoxically, Ives, nevertheless, had tied himself more to the tidal pull of the European composers' more substantively complex weight of expression, even as soon he would consciously rebel against it. What he found to replace it hardly was less complex and weighty—the language he used often considerably *more* so— and speaks through an entirely different medium, in no way like anything heard before.

For his most conventional of symphonies, however, Ives's chose virtually the same orchestral forces featured in most symphonies of the period—such as those of Dvořák, Brahms, even Tchaikovsky—the latter only slightly expanding the percussion. Aside from the more direct links to existing symphonies that Burkholder attempted to establish (see next paragraph), one can deduce where Sinclair's unsupported assertion that Ives had studied the symphonies of "Beethoven, Dvořák and Tchaikovsky" with Parker came from.[328] Ives's symphony expresses something that stands apart from the more heavily weighted—even, at times, darkly burdened—

---

[328] See again, Ives, First Symphony, Preface, iv.

symphonies of the trans-Atlantic masters, its youthful, sunny perspective of Ives's upbringing during the newly energized America yet far from the gradually gathering storm clouds of the Great War soon to erupt in Europe in 1914.

In its relation to comparisons with other standard works of the genre, Burkholder isolated possible musical parallels. Other than a plausible reference to the third movement of Tchaikovsky's *Pathetique Symphony* in Ives's finale, and, perhaps, also paraphrasing its rushing scales, the examples cited are hard to determine with any certainty, or lacking a reasonable basis at all, seeming almost predeterminations in need of justification. (The writer includes in this assessment the supposedly "obvious relationship" of the admittedly similar theme of Ives's slow movement to that of Dvořák, which Sinclair also referenced in his Preface, and explained in greater detail, below.) Ives's theme for his scherzo, for example, hardly seems to reflect the scherzo of Beethoven's Ninth Symphony (the *Choral*).[329] It is yet more improbable to link Schubert's Eighth Symphony (the *Unfinished*) to the opening melody of Ives's first movement, although, Burkholder's link to *Beulah Land* does hold, even as the rhythmic feature that characterizes the link, however, is common enough in music. Insignificantly, in this instance, quoting such fragments of vernacular melodies was a commonplace practice at the time, no less so by Ives, and notably, of course, in his succeeding Second Symphony.

Burkholder's belief that *The Shining Shore* influenced its mid-section, actually, seems entirely subjective; to the writer it suggests only the stylistic and diatonic characteristics of hymns in general; if one must make a comparison with a hymn in particular, it is more reminiscent, perhaps, of *Dorrnance*. Rather, it is the larger effect of exposure to types of music in his early years that would seem to be an infinitely

---

[329] There are too many examples of the octave component announcing thematic material throughout musical literature to leap to such a conclusion and ascribe the comparison. An familiar thematic device, for example, in Chadwick's Second Symphony, almost countless placements throughout its length of the same prominent figure (the octave leap occurring in either direction) much more strongly evoke Beethoven's Ninth—especially at the Allegro con brio between rehearsal letters A and B in the first movement, or at twelve bars before rehearsal letter B—the same rhythm with repeated lower tone being notable. Chadwick's *Romanze* (1883), too, begins with the figure inverted as an ascending octave leap. It appears frequently in other musical works, such as the beginning of the fugal subject in the finale of Brahms's First Sonata for Cello and Piano, even concluding another—a 'period' in the emphatic concluding two-note motif of Mahler's First Symphony—which, again, reflects more the energy and character of Beethoven's Scherzo, or even the upward octave leap that begins the finale of Mahler's Ninth. In yet another instance, completely opposite in effect, the gentle opening theme of Wagner's *Siegfried Idyll* also features upward the leaping octave. However, a more remarkable, and almost surely unintended link to any of these examples, and certainly both symphonies of Mahler can be found in another work by Horatio Parker; see discussion later in this chapter on *Hora Novissima*.

more compelling source of the diatonic intervals in many of Ives's melodic choices, not to mention the dictates of their harmonic and rhythmic contours. Thus, despite the prevailing musicological 'consensus' of works and melodies that Ives is supposed to have modeled his symphony upon, any attempts to enforce as unequivocal those sources that are not readily demonstrable ought to be taken with a pinch of salt, being no truer of Ives's melodies and compositions than of many the works of other composers of the period.

Inasmuch as there are, nevertheless, some moments in which similarities between Ives's and, notably, Dvořák's symphonies spring to mind, at least from a technical standpoint, there is enough clarity, nevertheless, to propose an opposite scenario to any theory that Ives modeled his own first excursion into symphonic literature upon another—and notably—one that he categorically denied he had heard at the time. The music of the composers of the 'Second New England School' surely had much to do with introducing *Dvořák* to the vivid sounds of Americana in his *New World Symphony*, rather than the other way around. It is entirely reasonable to propose that Dvořák would have gone to great pains to 'sound' American, as he had championed Americans to do. In the absence of anyone yet having emerged as the 'Great American Composer,' Dvořák could not have intended to offend anybody; his instincts seem to have been entirely a byproduct of the culture of the time, which, musically, at any rate, was still dominated by that of the old trans-Atlantic empire states.

Regardless, Dvořák's proposal that local coloration could be 'tacked on' onto structures built according to the prevailing European musical methodology offended countless American musicians at the time (including Ives), who indignantly condemned any foreign composer who might try to impose himself on his countrymen and their music.[330] Ives considered the mere blending of materials identified with American nationality into any new composition to be hollow, entirely lacking the authenticity of personal experience. Thus, it was Dvořák who had become the copier, not the copied, not Ives, nor anyone else! The model Dvořák chose was based on the sounds of the immediate locale in New England, as well as everything he could glean from music of the American continent, notably spirituals, which he touted as a uniquely identifying hallmark of the country. Ives did not concur, stating quite clearly that spirituals were derivations of old Gospel hymns.[331] Authentic

---

[330] Ives, *Memos*, 52. Perhaps, however, the closest instance in which Ives expressed his sentiments—without mentioning Dvořák by name—can be found in *Essays Before a Sonata*, 91–96; the words, are directly linked to (by then) the age-old issue.

[331] Ives, *Memos*, 52.

sounds of the New World were represented, too, by the symphonic works of Chadwick, which, in turn, reflected many uniquely American melodic components; the difference was that Chadwick's idiomatic inclusions, not added by design, arose subconsciously from his lifelong immersion in them. Even Parker himself weighed in upon the controversy, causing for himself another in its wake by claiming that music, native to America, did not, as yet, exist![332]

An often-overlooked part of the equation relates to indigenous music in general; just as Chadwick's idiomatic sound reflected his cultural heritage and its indigenous melodies, the pentatonic nature of many of them exists, too, in many tunes of Bohemian folk music! The fact that Dvořák's melodies—within works written long before his sojourn in America—often shared the same pentatonic folk roots found in Chadwick's work has been missed all too often. The point at which all cultures merge and become diffusely joined or separated remains as intangible as ever. As Baron pointed out, similarly linked melodic phrases in countless simple diatonic melodies (such as can be found in the very symphonies by Chadwick, Ives and Dvořák under discussion in this section) occur no less readily in virtually any comparable diatonic source; these tunes frequently share vernacular-styled origins. Such intimate connections make one aware, additionally, that it is impossible to be completely original in anything, let alone within the confines of a mainstream late-Romantic symphony of the day. We are a product of our time and place in the ongoing march of human evolution, as the old is recycled into the new, something Emerson knew all too well.

Looking at the first movement of Ives's symphony, however—and critically separating his primary themes from the respective symphonies of both Chadwick and Dvořák—the differences in their opening melodic phrases are instructive. Chadwick's and Dvořák's themes are entirely diatonic to one key, moving through and across tones associated only with the tonic:

$$B\flat - B\flat\text{-}E\flat - B\flat \text{ (}\textit{Chadwick}\text{)}$$
$$Em - C - Em \quad \text{(}\textit{Dvořák}\text{)}$$

Ives's opening theme, however, shifts almost immediately; already, in the second bar, it has progressed into other tonal territory, also staking uncommon ground, passing through a whole-tone scale (over the course of an augmented fifth), one tone short of completing the octave:

---

[332] Kearns, *Horatio Parker*, 40.

142

Dm - A - F - Bm - Cm - E+ - A
^whole-tone steps in the melody

Comparing the themes, it is possible to appreciate the relative melodic ingenuity of each composer. Chadwick's theme, not only is stagnant, melodically and harmonically, but also fails to extend the substance beyond the simplest of melodic motifs. Dvořák's theme emerges from a similar mold, but is entirely more captivating, due to its attractive and extended artistic shape, more memorable rhythm, and musical impetus. However, of the three composers, it was Ives, who—by far—produced the most sophisticated and creative theme. Although it begins with the suggestion of having similar roots, it soon traverses a far more elaborate melodic and harmonic curve.

Chadwick's choice for his second theme is hardly more memorable than his first, nor sufficiently different, to disguise the fundamental weakness of his entire symphony; the limitations of his melodic gifts, consequently, impact its artistic value diametrically. In comparison, both Dvořák and Ives devised entirely contrasting, more busily intricate second themes, maintaining the variety of such divergent thematic choices throughout their respective symphonies. In relation to the transitions between these themes, Burkholder raised a matter concerning the common appearance of elements of the second theme in the transition in both Ives's and Dvořák's symphonies, commenting that doing so was an unusual practice.[333] Ives might just as easily have borrowed the idea from Chadwick,[334] because, in this particular instance, a similar design feature can be found, too, in Chadwick's symphony! Perhaps, a moral of the story is that greater truths revealed by wider-based observations render such commentary a risky prospect.

What led, in the first place, however, to the commonly held assumption today that Ives modeled his symphony on Dvořák's work? Burkholder maintained the strikingly similar setting of the English horn for the primary theme in both respective slow movements is "the most direct allusion."[335] With Parker's earlier association with Dvořák at the National Conservatory of Music, might it be, possibly, that the

---

[333] Appearances of materials form the second subject in the transition is not all that unusual. Mahler, for example, featured precisely this technique in his Sixth Symphony (first movement).

[334] Burkholder, "Ives and the European Tradition," in *Charles Ives and the Classical Tradition*, 23.

[335] Ibid., 23.

143

choice of instrumentation was made upon Parker's advice, instead? Might Ives, perhaps, have been familiar with Chadwick's symphony, rather than Dvořák's? Victor Fell Yellin remarked that the same instrumentation appeared some ten years earlier in opening of the first movement of Chadwick's Second Symphony, echoing Dvořák's respective slow movement. For the record, however, the English horn is *not* specified in the instrumentation of Chadwick's symphony, two oboes being maintained throughout.[336] Chadwick, instead, specified the solo *French* horn solo to open his symphony. Albeit, the theme is more of a fanfare figure than the memorable song-like theme Dvořák had created with *Goin' Home*, although it does sound curiously like it, nevertheless. The fact that the line lies within largely the same register, and sounds tonally quite similar, no doubt, explains why Yellin mixed up the instrumentation.

Tawa, however, noted the instrumentation correctly.[337] Nevertheless, one can find virtually the same thematic element that opens the finale of Ives's *First String Quartet* (1896–99), as if to underscore the fact that many diatonic tunes, and free melodic writing, feature shared components, especially in music so regionally influenced as that by Ives and Chadwick. However, the writer is unaware of any attempt to link *Chadwick's* symphonic theme to Dvořák's *New World Symphony*, any such accusation of musical hijacking again being held for Ives, exclusively, despite his disavowals.

One feature Burkholder appeared to miss, however, really *does* support his assertion, although it still does not discredit Ives's staunch denial of being influenced by Dvořák's symphony. The clue lies in the harmony. Ives's and Dvořák's melodies pass through a striking augmented chord in the middle of their respective second phrases—the fifth degree of the tonic chord being raised by a semitone, to escort a tone a major third from the tonic—before the harmony in each resolves to the subdominant added sixth. The effect upon one's emotive reaction of the chromatic progression and consequent placement against the melodic curve is sufficiently powerful to render it unmistakable.

However, were one to conclude, therefore, that Ives had, in fact, heard the *New World Symphony* before embarking on his own, it is worth noting that, mid-movement in the development of his symphony, Chadwick *also* included, though only as a passing harmony, an augmented F triad in the second phrase of a passage (for two oboes) that is built on the opening horn theme! The progression, thus, is

---

[336] Victor Fell Yellin, *Chadwick, Yankee Composer* (Washington, D.C., Smithsonian Institution Press, 1990), 93.

[337] Tawa, "Ives and the New England School," 62.

demonstrated to be anything but unusual within the music in late-Romantic works. Indeed, in the third movement of his symphony, Chadwick again utilized the technique (e.g., bar 10), the ambiguous nature of augmented chords allowing all kinds of tonal outcomes in the shifting tonal base. In one other instance in the same movement, Burkholder pointed to the mid-section of the respective themes, but once again, it is the harmonies chosen by each composer that call his conclusion into question; the context is entirely different. Dvořák, from m.13–15, again featured a static harmony, the chordal alternations acting as passing tones only:

$$G\flat - Fm\text{-}G\flat\text{-}|\ G\flat\text{-}Fm\text{-}G\flat\text{---}|\ D\flat\text{---}|$$

The comparable place by Ives (m.4–7), however, seems quite different, the critical comparison being in the moving harmony, an underlying perfect cadence, versus Dvořák's static, harmony:

$$F\ -\ F+\ |\ B\flat\text{---}|\ C7\text{-}F\text{-}|\ F\text{---}|$$

Can these instances of similar, but not matching, melodic and harmonic choices be claimed by anyone to represent essentially the same thing? Other common features, such as the cyclic emergence of thematic materials in both Dvořák's and Ives's symphonies, even more, their appearance at comparable points in both works, have been taken to lend weight to the supposition that Ives used Dvořák's symphony as a model. However, it should be pointed out that Chadwick's symphony is entirely cyclical in its thematic structure, too, the material being subject to transformation throughout, and cannot be considered, thus, unique only to the works under examination.

Cyclical structure occurs frequently enough in various works by composers, such as Brahms, Beethoven, Berlioz, Liszt, Schubert, Mendelssöhn, Schumann, Saint-Saëns, Bruckner, Mahler, and Franck, to name just a few. Regardless, if the argument that Dvořák influenced Ives cannot, overall, be more than proposed, some striking parallels undoubtedly exist between them. It is only when one compares the first three symphonies featured in this segment, however, does the attempt to tie Ives's and Dvořák's symphonies together directly begin to take on water.

Chadwick's complexly orchestrated score also is the largest work of the three; in a straight comparison, despite its sunny, eminently listenable aura, however, it features the least substance, and, thematically, is built, cyclically, upon the same uninspiring, blandly bald diatonic material throughout. Although Dvořák's

145

symphony is noticeably much simpler, basic and compact, it is full of contrasting and memorable themes, strikingly handled in their development. Ives found a happy medium; while creating an intricate work, it is less massive in scope and intricately scored than Chadwick's, though built of hardly less memorable and interesting materials than those Dvořák utilized. However, Ives revealed whom it was, surely, who had the most inventive compositional mind.

Ultimately, the idiomatic similarities between the symphonies probably owe more to the absorption of the dominant grand pattern among Romantic symphonies than to any other factor. The distinctive 'local' sounds of music in New England were familiar, too, to all three composers at the time. With claims of uncovering borrowed ideas from well-known masterworks easily becoming contrived, it is uncanny how elements of one composer's sound or style can be 'found' with regularity in the works of others, with apparently no discernible relationship between the composers, whatsoever.

There is no way to explain phenomena common to other contemporary figures—Mahler, for example, being the composer, perhaps, most often raised in conversations about Ives—such as the sharing of the identical thematic motif at the beginnings of Mahler's First Symphony and Parker's *Hora Novissima*, for example (see later this chapter), or the sudden appearance of Mahler-like writing by Ives in his Second Symphony (e.g., in the slow movement from m.80); there are no known links between either of these figures to Mahler at the respective times of the compositions. Maher's First Symphony had only received its final revision for its second performance during the same year (1893) that *Hora Novissima* was written. As additional curious parallels to other works indeed can be found in Ives's symphony, to attempt to clearly link them specifically, as Burkholder did, to moments throughout the *New World Symphony* seems hard to justify.

Although efforts to find parallels between Ives's and *any* other music, in order to understand Ives's better, are, of course, to be lauded, would it not have been preferable had direct comparisons been more *objective* about something that is ultimately, *subjective*, rather than being the slave of foregone conclusions? Again, it is the proverbial answer in search of a question. Why Ives, however, is routinely singled out for the kind of dismissive characterization, which posits that his music is fundamentally built on someone else's, is the real unanswered question.

Verdict: In relation to evidence of Parker's role, Ives's symphony reveals, perhaps, more about his own familiarity with the prevailing Romantic literature of the day than it does Parker's direct teaching. Aside from what is known of his classes, there is little that Parker composed that resembles the symphonic writing found in either Ives's or Dvořák's respective symphonies. Consequently, it is reasonable to further propose that Ives was thoroughly grounded in the musical language and traditions of the day long before he attended Yale; in the circumstances of his upbringing, it would be surprising to expect otherwise. The fact that Ives's immersion in the music of his immediate surroundings, quantities of organ literature, and transcriptions of symphonic literature was more substantial than has been allowed in recent musicologically correct times is an inconvenient truth. Even as Ives's symphony appears to owe few substantial allegiances to any particular work or melody, it shares more than a few ideas with several. Regardless, to believe that Ives could have amassed the ability to produce such a masterful, elaborately and intricately orchestrated, *mature* work in a mere two years of actual direct studies with Parker—especially in light of the fact that work on the first movement might have taken place as early as 1895—defies all reason. Further, revisionism requires one to take the position that it was possible to compose such an elaborate work in the absence of any substantive background prior to entering Yale, and then—if we must take the revisionist line that Ives could not have become a composer of substance without formal studies—to absorb the breadth of knowledge to advance within an impossibly short timeframe to the level necessary to produce a work that could only be considered of *post-doctoral* quality stretches the bounds of all reasonable argument.

So again we ask, what, exactly, did Parker bequeath Ives? The clues lie in the types of music he wrote before and after Yale. Though he knew great symphonies, he had not contemplated composing one of his own, nor did he have the organizational scope to build large compositional structures before Parker drilled into him the mental discipline to do so. Parker, it seems, caused Ives to think 'big,' to see himself writing large-scale works of his own in the molds of those of the major composers long known to him. Certainly, Parker must be credited with providing the level of constructive criticism necessary in order for Ives to compose a four-movement symphony. Parker, however, also bequeathed Ives hope of an old dream.

Two Cantatas Compared

by Parker: *Hora Novissima*
by Ives: *The Celestial Country* (1896)
   (with *The All-Enduring* [TTBB & orchestra, arr. piano & voice])

The quality of Ives's First Symphony points to the seriousness with which Ives approached his truest passion; in truth, he still harbored a quiet aspiration for him to a career in music. Parker had actually provided what Ives considered the perfect model! Looking to emulate his teacher's ascent to prominence, it is readily apparent that he considered his best chance was with a work in the same vein as Parker's celebrated cantata, *Hora Novissima*, which had brought him to fame. The fact that Ives arranged and paid for a performance of his own work in New York City speaks to the fading hope that fate would look on him kindly and allow his dream to come true; fate, however, had other plans that would ultimately lead Ives to real greatness.

As it turns out, fate already had interceded years before; in a near coincidence of fate, Parker's celebrated *Hora Novissima* originally had been intended to debut at the 1893 Columbia Exposition in Chicago that Ives had attended; instead, it had to wait until 1894 to premiere in Cincinnati.[338] We can never know if Parker's and Ives's paths had crossed at that time would their future relationship have been different. Regardless, *The Celestial Country* was directly modeled on *Hora Novissima*, and clearly was cut from a similar—if not the same—cloth, even sharing the same essential, late-Romantic, musical language and, even more, the subject material. Although Ives's cantata likely was begun only in the closing days of his Yale years and completed after graduation, its language is so closely intertwined with Parker's— probably more so than other examples of Ives's work during his time in New Haven—that *The Celestial Country* can be included in this comparative discussion. Ives mistakenly believed his text was based on part of the same larger historic text his teacher had used in his own cantata—the oddly-titled *'rhythm of St. Bernard de Morlaix, monk of Cluny, on the celestial country'*—a three thousand-line twelfth century poem. Unwittingly, Ives had selected the much more manageable ninety-six-line *Forward! Be Our Watchword*, actually written by Henry Alford (1810-1871) in the last year of his life, just three years before Ives was born.

Ives's cantata is not quite of the scale of Parker's generally acknowledged masterpiece, though features more extensive and intricate instrumental sections than his teacher had utilized. Attempting to showcase his own abilities, Ives hoped it would inspire critics and audiences alike in much the same way that audiences had enthusiastically embraced Parker's *Hora Novissima* and—thus, subsequently launch, too, his own career as an important new American composer. At the time Ives had completed his cantata, he was almost the same age Parker had been at the time he was catapulted to fame and success; however, Ives's chances for recognition, in the absence of the social connections, European background, even less, prior track record, such as his distinguished professor enjoyed even prior to his success with *Hora Novissima*, were infinitesimally smaller. In short, it was a pipe dream.

---

[338] Kearns, *Horatio Parker*, 18, n.41.

Comparing the two works, Parker's cantata is broader in style, and substantive in scale. Musicality, too, it is grander, more dignified and mature. It is even, at times, somewhat Wagnerian in effect (even, perhaps, a little reminiscent of Brunnhilde's Immolation Scene in *Gotterdammerung*), its orchestration, heavily weighted toward the brass, hardly is indicative of the more lyrical sound of Ives's cantata. *Hora Novissima*, thus, does not seem to be an ancestor of the intricate and sprightly orchestration found in Ives's First or Second Symphonies. The lack of similar orchestral works by Parker from the period (1894–98), in which he was likely to have been of most influence upon Ives, again reinforces the likelihood that Ives already was long familiar with the symphonic models of the day.

In style, if Ives's cantata, at times, still reflects the barbershop sounds and chromatic harmonies of Dudley Buck, its distinctive Victorian attitude—one might say, almost reminiscent of the best parlor music—it does not, nevertheless, overwhelm the power of its artistic invention, disciplined design, fluent technique, even the scope of its occasional adventurism, even if there is something, notwithstanding, about its spirit that sounds reminiscent of a Yale 'good fellow.' In this respect, its naïveté might be charming, but Ives would have been far from happy to know his music had created such an impression. Regardless, the work's greater attributes—notably, the pure sophistication of its technical prowess—are again remarkable to find in a large work from a composer so young.

It is not known if the interludes, in any form, which separate many of the numbered movements were included as part of the original performance edition, more especially if Ives might have improvised them on the spot at the premiere. The matter of dating the formal composition, however, of the interludes has been a point of contention, in that they are constantly bitonal, reflecting the polytonal chordal blocks of thirds found in his father's copybook, if not their wedge-like structures.[339] In Sinclair's catalog, the years 1912–13 have been assigned them, although it required a visit to the archives to examine the manuscript to correct the record. In fact, the manuscript places them around 1902 (the year of the premiere—though late additions, indeed—does not preclude their composition in time for the premiere), in one of the few instances where the writer agrees with Magee in regard to dating Ives's music.[340]

---

[339] George Ives's Copybook (Irving S. Gilmore Music Library, Yale University: The Charles Ives Papers MSS14), 68, 100, 168.

[340] Burkholder, 432, n.25. However, if Burkholder misstated the date, it seems either Magee later changed her mind or Sinclair was mistaken, because in his *Descriptive Catalogue*, Magee's date assignment for the Interludes appears as 1909!

149

Ch. 6 Works from Ives's Yale Years

Ives, in *Memos*, did imply that the interludes were added after the composition of the primary work, not by expressing anything specific, but rather with his comment that he had played a "short organ Prelude" that was built two dominant chords, a semitone apart, under the main theme. He made no reference to their brazen bitonality, so contradictory to the main work, itself, that it is logical to assume they were written as an afterthought, though, not necessarily years later. As the surviving polytonal exercises in George's copybook demonstrate, nothing about them falls outside the polytonal harmonic language Ives had explored with his father many years earlier, and clearly evident in the copybook.

Perhaps, in one of the oddest of coincidences, *Hora Novissma* opens with the same descending cycle of perfect fourths (each a diatonic third lower, respectively in, essentially, a series of T7 cycles) that Mahler had used at the beginning (his 'Nature Theme,' as if awakening) and ending (in triumph) in his First Symphony.

Hora Novissima:

Mahler: *First Symphony*:

In *Hora Novissima*, when the figure is stated for the *second* time, in the aspects of its scoring, it sounds almost identical to Mahler's symphony! No less startling is the sudden, and solitary, reappearance of the identical figure on page 137 in Act III, Scene II of Parker's *The Legend of St. Christopher* of 1898!

150

However, any possible connection between Parker and Mahler is non-existent, although Parker's teacher in Germany, Josef Rheinberger, also taught a close friend of Mahler, Hermann Behn (1859–1927), best known for arranging existing works for keyboard instruments, including Mahler's Second Symphony for two pianos. Although no actual connection between Mahler and Parker is known, whether either composer was familiar with the other's music cannot be determined, though it seems unlikely. So, just when it seems we have reached the end of the trail, suddenly the exact motif appears again in the *Piano Trio No.4* in F, Op.191, by—none other—than Josef Rheinberger! It can be found, prominently written in octaves, in the violin and cello parts at mm.11–12 of the fourth movement, Finale.

As if to underscore the mysterious musical coincidence of the times, the same momentary shared thought suddenly jumps out of the texture in the finale of no less expected a work than the Second Symphony of Brahms! Although the interval is part of the primary theme, it is only in its development (six measures before Rehearsal Letter "L") that, in a momentary similar context, the fragment is unmistakable. Parker utilized this coincidence of late Romanticism, modelling many of his themes on the perfect fourth throughout the eleven-section *Hora Novissima*. Literal cyclical sequences (often at T10) appear in it with regularity (even, too, in *The Legend of St. Christopher*), as well as numerous passages featuring near-cycles, or other sequential writing. Although it is, of course, possible that Ives was triggered to explore the idea of cycles, per se, by Parker's music—an attribute of his writing being his extensive use of transposition cycles—developing it to the next level,[341] the fact, however, that cycles and sequences are closely related raises, again the prospect that Ives's use of cycles involves nothing more than his familiarity with baroque organ music.

Another possible link between Ives and Parker can be heard in Movement *No.3* in *Hora Novissima*. Amazingly, Parker's theme is remarkably suggestive of the opening theme of the first movement of Ives's First Symphony, sharing not only its key (D minor), but also its range and initial ordering of pitches; the wandering harmonies, although different in each example, nevertheless, suggest something of a common shared character, although Parker's theme is far less daring in its overall design (whole tone scales, notably, were not in his lexicon). Instead of looking to Dvořák, perhaps Burkholder, Sinclair and others might have sought such links that are closer to home.

In his initial preamble in the chapter that he contributed in *Charles Ives and the Classical Tradition*, Nicholas E. Tawa appeared to offer a more encouraging view relative to uncovering connections between the cantatas.[342] Despite his acknowledgement that direct associations are "elusive," Tawa attempted to draw firm comparisons between both Ives's and Parker's cantatas. However, most of what he claimed to have isolated as direct links do not hold up upon inspection, especially in relation to drawing definitive conclusions. Citing the primary melody of Parker's movement *No.10*, 'Urbs Syon Unica,' and Ives's melody at bar 93 in *No.5*, 'Double Quartet,' the key might be the same (C), but the context is not. The segment, however, of *The Celestial Country* that Tawa compared is not the melody, but rather a free segment derived from it that occurs late in the movement. It does, however share a few attributes, even though its outline, as an extended line, takes a different shape. Moreover, its purpose is utterly different to the four-bar figure in *Hora Novissima*— which is part of a fugato—and thus, hardly comparable.

In the rush to link Parker to Ives, Tawa's contention that Ives modeled the "overlapping" chords in his 1914 song, *The Rainbow*, on those harmonies accompanying the motif is still less merited. In Ives's song, the chords do not move 'en bloc' with the vocal line, nor do they descend in diatonic perfect fourths. Any

---

[341] A good example of cyclical writing can be observed in the structural form of Ives's final version (c.1912) of *The Pond*, in which cycles play a circular role, too, shifting within a systemized design, the culminating B tonality implied at the start (d#6, c#5, and b3) being subtly confirmed as the root in the final chord (see detailed analysis in the writer's volume, *Charles Ives's Musical Universe*, 65–68).

[342] Nicholas E. Tawa, "Ives and the New England School," in *Charles Ives and the Classical Tradition*, ed. Geoffrey Block & J. Peter Burkholder (New Haven, CT: Yale University Press, 1996), 65–67.

other similarities, which are hard to demonstrate, are the result of conventional piano writing and the limitations of the hands, rather than of any obvious influence from Parker.[343] Tawa also maintained that Ives had followed a similar rhythmic trait in *The Celestial Country* to one his teacher had featured in *Hora Novissma*: a dotted rhythm that appears at the outset of many of the second bars of Parker's melodic phrases.[344] Examples of this feature in Parker's cantata are fairly common, appearing in the choral entry in *No.1*, the instrumental introduction to *No.2*s and *3*, the tenor solo in *No.7*, the alto solo in *No.9*s and *10*, the opening of *No.11*, as well as many points within the movements, themselves. In *The Celestial Country*, they appear, however, not nearly so often, although, undoubtedly, there are enough examples to justify the claim; for example, see Ives's opening Introduction (the first bar, however, beginning mid-bar), *No.5*, not quite literally in *No.7*, with other occurrences of only the dotted rhythm itself within the movements seeming quite typical among most works of the period.

In other words, in *The Celestial Country*, the figure is far from the prevailing feature that Tawa posited had been so strong an influence from Parker that Ives continued to use it even in his later compositions, such as his 1912 song, *At Sea*. In fact, the very same rhythmic feature occurs in a number of hymns that Ives quoted with regularity, including *Bethany*, *Lambeth*, *Woodworth*, and *Something For Thee*. One cannot build a sustained case, such as Tawa's, therefore, on a well-trodden musical feature of many melodies throughout Western music, even more, the types of melodies that featured so prominently in New England during Ives's most impressionable years. However, it does seem reasonable to believe that Ives did feel some subconscious—even deliberately intended—allegiances to Parker's cantata at many levels, especially because he was trying to emulate its style, and, apparently, its model toward his own success. Regardless, the feature could not be considered to be a stereotypical trait in Ives's music, and certainly nothing identifiable as a product of his years at Yale with Parker.

Tawa, nevertheless, strained in other ways to find direct parallels between the two works, isolating specifics that can be made to illustrate a predetermined point. The progressions Tawa cited in *Hora Novissma* feature alternating progressions between tonic and harmonies, other than the dominant. Not necessarily unusual in music as a whole, though not commonplace, the specific usage he cited, in which alternations with the tonic of several, non-dominant, chords, form a kind of

---

[343] Tawa, "Ives and the New England School," in *Charles Ives and the Classical Tradition*, 65.

[344] Ibid., 63–65.

harmonically suspended repeating 'cell.'[345] In the example for comparison that Tawa selected in *The Celestial Country, No.5* ('Glories in Glories'), however, neither Ives's primary melody, nor its harmonic alternations, feature the same harmonies as Parker's (I-VI-I-II-I). Instead, they rock back-and-forth through the supertonic chord only (I-II-I-II-I), *before the harmony eventually moves to the dominant.* The identical feature, however, can be found often in other works of music, such cadential avoidance often a means of extending a phrase. For example, in mm.34–35 in the Overture to Wagner's *Die Meistersinger*, the harmony briefly alternates (II-I-II-I); Wagner, too, moved from there to the dominant (transitioning through diminished seventh harmony). Although not too dissimilar an idea in the totality of its static nature, the specific application by Parker to form a type of repeating cell is not, however, "obvious" in respect to Ives's work, and especially in this instance within it that Tawa cited for comparison. Moreover, Ives's use of the technique seems distinctly more like Wagner's application than Parker's!

Another later example, Ives's 1901 song, *Elégie* (discussed in Chapter 2), contains two such repeating 'cells.' The first occurs between mm.21–25, in which the chord of the flatted leading tone alternates with the subdominant minor from bar to bar. The context is as unusual as is the harmonic context:

$$♭VII-IVm-♭VII-IVm-♭VII$$

The other instance, less harmonically interesting, appears at mm.39–40, in which two sets of alternations occur on each half-note:

$$VI-IV6-VI-IV6$$

Even though Ives's song was written in 1901, five years after his graduation, it does bear some greater similarities, however, to a different work by Parker: the opening of his *Concert-Piece No.1.* In its diatonic hymn-like inference, the use of pedal point, together with a highly similar pacing, this song might have been a better example to examine for possible influence by Parker. Although, in this example, Parker avoided true perfect cadences—with the exceptions of leading to the second phrase, and the conclusion of the sixteen-bar, two-phrase segment—nothing would describe the harmony as unusual or particularly interesting. In this sense, Ives and Parker were poles apart.

---

[345] Tara, in "Ives and the New England School," cited in *Hora Novissima* at nineteen bars from the end of *No.1*, and eighteen bars before the end of *No.4.*

Yet more tenuous, however, was Tawa's attempted linkage of the respective third movements of each work, positing again that Ives's work was deeply "indebted" to Parker's. With the possible—even likely—exception of the use of alternating meters (more later), and the shared D minor key, the case seems hard to substantiate. Tawa implied the harmonic progressions are virtually identical in both works, although, in fact, they hardly could be described *even as similar* by objective scholars. Moreover, the opening bars of each (the 'preludes,' according to Tawa) are not cut from the same cloth, as he claimed. In *The Celestial Country*, the progression is:

I–IV–I–VII°7–I

In *Hora Novissima*, it is:

I–IV–V–I–Vm–#IVø7–IIM–I

Aside from beginning and ending on the tonic, and progressing immediately to the subdominant, these progressions do not look or sound much alike. The respective entrances of the bass (Parker) and vocal quartet (Ives) do not alter the situation. At this point in *The Celestial Country*, the harmony is much simpler than in its counterpart:

I–#VIø7–VI–I

In *Hora Novissima*, it is:

I–I7–IV–Vm–#VIø7–IIM–V(#7)-7–I

Again, with the exception of a few obvious mutual chords—the raised submediant half-diminished mid-way in both, and that they both begin and end on the tonic—it is hard to find anything obvious, or so persuasive that one would conclude there is much in common between them. Tawa further posited a link through the instrumental motion that characterizes both 'preludes.' Indeed, finally, he might have been onto something; the rising eighth-note scales in both might indicate a direct influence. However, Tawa missed a *much* closer link at the beginning of *No.2* of *Hora Novissima*, in which almost identical rising eighth-note scales seem almost to belong to Ives's *No.3*.

Whether Ives borrowed the prominent alternating meter for his 'parallel' cantata, there seems to be, however, little room for doubt. Appearing in *Hora Novissima* in *No.3* between mm.33–51, 4/4 bars alternate with 3/4 bars to create a remarkable sense of urgency. Apparently, Parker's innovative idea strongly impacted his student, who likely borrowed it for his own *No.3* (between mm.33–75), as Kirkpatrick also noted.[346] Although it seems to confirm Parker's influence, it appears no less directly to reinforce George's thinking, according to commentary by Ives.[347] Indeed, a similar switching of meter occurs in the 1894 song, *At Parting*, in which irregular meter is a feature, if not quite a comparable alternation; Ives had not yet studied composition at this stage with Parker.

Ives, however, in *The Celestial Country*, not only utilized this rhythmic feature more extensively than did Parker, but also, consciously or not, revisited it again in *Scherzo: Over the Pavements* (mm.73–80). Appearing not to associate it with *Hora Novissima*, Ives used it only for a short segment; the context is so different that one can only speculate about what lay behind it, because the idea of creating musical expansion through evolving meters—as a central feature in the piece—seems to speak to a different origin that is entirely serialistic in design. Tawa, however, seemed to presume that Ives had deliberately failed to acknowledge Parker's role, having assumed there was one. Even if so, it is possible for someone to remember every detail about events from many years in the past? Is it always necessary to enunciate everything that has influenced one's decisions and choices? As always, Ives is held to different standards than other composers. Tawa, effectively, though probably unwittingly, had just added fuel to Maynard Solomon's fabricated charge that Ives altered many details of his life in order to establish unwarranted priority.

Regardless, even at about the same time, Ives would expand the idea still further. Toward the end of the finale of his First String Quartet, he *combined* both meters together over the equivalent of a nine-bar 4/4 span, while featuring the hymns *Webb* ('Stand up, Stand up for Jesus'), *The Shining Shore*, and his own starkly "New England"-styled melody (that avoids the dominant harmony) from earlier in the movement; Ives might have built that melodic element, however, on part of the mid-section of *Wake Nicodemus*:

---

[346] Ives, *Memos*, 62, n.8.

[347] Ibid, 140.

"Wake me up!", was his charge,

Tawa, again, was incorrect in stating that Ives's Melody at m.50 in *No.3* closely resembles Parker's melody in *No.7* of *Hora Novissima*. Although Tawa's asserted that both Ives's and Parker's third movements share characteristics, it is, nevertheless, problematic to demonstrate it; ultimately, there is no obvious connection between them, other than some superficial similarities at the outsets of each. These features function, musically, in quite different ways, the resemblances, such as they are, dissipating early in each instance. Far closer, however, are the similarities Tawa missed between Ives's *No.3* and Parker's *No.5*, which, rhythmically, are of the same ilk, maintaining the similarity through much of their respective lengths. Both of them feature, too, similar increasing instrumental motion to and during their highest points.

Another parallel with a different work by Parker (*Melody and Intermezzo*, Op.20, No.1) can be found in relation to the tenor aria *No.6* of *The Celestial Country*. In Parker's piece, for about six bars, from the last two systems of the second page, a passage appears that might as well have come from Ives's aria. Texturally and in articulation, the excerpt seems tellingly akin to Ives's introduction; unlikely to have been the result of intentional modeling—there would be no obvious reason for doing so—more likely it serves to shine light on Ives's exposure to Parker's music in general.

We cannot leave these two works without examining another work by Ives: the song, *The All-Enduring* (upon which the finale of his piano *Trio* was based), and which emanates from its original version of 1896. Ives arranged it for voice and piano, at much the same the period in time, surely, he was already contemplating *The Celestial Country*. Regardless, the song provides the ideal comparison of the relative original creativity of both Parker and Ives, as well as serving to refute any continuing claim that Ives was not entertaining much beyond the language of Parker in his own compositions. It is also a useful counter-argument to claims that Parker was almost as radical as Ives, rather than the reality that Parker was a composer whose efforts to advance his music into more innovative territory could not escape the gravity of his own choices and situation.

Aside from offering precisely the model that Ives followed in his cantatas, Parker's piano reduction of *Hora Novissima* contains passages that closely resemble some of the writing of Ives's piano score of *The All-Enduring*, except for the truly

157

striking departures from convention (in Ives's song) that separate them.[348] Originally scored for chorus and orchestra for the Yale Glee Club in 1896 (this version has been lost), as Ives recounted on an ink copy of the piano and voice reduction, "they wouldn't sing it." The entire song seems modern beyond its year, on the page, the segments so reminiscent of Parker's work, yet sounding, nevertheless, entirely different! Beginning with a chordal, half-note accompaniment reminiscent of a hymn, the tone of *The All-Enduring* gradually shifts through increasing rhythmic activity. Adding simple quarter-note motion between chords, soon it extends freely across the texture into moving lines that begin to resemble contrapuntal writing. With the introduction of eight-notes, and increasingly fractured lines, the music takes on a more rhythmically driven impetus; the chorale quality has vanished.

The key, however, to understanding how the harmony in Ives's song (even in a great deal of his music) is separated from many of his contemporaries lies within the use of carefully placed tones that fall just enough outside the primary tonality to create remarkably 'modern' sounds. Because he roots of the primary harmonies are subverted, *but not undermined*, the result is an effective homogenization of tonality and atonality.[349] In *The All-Enduring*, the 'alien' harmonic inclusions gradually enter the texture, though, in actuality, here they are a derivation of an imposed polytonality, except that the added tones do not constitute *complete* superimposed harmonies, defined by the dominance of more than one root. In these instances, the lower-placed root wins. However, the polytonal aspect does change the larger harmonic implications sufficiently to suggest the song belongs to music beyond 1896, although nothing in *Hora Novissima* resembles this kind of harmony in any way.

In the song, between mm.34–84, the harmony of the segment (defined by flowing triplet arpeggiations in the left hand and semi-chordal/semi-melodic writing in the right) accompanies the partly syncopated melody. Elements of *Hora Novissima* that seem possibly related—at least in providing a springboard, if not the specifics that separate them—may be found in *No.2*, 'Hic Breve Vivitur,' mm.61–67, in *No.5*, 'O Bona Patria,' mm.23–39, and also mm.72–81. Similar writing, perhaps not quite so closely aligned, also appears within the finale, *No.11*, 'Urbs Syon Inclyta,' not to mention at other brief points throughout the cantata. In comparison, the melodic line of Ives's song, far from anything Parker would have entertained, is an especially

---

[348] There is also, in mm.31–33 of the song, a syncopated segment that culminates in what can only be described as ragtime inspired, at least in part, and possibly more evidence of the effect that pianist George Felsberg had upon Ives at Poli's Theater in New Haven.

[349] The writer demonstrated Ives's use of the technique in his analyses of *Thanksgiving*, and also of the Fourth Symphony, in *Charles Ives's Musical Universe* (W. Conshohocken, PA: Infinity, 2015), e.g., 220, 357.

158

interesting and creative hybrid. Immediately, one can see manifestations of George Ives's influence—an all-enduring spirit to be sure. The opening introduction begins with jagged intervals, its curve featuring two sweeps at the extremes (across a major seventh and minor ninth) respectively. The voice enters, echoing the second part of the introduction. With a line built on a descending scale that reverses course into an ascent between mm.20–22 and, with similar jagged characteristics that pass through three major sevenths and extreme chromaticism) eventually it settles down to take the rhythmic character of the accompaniment, as well as a somewhat more conventional attitude. From m.34, over flowing triplets, George Ives's influence remains within the larger contours of the melodic line, major sevenths often comprising parts of its travels across multiple bars.

Although it is not unreasonable to credit Parker with the fundamental writing style found in this song, it is Parker's work, however, that is constrained entirely by convention. After Ives's four years at Yale, it is George Ives who appears to be the greater influence. Despite the near-identical flowing motion and traditionally based writing common to most of Parker's and Ives's music during these period, nevertheless, and efforts by Parker to escape his better-known role of 'conventional' composer appeared not soon enough to have influenced his young student—nothing being so extreme in Parker's work before 1896 that resembles, or even suggests, what Ives devised for *The All-Enduring*—Parker's own more 'radical' compositions belonging to the years after Ives had departed from New Haven, and always being limited by his essentially staid Victorianism. It can be comfortably assumed, therefore, that Ives's adventurism was entirely his own, inspired, encouraged and enabled by the impetus generated by his father's freewheeling musical spirit; while emulating Parker's technique, Ives had added to it his own ideas, indicating, once again, that by the time he attended Yale, Ives was already far in advance of many recent projections of his compositional acumen.

Finally, almost fittingly at that, on the title page of the last movement (No.7, "Chorale and Finale") of *The Celestial Country*, Ives "doodled" a couple of charts that speak more to his musical being than any comparison with anyone ever could do. One of them, a study of quarter-tones, was noted by Kirkpatrick in his catalogue; the other, markedly fainter, even Kirkpatrick appeared to miss: a chart in *eighth-tones*. Somehow, *neither* of these remarkable indicators of Ives's impending ultra-modernity (in his handwriting of the time) was considered important enough to be mentioned by Sinclair in his *Descriptive Catalogue of the Music of Charles Ives*.

Verdict: Although *direct* comparisons between both cantatas examined here remain relatively few, even with many hypothetical links easily disproven, for anyone to propose, however, that the two works are entirely independent would be as inaccurate as those that have considered them matched. Quite aside from what can reasonably be demonstrated, the problem of determining the degree of Parker's influence (assumed by many to be virtually total) remains challenging and subjective, however. If it cannot be known how many of the skills necessary to compose such a cantata Ives possessed *prior* to entering Yale, he already had demonstrated that knew well how to write for chorus. It is possible, however, to state with reasonable certainty, all

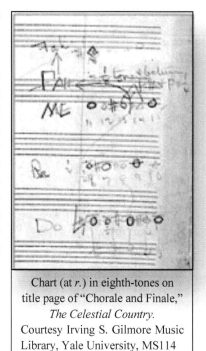

Chart (at *r.*) in eighth-tones on title page of "Chorale and Finale," *The Celestial Country.*
Courtesy Irving S. Gilmore Music Library, Yale University, MS114

comparisons aside, that Parker did provide the model for a successful work of this nature; indeed, his influence, musically, can be heard and seen often on the page. That same steadying presence is on display in other works from the time, too, even as illustrated in the larger discussions in this book.

However, it would be foolhardy to propose that Ives could *not* have composed some type of substantive choral work in the absence of his educational experience during these years, had he aspired to it. His own professional situation in church positions, and frequent work with his father's own choir during his years in Danbury had made the medium as comfortable to him as any. In *The Celestial Country*, in relation to his newfound ability to conceive and assemble large-scale works in general, not to mention his growing powers of musical invention—no less clear than in the expertise demonstrated in the composition of his First Symphony—seems far beyond anything that might be reasonably expected of an undergraduate composition student at the bachelor's level, of even at the most notable of institutions.

Songs

by Ives:

Nature's Way (1892/1901/1911; No.61 in *114 Songs*)
My Native Land (1893; No.101 in 114 Songs)
A Son of a Gambolier (1895; No.54 in *114 Songs*)
An Old Flame (1896; No.87 in *114 Songs*)
Memories: A, "Very Pleasant"; B, "Rather Sad" (1897; No.102 in *114 Songs*)

by Parker:

Evening (1891; from *3 Sacred Songs*)
Pastorale, Op.8, No.3 for organ (1891)
Wedding Song (1891; from *4 Compositions for Organ*, Op.20, No.1)
The Lark Now Leaves His Watery Nest, Op.47, No.6 (1899; from *6 Old English Songs*)

The effects of Parker's guidance seem clear enough in aspects of many of Ives's songs from 1895, or so, especially in more of his more conventional settings. It must be emphasized, however, that virtually any example put under the microscope reveals the enormous differences—many subtle, though no less substantive, regardless—between teacher and student. Ives's creativity and variety are remarkable, so much so, that few direct comparisons are readily evident, even in examples that might be considered to have been modeled on one (or more) works by Parker. Contrary to impressions one might gain often in general commentary, and which might not appear absolute even during the reading of this chapter, Ives was no mere imitator. It explains why there are aspects to the *sound* of his work that stand apart from the pack, even when the larger musical language and design are directly beholden to any particular long-established tradition.

Regardless, it is illuminating to tease out clues in the search for links between teacher and student. In *114 Songs*, among examples that Ives counted to be best avoided is a song from college days, *An Old Flame* (1896). That song, plus another, having roots from Ives's pre-Yale years, parallel at least two others by Parker: *Evening* (1891, one of the eight sacred songs he would pen by the end of the decade), and the other, *The Lark Now Leaves His Watery Nest* (1899), the year after Ives had graduated. The style of the latter, however, does not deviate from the familiar language of Ives's teacher to any perceptible degree, so that its style is not rendered irrelevant by the comparison. Many common traits in all three songs are apparent at

Ch. 6 Works from Ives's Yale Years

first glance. Revealing harmonic similarities, as well as occasional surprises, the most significant are their mutual reluctance to comply with the widely accepted (and often borne out) premise that an avoidance of the dominant harmony was entirely characteristic in the chosen melodies of the New England composers! Each song gravitates toward tonic and dominant, traveling little between their continual affirmations of a central tonality.

Surprises appear in *An Old Flame* at m.15, for example (a passing raised seventh appears in conjunction with a C7 harmony), and in *Evening* at m.2 (the dominant tone is maintained in the top line of the supertonic minor seventh chord); tones at odds with the prevailing simpler harmonizations demonstrate that, even here, the composers' innate creativity still was engaged. It is noticeable that *The Lark*, however, probably Parker's most successful song, does not venture beyond its all-too-familiar harmonic confines, although, in mm.28–29, the vocal line—with a fast ascent and dip over an octave span—negotiates a line almost worthy of George Ives's 'Humanophone'! Excerpting from each the harmonic outline of the respective first eight bars (from m.7 in *The Lark*, where the voice enters) reveals, however, how much the songs share:

Ives (*An Old Flame*):

I-V7- | V - | I- VI- | V- 7(add sus)- |→

I-+-VI-IV-| I-+VI-II7-| I-7-IV- | II7- V9 - |→ (m.9)

Parker (*Evening*):

p/u| I - | II7(add sus)-V7- | I- V7- | I-V-VI-V-|→

I-7-#IV-I-| II-VI-II-7-| V7- I- | #IV(#7)- VIIm- |→ (m.9)

Parker (*The Lark*) from m.7 (vocal entrance):

p/u| I - | V - | VI7 - IIM-| I-V-VI-II-|→

V - VI-IIM-| V - | I - | V - |→ (m.15)

The general pacing of the songs is similar, the basic common-time meter and unadventurous, and the largely four- and five-voice chordal harmonies of their respective layouts are entirely compatible. Parker's *Evening* offers, perhaps, the most variety, especially by its use of a larger three-part form, and a middle section that injects a sudden change in coloration (to minor) with the words, 'half-hearted,'

162

followed by ongoing chromaticism. The middle section is somewhat more active in its inner motion, too, passing through numerous diminished seventh harmonies and, mid-way, octave movement in the right hand, and harmony exclusively in the left. By comparison with his student's work, in this instance, Parker wrote a more interesting song—though Ives's rejection of his own similarly styled work speaks, perhaps, to a disdain for his teacher's work. Connections to other songs that Ives wrote during these years, of course, are not hard to find.

The tenor of Parker's setting of *Evening* is not unlike other songs by Ives, too, which can be illustrated readily. Cross-referencing the middle section of Parker's with Ives's *My Native Land* (1897) reveals similarities in their overall settings. More specifically, a closely shared moment with Ives's song can be isolated at m.16 in *Evening*, and in many even-numbered bars in *My Native Land*, both from a technical standpoint, as well as in the voicing. Most notably, echoes of the left hand accompaniment in *Evening* can be seen in a *Nature's Way* at mm.12–14. Ives's *Nature's Way* (1892) also shares a number of general similarities in overall style, despite the greater fullness of Parker's setting. Not inconsequentially, such isolated similarities can be found in countless places in music that has a common cultural ancestry. For example, compare even Parker's *Pastorale* (1891) for organ, between mm.77–90, and the second section of Ives's *A Son of a Gambolier* (1895). To what degree Ives was directly influenced by his teacher in any work remains speculative, although surely some relationships cannot be denied. Regardless, little of whatever Parker or Ives contributed in this genre was unique to them, the style of song writing, even his overall compositional style, essentially, fitting the established mold of the time.

Looking further for connections between teacher and student, in Ives's *Memories*, the humor of the first part (A), 'Very Pleasant,' resonates, true to the composer, his character so very familiar to anyone who knows his writing. The setting seems, however, to invoke the style of his early music, the immediate surroundings and innocence of his bygone childhood depicted with such deceptive simplicity that the listener is drawn directly into it. The accompaniment alone is so simple that it seems hardly the work of the more experienced composer, the song's small, repetitive phrases seeming to speak more to those of *Holiday Quickstep*—more like a work from Ives's Danbury years than from the composer of the First Symphony—than they do to Ives's contemporaneous *The Celestial Country*. The simple style and slow harmonic pace of the accompaniments of both parts—in (A), being entirely of the march 'stride' variety, is so fleet-footed that it suggests, perhaps, Cakewalk or Ragtime and, of (B)—simple undulations of arpeggiated chords—make comparisons in Parker's own music hard to find. If anything so undistinguished as the simple 'oom-pah' of part (A)—also seen in a similar context in Ives's 1895 *A*

163

Night Song, No.88 in *114 Songs*—is hard to find in anything that Parker would have deigned to write, though perhaps, part (B) owes something in style of the middle section of his 1890 *Wedding Song*, Op.20, No.1, despite being written for organ.

The pace of part (A) suggests Ives's youthful impatience and enthusiasm. even as the simple diatonic, though fairly wide ranging, melodic line suggests, more, folk origins, such as a jig or hornpipe. Although set in 6/8 meter, the only real consequence of that meter, versus 2/4, is the sense of near 'swing' imparted to the vocal line, which carries the entire burden of the tune alone. The song falls, thus, within the parameters of the prevailing and emerging popular idioms of the day. The childish glee with which Ives depicted awaiting an impending production at the local opera house (which, one might assume, was not 'opera'!), counterbalanced by the eager energy of the setting, are a perfect match, and a realm of expression largely outside Parker's world.

Harmonically, the first part travels very little, mostly I, and V7 (often substituting VII), almost for the entire first page. The melodic attributes, however, dance across a fairly wide range (a maximum of an eleventh)—which is not so unusual in itself—but the speed at which it traverses most of the range at a time places demands upon the skills of the singer that might come as a surprise. Near the end of the page, the key shifts to the mediant tonality with an implied cadence, and part 'A' continues accordingly, periodically injecting the flatted leading-tone harmony in alternations with the tonic (E). Briefly returning to the tonic (via its dominant, B) in the second system, the harmony centers on the dominant in the third (B7-Bø7-C-Bø), and, finally, the dominant seventh of C—the opening tonality—in the fourth, confirming it at the top of the third page. The music proceeds as it began for four more bars, until it reaches a repeating harmonic 'cell'—not unlike those discussed in relation to *The Celestial Country* and elsewhere—in this instance, rocking between Gø9-G7 for four bars, then another briefly (implied) polytonal variation for two more bars, D°/G7♭5-G7/Bø7, before reaching a fermata on G7 to conclude the first part of the song (A).

Part (B) is set in E♭, a sudden jolt from the commonplace C of the first part. Of an altogether different character, the melodic line is set atop only tonic (I) harmony for the first five bars, dominant (V) for four more, (I) for another four, and subdominant (IV) for the next two-and-a-half bars, before a short-lived return to the tonic (E♭) for the balance. This simple harmonic foundation is followed by the only moment of more elaborate progressions—the first four chords occupying just an eight-note each:

I7-IV(#7)-IV°7-#IVø7-VI7-V7-I

164

With the tonic harmony continuing for the final three bars, the last portion of the song reflects the true sense of nostalgia for which Ives has often been incorrectly tied in all his works.

Who, then, influenced Ives in the style of his songs? It is hard to find close parallels in Parker's work. Because the fast "stride" accompaniment of part 'A' resembles the style *The Circus Band* (No.56 in *114 Songs*), and the left hand accompaniment of Part B of *Memories* suggests that of *Karen* (No.91 in *114 Songs*)—both from before, or after just the beginning of Ives's time at Yale—neither song is, thus, hardly likely to reveal much of Parker's influence on him as a teacher.

The scenario does not, however, negate what happened between 1894 and the time at which *Memories* was composed in 1897, however. If the direct influence of Parker remains nebulous, it is visible, however, in the sophisticated elegance of the song; it seems clearly more the work of a practiced hand than that of Ives, even more yet, the even younger Ives of just a few years earlier. Now, his music—more assured in its simplicity than contained by it—speaks from another time, and closer to the present.

For piano

Ives, equal as a pianist as an organist, nevertheless, spent years of his life as a professional organist. The absence of any work for organ emerging from his mature years is surprising, however, the plethora of his piano compositions standing in remarkable testament to his keyboard skills, and clearly, his own view that he was a pianist, first and foremost, who also happened to play the organ.

Because Parker, however, though comfortable on the piano, was, nevertheless, first and foremost, an organist, it should be easy, therefore, to understand the lack of each composer's output relative to their instrumental preference. Although Parker wrote nothing for solo piano after 1900, despite the relative paucity of such literature in his catalogue (just twenty short pieces, usually in ternary form, many grouped into sets), it is possible, nevertheless, to arrive at a reasonable appreciation of his writing style—especially when examining works other than those purely for the piano alone (see next chapter).

by Ives: *Invention in D* **(1896)**

by Parker: *Valse Gracille* **(1899) [from** *Trois Morceaux Caractéristiques pour le Piano*, **Op.49]**

Although Ives's little *Invention* was written two years prior to Parker's *Valse Gracille*, it is possible to see evidence of the approach of writing for the instrument that might have influenced his student. Both pieces exhibit the same effective meter (3/8 vs. 3/4) and similar flowing streams of even-duplet divisions of the beat in the right hand. They differ in regard to substance and treatment: Ives's *Invention* continues with regular interchanging of motion from the left to right hands, and more varied accompanimental writing. Parker's *Valse*, however, is an altogether more commonplace statement, with very little, other than superficial, differences in its structural makeup from bar to bar.

The most notable aspect of both pieces is the identical approach taken in the treatment of a fundamental idea of linear motion maintained in ascending and descending patterns, typically scalic in basis. Of course, these types of cascading passages, so frequently involving sequential structures—usually from bar to bar—date back to baroque times, and notably to Bach's keyboard works. Despite the fact that Ives already would have been well versed in such techniques long before he encountered Parker, it is no less likely to be true that Parker's rigorous course requirements imposed an additional strengthening influence on Ives's student works and beyond.

Chapter 7
How Ives's Mature Music Reflects His Influences

*M*any of the same forces that had so profoundly impacted Ives's early life continued to linger within him throughout his most mature compositions. Even when developed and expanded his range by his increasing exposure to other influences, his earliest influences remain detectable in virtually everything he wrote.

Tuning

Often little taken into account are the many indirect clues to Ives's musical background under his father's guidance and influence. Among them, the highly specific note 'spellings' throughout Ives's output can be traced to his father's struggle between 'just' and 'tempered' intonation. The reworked third movement of the Fourth Symphony—long post-Parker—for example, full of such variances from the original string quartet version, and also some harmonic 'adjustments' of doublings, or omissions (per George's admonition in his teaching notes), makes Ives's sense of subtle pitch shadings quite apparent, although such obvious signals seem never taken into account, or even mentioned. The late-period *Universe Symphony*, too, features many such alternate note spellings, microtones and scales, even a 'Just Intonation Machine,' as Ives specified in the sketches, along with the various tuning protocols raised in *Memos*.[350] More important for this discussion, in his recollections, Ives also connected these tunings directly to his father, making it clear, therefore, where his ideas originated.[351]

Ives referred to his father's experiments in microtones as "quarter and other-tone divisions," and mentioned efforts with a slide cornet (George had used this instrument to accompany his choirs better—composed of local musicians who frequently had difficulties maintaining pitch), glasses filled with different amounts

---

[350] Ives, *Memos*, 108–10.

[351] Ibid., 45.

of water, a piano specially re-tuned in partials, and various other types of unconventional scales. It was here in *Memos* that Ives elaborated a little on George's experimentation, and what sometimes likely had given rise to being viewed in Danbury as a "crank." To the degree that Ives remembered his father's work, these recollections seem convincing enough. Unfortunately, and hardly surprisingly, not much about George's work was documented, or is provable, although, considering how often ideas Ives attributed to his father appear in his music, there seems little reason to doubt their origins; why would he, otherwise be reluctant to take credit for his own innovations?

Melodic and Linear Choices

We have already discussed the wide and disparate leaps to be found in the melodic lines of many of Ives's works, and how these, too, are directly traceable to the influence of George—at very least—revealing his tolerance, even encouragement of musical exploration.[352] If the kernel of the idea indeed had been hatched by Ives's wild-leaping keyboard exercise,[353] even George's novelty 'contraption,' the 'Humanophone'[354] (by which, extreme leaps became more practical with multiple singers taking individual notes only), Ives discussed in *Memos* borrowing the idea for his music, if not the means to its practicality. Recognizing the awkwardness and near-impracticality caused by such intervals when employed at their greatest extremes of range, Ives mentioned that, in *114 Songs*, he had omitted most examples that featured such intervals particularly "annoying" to the performers.[355] He readily commented, too, on the challenges of execution he shared with performers. As late as 1916, in the *Universe Symphony* sketches, such angular and linear attributes largely defined the melodic attributes of the entire work. They show up, too, however, in works extending across the entire range of his output:

---

[352] Ives, *Memos*, 44. Additionally, for those musicians who maintain that Ives was oblivious to the difficulties he was imposing, his words make clear that it was not the case. Moreover, he discussed the challenges that he, too, experienced in playing or singing them, but, nevertheless, maintained that he never had written anything *he* could not play, regardless of the degree of practice it required. Needless to say, Ives had the advantage of knowing the music from the inside-out—not quite the same thing as a musician struggling to get hands and head around one of Ives's works for the first time.

[353] Ibid., 44.

[354] Ibid., 45, 142.

[355] Ibid., 141–42.

- Even in the First Symphony, a work wholly couched in the conventional, certain examples of extravagant linear contours can be found. If the accompanying figure that begins in m.82 of the finale seems innocent enough, appearing initially divided among players in more manageable rhythms, it evolves into two cyclic bars (at T10) written around quite awkward leaps for the violins at mm.90–91 and 94–95, respectively. Can it be pure happenstance to find such technically ungainly (though highly attractive) intervals here, even in a variant for the flute at m.108? And, note the similarity of the figure to that Ives used again in *Thanksgiving* (1904) at m.76; albeit appearing now progressively altered chromatically, it is still no less awkward. Could Ives have been any less influenced by the idea, even in the gentle Third Symphony in the second movement, at mm.70–73, or in mm.144–45?

- In *114 Songs*, such angular, leaping lines can be found in *Hymn* [100], *Nov. 2. 1920* [22], *From "Paracelsus"* [30], and *Tolerance* [59], for example, to name just four. Ives further discussed and illustrated the idea in *Memos*, in which he quoted a short theme from sketch (apparently from pages now missing) of his song, *Aeschylus and Sophocles*.[356] In a footnote, Kirkpatrick also listed *Emerson*, (from the *Concord Sonata*), and *Varied Air and Variations*, as works that further demonstrate this type of linear contour.[357]

- As early as 1901, in *From the Steeples and the Mountains*, the trumpet and trombone lines—quite aide from appearing essentially in 12-tone rows or near aggregates—feature the same type of wide-leaping angularity found in throughout. Again, a similar type of line (in both instances, in near 12-tone writing) can be found in the trumpet and trombone parts of *The Gong on the Hook and Ladder* of c.1911.

- Taken now literally, a variation of the challenge appears in *Scherzo: Over the Pavements* in the cadenza, for the piano (from the earliest sketch materials, likely dating from c.1906), in which every tone in the rapidly rising and falling waves are set a major seventh apart. The idea originated with George Ives. Kirkpatrick recalled that Ives had told his friend, George Roberts, that his father had prescribed an exercise for playing a type of rapid chromatic scale, each succeeding interval separated by a minor ninth.[358] In the *Scherzo*, the overall rhythmic context also shrinks and expands by subtle alterations of the

---

[356] Ives, *Memos*, 127.

[357] Ibid., 44, n. 5.

[358] Ibid., 44.

meter each bar that respond to a systematically controlled written acceleration in the orchestra. The piano 'waves' cross these meter changes independently, largely unaffected. Combining George's exercise with multiple meters that Ives attributed to George seem to be the only explanation.[359] The idea for such musical adventurism surely did not originate with Parker.

- In *Memos*, Ives demonstrated the idea behind a piano part built in patterns of ascending minor ninths, and claimed to have used this specific unit in *The Fourth of July* and *The Masses*. If they cannot be found in these pieces, his ease with writing wide leaps is clear.[360]

- In Section A of the *Universe Symphony*, George's presence is ever-present, not Parker's, and well-illustrated by a few examples: from Section A, mm.7–8 (tuba), bars 9–10 (first cello), or mm.33–34 (trumpet).

- In many other examples of Ives's angular melodic lines, they sometimes appear as complete (or near-) twelve-tone rows, even if he did not see a musical benefit to developing totally systemized melodic organization.

Polytonal 'wedges'

The polytonal 'wedge' formations, detailed by Philip Lambert, which had clearly caught the young composer's imagination from an early age, reappear with regularity in Ives's music across the years.[361] The satisfying effect of contrary motion surely emanating from the same place among musical minds throughout the ages, the 'classic' Ives polychordal 'wedge' surely was one of the youthful 'discoveries' that led him toward polytonality. The feature is often evident in the collection, *114 Songs* (and others), although not all can be considered strict representations of the idea. Among the most striking examples appear in *Majority* [1], *Religion* [16], *"Nov. 2, 1920"* [22], *Premonitions* [24], *From Paracelsus* [30], *Ilmenau (Over All the Treetops)* [68], and also in other works, such as the First Piano Sonata, (e.g., page 8 [system 4], and page 12 [systems 3 & 4]). In the song, *A Son of a Gambolier* [54], they are wholly tonal, with octaves rather than chords in the bass—the idea, rather than its polytonal representation being the idea.

---

[359] Ibid., 140.

[360] *Op. cit.*, n. 8. In the *Fourth of July*, there is a passage from mm.94–98 that features a pattern of *descending* minor ninths in the right hand, however. In *The Masses*, too there are several places in which *descending* chords spread over a *major* ninth appear.

[361] Philip Lambert, *The Music of Charles Ives*, 19–21.

The Dawn of Dodecaphony

In his lesson notes, *anticipating integer notation*, George assigned numeric organization to the twelve possible pitches (*1–12*);[362] almost identical to what actually occurred in the twentieth century, the equality of each pitch class speaking to Charles Ives's early use of tone rows and aggregates. As early as 1901, *From the Steeples and the Mountain* featured numerous 12-tone rows (e.g., in the trumpet, between mm.17–20, allowing for some double articulations). Even Ives's *tonal* works hint sometimes of dodecaphony, the sinewy, chromatic linearity of the individual parts in the finale of the Third Symphony, for example, being studded with many lines that threaten to become twelve-tone rows, their very tonality almost undermined by their unlikely, at times almost tenuous, link to the fundamental tonalities.

George's influence and adjustments of the 'rules'

In playing an acep't try not to play a third of a chord if you hear it in the air. The other part of the rule is easily understood if you try a few chords without any third. Notice Pattern chord and see how many octaves and fifths before you come to a 3d. You may wonder why we can omit the 3d in the Dominant 7th chord. There are several reasons, one is by adding the 7th to the 5th, we gain a third and that is enough for any chord, and the chord of Dominant 7 stands in better relation as to the tonic with 3d or 5th, omitted, as you can see-

Excerpt from George Ives's teaching essay
Reproduced Courtesy Irving S. Gilmore Library of Yale University MSS 14

George Ives's keen awareness of the all-defining role of the third (see again p. 94)—often 'heard' as present *even when not*—is frequently exemplified in Ives's music. Because actual polytonality in many of Ives's early works reflects harmonic blends that accommodate the third, in the last of *Three Harvest Home Chorales*,

---

[362] Carol K. Baron, "George Ives's Essay on Music Theory: An Introduction and Annotated Edition," *American Music* (Fall, 1992): 239–88.

Ch. 7 How Ives's Mature Music Reflects His Influences

for example, their repeated omission in *both* harmonic levels between **mm.13–24** allowed further tonal blends of otherwise more harshly conflicting chords. Arguably, such simple combinations introduced Ives to the possibilities of combined chords (something he referenced directly in *Memos*),[363] and surely were forerunners of the exploration of their possible combinations in works of music.

Demonstrations of the effectiveness of George's philosophical stance on music theory can be found featured prominently in Ives's extraordinary setting of *Psalm 67*. It is a composition that, at least in some form, clearly existed before Ives entered Yale and, apparently, was written under George's guidance. In Ives's psalm setting, careful combinations of major and minor chords imply extensions of the major in a *singular* key (Ives's stated intent)[364]—the third of the major never being challenged by the presence of conflicting tones a semitone distant. Ives's recollection, thus, that prior to 1894, his father's Danbury choir could entertain singing *Psalm 67* is entirely plausible. In reducing **mm.1–4**, for example, to conventional chords and occasional polychords, only when an increase in tension was needed did Ives deliberately allow true polytonal conflict (highlighted below), in which the third of C clashes brazenly with the tonic, E♭, of the adjoined chord:

C/Gm–G/Dm–C/Gm–**C/E♭**–F/Cm–E♭/B♭m =

C9/g–C9/d–G9/d–C9/d–**C/E♭**–F9/c–E♭9/d♭ =

V9–II9–V9–V/♭VII–I9–♭VII9 (it can be seen
that every *blended* chord forms a dominant ninth.)

Such harmonic structures were only part of something larger, however. As Philip Lambert pointed out,[365] they were part of the systematic thought processes to which Ives was drawn early on—the organization of musical language according to organizational code—having always been part of music, after all, from the very beginning. Ives new methodologies throughout his output are directly linked to George's questioning of the status quo.

---

[363] Ives, *Memos*, 47.

[364] Ives, *Memos*, 178.

[365] Philip Lambert, *The Music of Charles Ives* (New Haven, CT: Yale University Press, 1997), 15–22.

Father and teacher: mutual influence

Ives: *Trio* (1904/1911): first movement

In 1904, when Ives composed most of his *Trio* (completed and revised in 1911), the first movement shows the influence, again, of George's 'Humanophone.' The atonal, jagged lines starkly demonstrate Ives's early advances, again even touching upon many near rows and aggregates. On the score of *Majority*, Ives dismissed the wholesale usage of dodecaphony: "It's too easy, any high-school student (unmusical) with a pad, pencil compass and logarithm table . . . could do it."[366] In spite of the implication of pure atonality the substantially independent parts of all three instruments, they occur within a tonal harmonic order, a descending semitone (in terms of pitch class) being the most prominent motif. The avoidance of chordal thirds, which otherwise would conflict with implied tonalities, also reflects George's teaching, as elucidated in his essay.[367] Just as Ives handled polytonality in *Psalm 67* (1893), thirds in the violin and cello parts do not contradict the implied major or minor harmonic blend with the piano.[368]

The movement follows an interesting contrapuntal structure, built of four linear components: those of the violin, cello, piano left and right hands (the number of parts superficially tying it to standard baroque counterpoint, such as employed in fugues). These components, introduced in pairs and finally all together, total three distinct sections —in a latter-day manifestation of the ancient technique of *successive composition*, in which the compounding and layering of multiple separate elements eventually coexist, as described in Chapter 3,[369] each of the three linked segments comprising the movement having different harmonic implications, affected at every turn by the different combinations of tones. One has to wait for the final segment to hear the intended harmonic design. Each segment seems to gravitate toward C and G, or C7 and G7, the first hinting at the larger final tonal outcome (C) almost from the start.

---

[366] Ives, *Majority* (*The Masses*), 1915, 11.

[367] Carol K. Baron, "At the Cutting Edge: Three American Theorists at The End of The Nineteenth Century," *International Journal of Musicology*, 2 (1993): 193–247. See also Baron, "George Ives's Essay in Music Theory: An Introduction and Annotated Edition," American Music (Fall 1992): 239–88.

[368] Cooke 2015, pp. 36–39.

[369] Scott, "Horatio at the Bridge?": 448–78.

At the outset, the cello and piano (*right hand* only—a 'low' and 'high' part together) appear together, to form the first section. Both parts follow freely atonal lines, yet it is by tones common to standard chords, or those lying just outside them, that one can detect the harmonic motion. For example, opening in A minor, a clear implication established by the low 'a' in the cello and high 'c' in the piano, the various melodic tones that follow skirt around the tonic (A) as major and minor sevenths, and with a contraction of the major seventh, too, into minor seconds. By the middle of the third bar, D7 harmony is implied, and through other close tonalities, leads to C through the dominant (G) in m.6.

Continuing to skirt around the primary tonality, the roots of these harmonies outline a melodically ascending and descending curve to and from the mid-point (m.9), falling back with more frequent progressions, to reveal, imply, and ultimately confirm C as the primary tonality. It will be re-confirmed at the end of the movement. It can be seen from the graphic that the first segment of the section (mm.1–19) is dominated by three primary harmonic regions that seem to point toward an overall cadential motion of dominants, substitutes for dominants, and like-chords that, ultimately, gravitate toward C.

- The *first*—for cello and piano right hand alone [Figure 1, bars 1–19]

- The *second*—for violin with piano left hand [Figure 2, bars 28–51] differs in its tonal implication

- The *third*—for cello, violin, both piano hands [Figure 3, mid-bar 51–conclusion] reveals the full harmonic design

In the first segment, a descending semitone, sometimes inverted as a major seventh, is the primary motif throughout; identifying and projecting its multiple appearances is crucial to establishing coherence of the tightly structured form. Beyond m.19, the tonality is less diffuse, leading to the larger tonal destination for each segment (C):

The *first* segment: bars 1–27

mm.

1.	2.	3.	4.	5.	6.	7.	8.	9.
|Am - |Am- C- |C-D7-|D7 - |D7 - |G-G#°7-|C#°7 -	C#°7-D9-|F - |→							

10.	11.	12.	13.		14.	15.	16.	17.	18.	19.	.
Em - |B - |G - |G-G♭ -F-E-|Dm - |G6 - ‖|D+ -A-|E♭ -C-7|C7-D-7 |E-D-G-|→								

20.	21.	22.	23.	24.	25.	26.	27.
A♭ - |A♭ -B♭ -|E♭ -B♭ -| C-B-C-|B-C-F-|Em-B-C-| E♭m-F-C-F	G7-C-|			

The second segment (bars 47–51), though of a similar vein to the first, takes on a new identity; the latter portion, bridging to the third segment (though structurally still part of the second), features ragtime-like syncopations in the violin, centered on C/C7 tonality:

The *second* segment: bars 28–51

mm.

28.	29.	30.	31.	32.
Dm -	G (add 6) -	D+ - A (add 13)	E♭ (add 9) - C-3 (add 13) - 7| C7 - D - 7 |→

33.	34.	35.	36.	37.
E-3 - D-G+(#7) Dm7/G| A (♭5 #7)	(cont'd) - B♭ (♭5)	C(♭5#7) - F	F7 - C - 7 |→

38.	39.	40.	41.	42.	43.
B♭° - Am-F	Gm7-G°-Fm-F#°	G7-Dm/G-	Am7-A7-#7	C-C#7-C	C#-C-F-	→

44.	45.	46.	47.	48.	49.	50.	51.
C#- C- Em-	Fm-F#m-G	Am-G-C7	C - C7 -	C - C7 -	C - C7 -	C7 -	C7 -	

Finally, all four independent lines appear in grand concert in the *third* and final *polytonal* segment:

mm.

52.	53.	54.	55.	56.	57.	58.	59.	60.
Am -	Am-C-	C-D7-	D7 -	D7 -	G-G#°7-	C#°7 -	C#°7-D9-	F -	→
Dm -	G6 -	D+-A-	E♭ -C-7	C7-D-7	E-D-G-	A♭ -	A♭ - B♭ -	C-F-	→

61.	62.	63.		64.	65.	66.
Em -	B -	G -		G-G♭-F-E-	E♭ - B♭ -	C- B- C-	→
F7-C7-	B♭-A-F-	Gm7-G°-Fm-F#°	G7-Dm/G-	Am7-A7-#7	C-C#7-C	→

67.	68.	69.	70.	71.	
B - C - F -	Em - B - C-	E♭m-F-C-F-	G7 - C-		→ *coda in C7...*
C#-C-C#-	C#- C- Em-	Fm-F#m-G-	Am - G - C7-	→	*to end in C.*

The segment (third and final) leads to the conclusion and tonal confirmation of C—implied all along. Despite the apparent completeness of each of the three 'segments,' it is only here that Ives's larger polytonal design is revealed, as well as the final united tonal resolution. A Schenkerian-like approach to the piano bass line of the final segment reveals a more telling, inner, tonal design. Omitting smaller

Ch. 7 How Ives's Mature Music Reflects His Influences

chromatic motion, diatonicism revolves around the tonic, supertonic, subdominant, submediant, and dominant chords—resembling the hymn-like bass lines at the heart of much of Ives's music:

```
 II      V      II  VI  III    I   II   III II  V ( ♭)VI ( ♭)VII  I   IV
 D  -  |G  -  |D -A-|E♭-  |C -D-|E -D -G |A♭  -  B♭ |C -F-|→

 IV  I  VII   VI  IV  V   IV  (#)    V  - II/V VI      I  (#)  I
 F  -  C |B  - |A - F  |G  - F  - (F#)  |G  - D/G |A  -  |C (C#) C |→

 I     (#)I  (#)I   I  III  IV     V  VI  V I
 C  - (C#)  |(C#) - C - E  |F (F#) - G |A   G C|→
```

The implications are clearer by beginning a hypothetical bass line:

Overall, the movement is remarkably complex; much of the time, each instrumental part seems unrelated with no obvious common pulse or shared tonality, entirely independent in character and motion. With many of Ives's defining cues absent—the quotes, programmatic associations, even traces of his famous humor—likely Ives conceived it as a 'take-off': a short exploratory excursion. The rest is for the players to discover and entice off the page. Not likely consciously made choices, nevertheless, Ives's melodic instincts, buried within his New England roots, seem to have dictated his thought processes, no less than Parker's, Chadwick's, or any of the other composers of the era working in that region of the country.

Verdict: If Parker caused Ives to dig deeper into counterpoint in baroque counterpoint, he probably was responsible, too, for some of the expansion of Ives's methodology into this unusually striking form. However, the presence of George Ives seems to loom larger in relation to applications of integer notational thinking, the atypical, jagged linearity, as well as the effective conjoining of harmonies.

Myth vs. reality: Ives's "simulations" of George's clashing bands

(*Putnam's Camp* from the First Orchestral Set: *Three Places in New England*)

George Ives's fascination with separate bands clashing on Main Street has long been at the center of Ives lore. Does the reality, however, match the legend? *Putnam's Camp*, the second movement of Ives's *First Orchestral Set* (otherwise known as *Three Places in New England*), is the best-known instance of its supposed recreation in an actual work by Ives. Perhaps, not quite what the uninitiated might have expected, the clashing bands appear as ghostly entities rather than the stark conflicts one might have expected. The gentle march rhythms with short interjections of *The British Grenadiers* by a solitary trumpet constitute all the instrumentation and music of the faster 'band,' which, by nature of its tempo and prominent percussive rhythm, takes a separate 'street beat.' Seeming almost more prominent in the texture than the larger primary unit, which, remaining in the original speed, accompanies the faster unit with ghoulishly eerie chromatic harmonics in the upper strings.

Although commonly taken as George visiting 'from the other side,' what Ives actually had in mind were the ghosts of Putnam's soldiers in their harsh winter encampment of 1778–79. Furthermore, in *Putnam's Camp*, the scoring of the faster 'band' hardly can be considered a complete representation of such an ensemble, nor is it in any way clear how the oft-touted 'crossing' of two bands now immortalized in *Putnam's Camp* was originally determined as such. Indeed, the entire, long accepted, basis that it is a recreation of the effect of 'clashing bands on Main Street' associated with George Ives is, in fact, nothing of the kind. Ives provided the definitive answer in his program notes: the faster material merely represents the soldiers marching out of camp. There is no mention of clashing bands, let alone anything inspired by events on Main Street. The fact that the segment features two independent speeds should not be taken to demonstrate the faulty hypothesis, either.

Ives already had broached multiple speeds long before composing *Putnam's Camp* (e.g., *The Unanswered Question*, *Central Park in the Dark*). If these efforts have never been similarly held up as representations of 'clashing bands,' it is only because they do not feature any band tune. Looking further, although more in line with the effect one might expect to hear by the description, the multiple conflicting clashes of band tunes in the *Scherzo* of the *Fourth Symphony* still do not represent the changing of physical positions of one ensemble relative to another. Neither does the typically unaccompanied instrumentation of the quoted tunes actually suggest any motion at all, nor generally complete independent ensembles, even when one of the quoted tunes appears in reasonably full scoring. If the locomotive, too, of Hawthorne's description is vividly portrayed, even imparting the sense of motion that suggests its progress along the tracks, there is still nothing, nevertheless, to suggest conflicting *physical* motion by the accompanying cacophony, such as might have been inspired by George Ives's experiments with marching bands.

Looking further afield, representations of separate conflicting ensembles can be found in *Washington's Birthday*, in which small groups of players break away from the main group. However, once again, the separate tunes (and break-away ensembles) are quoted only as unaccompanied melodic fragments, still with no suggestion of any group actually *crossing* each other's paths in the depicted scene. Similarly, the final conflagration on Main Street in *The Fourth of July* conjures up a vivid portrayal of more than one group of players; however, other than the larger town band, they are little more than parts of the fabric—again, not more than skeletal, unaccompanied fragments of tunes, amid representations of chaos—there is still no suggestion of the kind of kaleidoscopic musical settings that had captivated George Ives. However, at least *part* of another phenomenon that fascinated George is depicted: sonic entities in the open air.

Was Ives still heeding his father's admonition not to inject too much experimentalism into actual works of music (despite the other radicalism on display!)? Even if no one ever hears George's clashing bands crossing Ives's works, perhaps Ives considered depictions of relative physical motion worthy of a different medium than mere bands in a parade. We do hear truly independent relative motions in the rhythmic patterns of foot traffic in *Scherzo: Over the Pavements*, for example, although only at virtually the end of his output did Ives capture, in the virtually complete first section of the *Universe Symphony*, a portrayal of actual true relative physical motion—clouds floating across the sky over the earth below—even as only *one* component (the clouds), nevertheless, was moving. However, referencing "orbital harmonies" in the symphony,[370] even in the absence of obvious depictions of such explicit physical motion, one can posit, however, that Ives captured, in its multiple levels, something of the independent processions of stars and planets, and time, itself.

---

[370] Ives, *Memos*, 107–08.

178

Verdict: Too much attention has been paid to the actual representation of motion of physical bodies in Ives's music, though it is partially present. Although clashing entities are common enough throughout his work, the musical portrayal of motion itself, especially *crossing* entities—in the manner of changing relative position—in reality, occurs only in the *Universe Symphony*, and only in the admittedly highly esoteric motion of orbiting planets in the cosmos.[371]

Depictions of water:

The Housatonic at Stockbridge
(mvt. No. 2 from the First Orchestral Set: *Three Places in New England*)

With the depiction of running water at the heart of this movement, it is instructive to look at other works of the period that might have influenced Ives's sound painting. Although the subtle shimmering of the Housatonic River is depicted with a realism and beauty seldom paralleled in virtually any other work of music, certain features of its content do seem, fleetingly, reminiscent of Debussy's *La Mer* of 1905. The American premiere of *La Mer* in Boston in 1907, by Karl Muck and the Boston Symphony Orchestra, was met with mixed reactions. In a review, no more enthusiastic than at the 1905 premiere in Paris, Louis C. Elson summed it up with the rebuke, "If this be Music we would much prefer to leave the Heavenly Maid until she has got over her Hysterics." Nevertheless, *La Mer* would prevail, soon to become a concert favorite; popularized by Arturo Toscanini, he programmed it regularly after 1909. Because it is known that Ives heard Toscanini, due to his sarcastic appraisal of his conducting,[372] it seems plausible that he might well have heard *La Mer*, and even been influenced by it

Although, according to Ives, the roots of *The Housatonic at Stockbridge* can be traced to 1908 (a date routinely altered by revisionist scholarship),[373] it is

---

[371] Cooke, *Charles Ives's Musical Universe*, 455–56. See also Ives, *Memos*, 107–08.

[372] Ives's condemnation of Toscanini's rhythmic rigidity paralleled that of Giuseppe Verdi, as evidenced in his letter to Nicolas Slonimsky of June 18, 1936. The Charles Ives Papers, Irving S. Gilmore Music Library, Yale University MS114.

[373] Sinclair, *A Descriptive Catalog of the Music of Charles Ives*, 40; in that Carol K. Baron demonstrated that the dates of *Putnam's Camp* are entirely in one with Ives's, there is no reason to suspect otherwise for *The Housatonic at Stockbridge*. See again, Baron, "Dating Charles Ives's Music," 32–49.

entirely probable that the entire composition, even, perhaps, the water's glistening texture, was not set finally in place until 1914. Ives's dislike of Debussy's music, however, might not have been enough to prevent him from reacting to some facets of its sonics. The conclusion of the first movement ('De l'aube à midi sur la mer') of Debussy's masterwork reveals some fascinating parallels to the ending of Ives's movement: the shimmering tremolo strings—in register, too—the effect of the motion in the woodwinds not entirely unlike it, the wavy footsteps of the low instruments; most of all, even the similarity of Debussy's theme at rehearsal No.14 to Ives's selection of *Dorrnance* is remarkable.

The last bars of *La Mer* (the third movement: 'Dialogue du vent et la mer') also seem to invoke something similar to Ives's sound painting in *his* concluding bars: the rapidly 'flying' scales of the high violins, the cross rhythms of the woodwinds occupying comparable ground, the powerful brass chords over two repeating bass notes, and the long sustained final chord (even as Ives completed his movement with a brief moment of introspection after it), the similarities continue to be striking. Although, of course, none of these comparisons prove that Ives modeled any of his movement on *La Mer*, especially because Ives's music is entirely more modernistic and wholly original in its major content. Nevertheless, one cannot ignore the possibility of the influences—as is the case in all music—of the work of other leading figures of the day. Indeed, such consequences likely point to the reason Ives eventually chose to stay away from concerts; his complaint he noted in keeping his own musical thoughts independent of anything recently heard—and remembered—is often aired by composers.[374]

Moreover, we cannot overlook other references to water in Ives's music that seem to have leanings toward the French impressionists. The depiction of Walden Pond in 'Thoreau' in the *Concord Sonata*, of course, immediately comes to mind, the gentle rippling effect of its opening suggesting something almost Ravel-like in quality. As it happens, within Maurice Ravel's piano piece, *Jeux d'Eau* (1902), can

---

[374] Ives, *Memos*, 137. Ives made the remark in relation to a concert he had heard, at which none other than Gustav Mahler was conducting. He also related how long-familiar music did not have the effect of interfering with his musical creativity, so it is remotely possible he was referring to a performance of a Mahler symphony or other contemporary composition, such as he would not have been likely to hear previously. In the same section of *Memos*, Ives described another occasion at which Arthur Fiedler had conducted music by Reger, Ives found his own inner ear had been disturbed. The writer, having at one time entertained the prospect of becoming a composer, is entirely sympathetic to Ives's comments, and can attest to having experienced precisely the same downside to hearing new music while engaged in composing a work of his own.

be found a passage highly reminiscent of it: located at m.55, the right hand features rapidly ascending groups of four thirty-second notes (with a wash provided by the pedal) that replicate almost the same passage—and certainly, the effect. The timing of *Jeux d'Eau* makes it quite possible that Ives was familiar with it, even though he probably made no conscious allusion to Ravel's composition, but the two moments are too alike to discount the possible connection.

There are further, even more stark, depictions of moving waters in Ives's song, between *from The Swimmers* (1915, rev.1921; No.27 in *114 Songs*), and one of a collection of piano pieces[375] by Ravel, *Ondine* (1908), and inspired by the nocturnal water nymph of Aloysius Bertrand's *Gaspard de la Nuit, fantaisies à la manière de Rembrandt et de Callot*. Although the roles of left and right hands are reversed in each respective piece, the single melodic strand set against a cycled loop of arpeggiated static harmony pervades the opening of Ives's song, and mm.43–44 of *Ondine*. Musically similar, if less so visually, was Ives influenced at all by the flowing right hand motion and the more articulated activity in the left hand on page 63, system 3 (first edition) versus m.53 of Ravel's work? On pages 64–65, Ives touches upon extremely similar turf, the chordal motion of the right hand over swirling arpeggiations in the left seeming to parallel *Ondine* at mm.63–66. It is impossible, too, not to be reminded again of *Ondine* (mm.24–28) on pages 65–66, the repetitively percussive chords seeming to have been cut from almost the same cloth.

Although there is no way to determine how one work might have influenced another—the types of writing common to these pieces being typical idiomatically of the piano—the prospect is tantalizing, and does fit the profile of their period.

Piano Music

by Parker: *Suite for Piano Trio*, Op.35 (1893)
***Trois Morceaux Caractéristiques pour le Piano*, Op.49 (1899)**

by Ives: Piano Sonata No. 1, mvts. IIa/IIb, IV & V (1899–1902)

The compositions in this section by Parker do not belong to Ives's time at Yale, although their proximity in context—by way of circumstance, origin and style—nevertheless, makes them hardly less suited to inclusion here. Moreover, it is difficult to find direct correlations between Ives and Parker within this category

---

[375] From the suite of pieces for solo piano by Maurice Ravel: *Gaspard de la nuit: Trois poèmes pour piano d'après Aloysius Bertrand* of 1908.

Ch. 7 How Ives's Mature Music Reflects His Influences

of composition; not so, the influence upon Ives of George Felsberg, the wild Ragtime pianist at Poli's. In comparison to the expansive radicalism of Ives's piano works, all of Parker's piano works display an entirely orthodox style of writing.

Two groups of short piano pieces (*Six Characteristic Pieces*, Op.7 [1882], and *Five Pieces*, Opus [1905]), by George Whitefield Chadwick, who probably was the most distinguished of Parker's predecessors, illustrate well Parker's direct lineage. In the words of Parker's biographer, William Kearns, Parker's late piano works, however, have "the conservative cast of the rest of his piano music."[376] At Yale, and shortly thereafter, Ives's piano music, too, falls within much the same musical category; Ives, no doubt preoccupied with his primary role and job as organist at the Center Church on the Green in New Haven, was yet to embark on exploiting the potential for the piano. Most of his writing for the instrument involved accompaniments to traditionally conceived songs, most notably, his eighteen so-called 'German' songs.

Parker's own group of three pieces, *Trois Morceaux Caractéristiques pour le Piano*, Op.49 were composed in 1899, just before he stopped writing for solo piano entirely. Notable for their well-written, if less-than-stimulating harmonic invention, other examples of such writing appear also in the Suite Op. 35 for piano trio. The Suite is a far better concert piece than generally has been allowed, Kearns's less than favorable comparisons to Chadwick's and Foote's chamber works finding little support here; the Suite is eminently listenable, with memorable themes and vitality—qualities starkly absent in the trios of his American contemporaries, despite the lack more extended development in the Suite.

Kearns, however, was less than accurate in his brief description; referencing the second movement, he featured the *third* as his example in the text. Moreover, the analysis of the harmonic design does not conform to the example. Kearns was partly correct in that the movement begins in G minor, but incorrect in stating that, falling back in bars 5–7, it emphasizes the sub-dominant, which would have been C minor. Rather, the emphasis is on B♭, which is, of course, the relative major. In turn, beyond the quoted excerpt, it progresses to C7, resolving to F. However, it does not end with a "weak cadence in the tonic key."[377] It confirms the shift to the subdominant, B♭—a logical, artistic and entirely traditional methodology to introduce a new, contrasting section. Instead, below is the actual harmonic outline of the segment:

---

[376] Kearns, *Horatio Parker*, 210.

[377] Ibid., 210.

p.18, m.1

B♭ - | Cm - | B♭ - | B♭ - 7 | E♭ - E♭m| E♭- A-C-F-7|B♭ - Cm-C|F-B♭ - |→

If such harmony reinforces the impression that it is cut from an exclusively conventional cloth, Parker injected a number of curiosities that prove exceptions to the rule—unexpected progressions, and, at times, surprisingly awkward enharmonic notation that reflects the continuing influence of Wagner's shifting tonalities. The adoption of modern-day equal temperament still was not yet uniformly set, of course, and much of the music of the time was notated in an entirely literal manner, rather with more practicality in mind. Parker, like many of his contemporaries, was thoroughly grounded in that very language, achieving in America, perhaps, the most proficient background in all aspects of late-Romantic music. The Suite, however, reveals the degree—within this kind of literature—to which Parker managed to exceed his teacher's (Chadwick's) ability, being one of the most effective domestic works of the genre to have emerged by 1893.

Examples of such writing appear, too, early in the Suite. In the opening *Prelude*, unexpected enharmonic progressions at high points take flight right from the outset, and sound almost startling:

m.[1]   **[5]**
A - | A - | A - | Bm - | A7 - | Aø7 - | G7 - | A7 - Bm7- |→

[10]
A#7(B♭7) - E7 - | A - | F#m - |Bm - Bm7 - |G#7 - |B♭7 - |→

Parker was fearless about pursuing such harmonies through all manner of enharmonic progressions, sometimes employing the technique unevenly between the various parts, making his writing appear illogical (e.g., in m.9 of the previous example). In the finale, Parker's usage of enharmonic writing across unusual harmony is the least practical of all. For example, beginning at m.22, such a series of progressions runs contrary to the kind of assessments that Parker, even in relatively conventional compositions, was averse to including anything outside the norm:

[22]
C°-C - B♭(Italian 6th) | A - | B - G - | C# - D+ - | B7 - A - | D#m7 - |→

183
Ch. 7 How Ives's Mature Music Reflects His Influences

Later in the movement, between mm.85–105, we encounter a strikingly harsh series of progressions, again, not the kind of harmonies one would expect from a musical "stick-in-the-mud":

[85]

G° - | A7 - | B7 - | D$^{(\#7)}$ - | →

[88]

A♭7 - |- D♭ - | A♭°7 - | A♭m7 - | E♭m7 - | A♭7 - | →

[95]

F♭7 - | B♭7 - | F°7 - | Dm - | D°7 - | F - | →

Standing out from the much more song-like surroundings, it can be seen that, even in the relatively staid context of high society parlor music, Parker did inject an element of daring. The Suite is a far better concert piece than generally has been allowed, and worthy of much more frequent airings than has been the case. Kearns's less than favorable comparisons of Parker's trio to Chadwick's and Arthur Foote's chamber works seem ill-placed and, especially, to those by Foote, whose two trios lack convincing melodic invention, interesting harmony, or even fundamentally attractive qualities. Parker's Suite is eminently listenable, however, with memorable themes and vitality, even dashes of the spirit of New England often captured so cheerfully in Chadwick's music—qualities all too often absent in the music of his American contemporaries—even if the lighter formula behind its structure causes it sometimes moments of weakness.

It should be emphasized, that when compared with Ives's post-Yale piano writing, Parker's 'radicalism' is limited essentially to unlikely chord progressions, rather than new types of innovation. Rhythmically, Parker's music stays within the tracks of the tried-and-true. It does, however, serve to illustrate that impressions handed down of a 'staid' composer are not altogether accurate, or even fair. There can be no doubt that Ives's own comments about Parker played the largest role in establishing the negative perceptions accorded his Yale professor. In this light, does Ives's maturing piano writing have *anything* in common with Parker's piano writing? It turns out that there are a few techniques they share and, in Ives's case, at least partly reflecting not only Parker's direct tuition, but also his demonstrations of well-structured piano writing, presumably in his music literature classes. Nevertheless, Ives's writing is decidedly advanced, increasingly fused with elements entirely external to his formal education; next to it, Parker's piano works look tame, the direct parallels few, and lacking new ideas.

Ives's maturing piano writing is nothing like anything by anyone else at any time. His major excursions for the instrument appeared suddenly in his early post-Yale works, as if from nowhere, though not in actuality. The second movement of Ives's First Piano Sonata (IIa/b), were sketched in the early years of the century—and, perhaps, begun even as early as 1899 (according to Ives's own documentation, and unpublished research by Thomas Warburton). Written in an idiom largely centered on Ragtime, it offers particularly useful parallels for the purposes here—Ives's first major excursion for piano (the sonata) having some of its origins dating from virtually the same time as Parker's last., even though, stylistically, they are far apart.

The strongly syncopated rhythms of the introduction ('ragged' in both hands), suggest regular 'stride,' though it is only alternating broken octaves. Appearing in the left hand to accompany the tangled rhythms of the right, the left hand also serves to anchor and stabilize the foundation. The music proceeds, and the 'stride' evolves, moving through modification to groups of three tones (the initial octave still being maintained), then adding upper dyads on the last of the group. At the start of the fourth system, one instance of pure 'stride' appears that effectively sets the idiomatic tone, the continuing distortions of which still maintain the character, nevertheless. Meanwhile, the rhythmic complexities in the right hand intensify. The music develops; any expected references dissipate—the idiom now so entrenched that the listener is carried forward on a wave of development, rather than the departures from it.

By the fourth page, fourth system, the writing in both hands becomes more conventional—more like Parker's piano writing, in fact; the most pronounced syncopations appear in the largely harmonized right hand, while the left hand plays octaves to maintain the rhythmic foundation. By the last two pages, allusions to Ragtime have mostly evaporated; the ending 'chorus' (a passage that shows up even in the *Second Orchestral Set*), once again, emphasizes the hymn-based melodies underlying Ives's roots, the distinctive links to near the end of the hymn *I Hear Thy welcome Voice* being clear, with a chordal 'cell,' much like the previous discussion in Chapter 5 (in relation to *The Celestial Country*). These alternating chords avoid the dominant, in this instance—I-IV-I-IV—and lead to the end, a plagal cadence, left unresolved.

Parker's group of three pieces, *Trois Morceaux Caractéristiques pour le Piano*, Op.49 (1899), is another well-written work, if mostly less-than-stimulating harmonically. However, some parallels can be found in portions of Ives's First Piano Sonata and *Trois Morceaux*, perhaps most notably, their frequently shared methodology of writing for the instrument. For example:

185

- In the first of Parker's *Trois Morceaux Caractéristiques*, *Conte Sérieux*, at m.10, a descending passage hints at something in common with a (far more complex) descent in Ives's first movement. Both examples were likely cut from much the same pianistic cloth.

- Even within the conventional appearing writing of Parker's movement, a similarity, pianistically, even musically, seems clear when comparing the first full bar and the second of Ives's movement IIa.

- The second piece of Parker's set, *La Sauterelle*, starts out with a segment compatible in many ways to another passage in the second movement (IIa) of Ives's sonata, at m.46 for five bars, its accompaniment and upper line seeming almost from the same mold, despite their idiomatic incompatibility.

- Again in *Valse Gracille*, can be seen ties to Ives's more advanced applications of similar ideas. In this instance, In Ives's mvt. IIa, at mm.38–39, the use of irregular grouped patterns is not unlike a simpler methodology by Parker, in which the triple meter features a four-bar bridge of hemiolas. Ives takes the concept further by grouping five 16th-notes in the left hand over groups of three 16th-notes in the bass.

- Later in *Conte Sérieux*, at m.48, and in Ives's movement, IIb—the First Piano Sonata version of the original first movement of *Four Ragtime Dances*—at m.102, similarly clad chordal writing also works largely in contrary motion.

- The third full bar of the same movement is reminiscent of another passage in IIb—at m.26—continuing for half a dozen, or so, bars, despite the obvious differences of rhythm and music context.

- The back-and-forth, largely traditional bass lines of Ives's IV at m.52 is quite compatible with m.57 of Parker's *Valse Gracille*; even in Ives's non-traditional setting, links to existing musical and technical roots remain.

- The opening of *La Sauterelle* also suggests another passage in Ives's movement IV from m.52 through the remainder of the page, in which frequent syncopations in the bass line, and certain melodic attributes in the left hand seems linked—at least in the type of pianistic writing.

- Later in the same movement, octaves in the bass, accompanying chordal motion in the right hand, pointing, even, to some similarities in Ives's fifth movement at m.208.

186

- The last movement in Parker's set, *Valse Gracile*, is deceptive, and interesting in its own right; appearing quite conventional, even tame, at a casual glance, in fact, its harmonic implications are surprisingly creative and evasive. A brief outline of the progressions (transposed to the tonic key) of its first page, alone, reveals again, that Parker, in harmonic applications, at very least, was not quite as sedate as his image (see again Chapter 4). Using nebulous tonality, the piece appears to be in C minor, leading oddly the next bar to in B♭, before the dominant of the true tonality (A♭) is finally established in the fourth bar. It is only with the repeat of the material at m.19 that one discovers that what had appeared to be C minor harmony actually is part of a larger sweep that creates E♭7(add13).

m.1   III   II V7   I   V7

       (Cm) - |B♭-E♭7 - |E♭7 - |A♭ - |A♭ - |E♭7 - |E♭7 - |→

m.8 **#I°7**   II   V7   I   **♭III**

       A°7 - |B♭ - |E♭7 - |E♭7 - |A♭ - |A♭ - |C♭ - |C♭ - |→

m.16 **♭VII**   V7   I

       G♭7 - |G♭(7) - |E♭7 - |E♭7-**(add 13)** - |E♭7 - |E♭7 - |A♭ - |→

Among other works involving piano in which Ragtime runs strong, is the song, *The See'er*, and its adaptation as the first movement of the First Set for Chamber Orchestra. It is also analyzed in detail in *Charles Ives's Musical Universe*.[378] Largely atonal, and, structurally, astonishingly cyclical, Ragtime again dominates its fabric. In just these few instances, one can appreciate how characteristically so complex and all-pervading the Ragtime idiom is in much of Ives's music that it seems impossible to decide where the idiom begins and another ends. It is also clear that it shares virtually nothing, idiomatically, with anything his illustrious teacher hade ever undertaken.

---

[378] Ibid., 240–42.

The direct influence of Parker's songs

by Ives:

Autumn (1902; No.60 in *114 Songs*)
Spring Song (1904; No.65 in *114 Songs*)
The World's Highway (c.1906–07; No.90 in *114 Songs*)
Old Home Day (1920; No.52 in 114 Songs)

by Parker:

Morning (1891; from 3 *Sacred Songs*)
Egyptian Serenade, Op. 24, No. 2 (1891; from *6 Songs*)
The Light is Fading Down the Sky, Op.24, No.3 (1891; from *6 Songs*)
The Lark Now Leaves His Watery Nest, Op.47, No.6 (1899; from *Six Old English Songs*)

In relation to song writing, Ives, perhaps, owed Parker a larger debt than is generally realized, especially in relation to those written during and shortly after his student years at Yale. Parker's songwriting, though never as prolific as Ives's, nevertheless, provided a perfect model of the Victorian musical genre of the day: well-conceived and written models during a time when soirées were socially fashionable as pastimes for the typically well-healed elite. In Ives's hands, the genre would evolve far beyond Parker's world to feature a near limitless array of styles and methodologies, becoming a window into his entire creative output. Parker's songs never assumed such importance, perhaps due to the limits of the expressive range of a medium that constrained him, professionally, despite his efforts to break with it. As became evident in virtually everything he wrote, no matter how rebellious his thoughts, Parker could not shed the dictates that defined him, and provided for his living. In comparison, as the years went by, Ives's songs increasingly broke with established convention, being received with scorn and derision upon his efforts to promote them in the now iconic self-published collection, *114 Songs* (1921).

Most of the New England composers were renowned as songwriters, their success in the medium assuring them of an income. Providing a few gems that have stood the test of time, notably among them, *To a Wild Rose* by Edward MacDowell, *It Was a Lover and his Lass* by Arthur Foote, and *The Miller's Daughter* by George Chadwick, still are sung today. As a songwriter, Parker is overshadowed by these figures; his output, however, though correspondingly smaller, is not necessarily inferior, despite their relative unfamiliarity to the public. He is, nevertheless, an important contributor to the emerging American art song, and consequently, part

188

of the seminal rise of greater musical sophistication in American society and its growing acceptance of homegrown composers.

Because Ives's song productivity took flight during his Yale years and never looked back, one would expect to find demonstrable traces of Parker's work within his work, too. With Ives's awareness of his songs' potential, his output in the genre is often considered among the broadest in scope and variety of any composer, Schubert included. Songs became Ives's workshop; sitting at the piano, daughter Edith at his feet, Ives would sing and expound upon his musical ideas late into the night, having already put in a full day's work in his business office. The huge range of styles and invention they cover is as interesting as their appearance on the page, the degree of their artistic attainment hard to overestimate.

By comparison, Parker's songs, overall, seem infinitely less interesting, much less creative, and staid in content. Before dismissing them as modest representations of his capabilities, however, one should look a little closer. Parker's songs are deceptive, the appearance on the page less likely to catch the eye than those by Ives: Parker distinguished himself largely through his harmonies. Though hardly expansions of the existing language, they contain unusual progressions. These attributes typify the flexible harmony of most of the post-Romantic composers, still struggling to find compatibility with the shifting tonalities left in Wagner's wake; Parker, however, utilized with greater ingenuity. As true 'equal temperament' became standardized, composers began notating less literally, recognizing that performers found it more practical to play music that was written according to the easiest mode of readability.

Parker's song, *Morning*, one of his sacred songs, appears to have provided a good model for a number of other songs by Ives, its stylistic cues showing up with regularity even many years after Yale. The triplet-triad motion of Parker's song, for example, can be found reduced to straight eight-notes in Ives's *Spring Song* (No. 65 in *114 Songs*), especially in the second part. The song was written during what Ives described as a composing 'slump' he experienced some six years after graduating from Yale. The simple bass lines of both Parker's and Ives's songs, though strongly chromatic almost at once, also have much in common, although Ives's work in this respect is the more remarkable. The harmonies during the primary statements are more straightforward than during their mid-sections, during which they become decidedly more adventurous, reaching across chromatic transitions that are entirely in accordance, nevertheless, with art songs of the period.

Ives's *Autumn* (1902; No.60 in *114 Songs*) is another example in which other attributes shared with *Morning* can be found. Although the voicing differs, and the accompanying chords are syncopated, the overall continuation of the pulsing harmonic foundation, as well as their linear climbing and descent, links them. Even the triplet chords that evolve in Parker's song may be found in Ives's at m.16. Ives's *Autumn* opens in an entirely diffuse setting. Although D flat is the nominative tonality, Ives avoids its firm confirmation assiduously throughout; even the final confirmation is not approached by a perfect cadence, and ends with the tonic chord in first inversion. Thus, the similarities lie largely within the song's mutual late-Victorian style of writing. We can compare the first ten bars of each:

Ives: *Autumn*

(p/u)E♭7| Cm - A♭(#7) - | B♭m7 - E♭°7 - | D♭ - A♭m - | E♭ - |→

D♭ - B♭7(#5)-E♭m°7| B♭° - E♭°7 - | D♭ - A♭m - | B♭7 - A♭m - |→

B♭7 - A♭m- | G♭ - D♭m - | Fm - (♭5) |B♭7 - (add9) - |→

Parker: *Morning* (beginning m.3 on vocal entrance)

D - Bm7 - | D - Am7| D - A-D| Bm-Em-A-m|→

Em-D-C-B|C#m-D#m-Em-C#°7| D - E7 - | →

A7 - D-(add9)|A(sus) - D - | Gm-7-C(#7) - |→

It can be seen that both songs tread relatively adventurous harmonic paths, the characterizations of Parker as an uninspired musical drudge is not always fair or accurate. However, it is Ives, nevertheless, who staked the more unusual and creative turf. In no better way is the yawning gap between Ives and Parker better illustrated than by his handling of the long-standardized tonic-dominant relationship alone—predictably present in Parker's *Morning*—but absent in Ives's *Autumn*.

At the conclusion of *114 Songs*, Ives wrote an elaborate and commentary, with a reference to eight of them he considered unworthy examples, best avoided, even better, never written. Including them only as demonstrations of the types of song that should not be written, one wonders how Ives thought his publication, intended to introduce his music to the world, would be received! An intriguing relationship between teacher and student again can be isolated between Parker's *Egyptian Serenade* (1891) and Ives's *The World's Highway* (c.1906–07, No.90 in

114 Songs, and one of the examples that Ives considered not worthy of performance!). The partial resemblance to fauxbourdon that begins both examples makes the prospect that Ives was well familiar with Parker's song plausible.

Both of these songs commence in parallel thirds in the right hand, virtually matched in register and character. Perhaps surprisingly, Parker's, however, is more harmonically interesting; starting in a loosely suggested B tonality that is never confirmed, the music ultimately winds its way through shifting harmonies to its true foundation in E major. The similarity of both songs, in accompaniment and melodic lines, is immediately noticeable, although Parker's work is more daring in its harmonic implications. Parker's song avoids a firm sense of the tonic key (Em) for as long as possible. Ives chose, however, a more straightforward path, beginning his song in the prevailing tonic key (G major). Maintaining its dominance in the opening segment, nevertheless, he continued in the middle portion with contrastingly shifting tonal ambiguity, leading to a third section that keeps closer to the opening tonic for the conclusion.

As compositions, both of these songs owe each other their mutual broken triadic bass lines, the ranges of both right and left hands, the eighth-note motion (almost exclusively featuring nothing smaller), the frequently ambiguous choices of chords, and generally standardized four-part voicing. The harmonic designs of the first part of each disguise their similarities:

by Ives:

p/u |I - IV | I - V-#IV°7 | I   -   VI - | I - |

G | G -C- | G - D-C#°7 | G6/4 - Bm - |G - |→

I - #IV°7   V7-VI°7-III7| C-#IVm7-IIm7/D | I

G - C#°7 | D7- B°7- B7 | C- C#m7-Am7/D | G6/4 - |→

         I - IV | I   -   V-#IV°7 | I   -   VI - | I

         G -C- |G   -   D-C#°7 | G6/4 - Bm - |G - |→

by Parker:

V   - |V - |V   - |V - IIm - |IVm - V7 - |

B6/4 - |B6/4 - |B - B6/3 - |B6/4 - F#m - |Am - B7 - |→

        I   - VI9 - |V(#7) - I/II - V|II - V - |Im   - VI°7 - | -

      Em - C#9 - |B(#7) - E/F#-B|F# - B - |Em - C#°7 - |→

            I - |IIIm -#I° -xVIm7| VII#7- |

            B - |G#m-E#°- Cxm7 | D#   - |→

Ch. 7 How Ives's Mature Music Reflects His Influences

Ives, however, did not follow nearly such an aggressive harmonic path as Parker, opting, instead, for a closer affinity to the primary tonic harmony (G major)—although in mm.5–7, Ives was closer to Parker.

Parker's best-loved song, *The Lark Now Leaves its Watery Nest*, belongs to his set, *Six Old English Songs*, of 1899. Although Ives no longer was Parker's student when it was composed, its fame at the time makes it quite likely that Ives knew it. Looking at those eight examples in *114 Songs* that Ives "disowned" begins, perhaps, to reveal an ulterior motif—was it a late backhanded 'slap' at such efforts by Parker, many years after the fact? It turns out that the celebrated *Lark* more nearly resembles these eight songs than most others in Ives's collection, being decidedly simple and harmonically straightforward—indeed, and having few of the sophisticated attributes of Parker's better efforts—though no doubt the real reason for its endearment to audiences of the day.

Such music, of course, was precisely the kind of work Ives, even Parker, sought to escape! Kearns admired *The Lark's* "clever descriptive figures, the clear-cut rhythmic sequential patterns, the transparent texture, and the virtuosic vocal line." In reality, the elements described are not all that interesting, the patterns are not sequences, nor are they patterns, nor are they clear-cut either way; the vocal line is fast, though not especially challenging. The texture, however, *is* transparent! In fact, it is downright thin, and its fabric dull—presumably the stuff of musically, if not societally, unsophisticated audiences. Of the eight "bad" songs in Ives's *114 Songs*, perhaps *On the Counter*, No.28, *Dreams*, No.87, and *A Night Song*, No.88, are closest to *The Lark*, their unadventurous language and routine harmonies only adding weight to their latter-day, unfashionable, redundancy.

Even in such an inventive song as Ives's *Old Home Day*, written in 1920, traces of his background still can be detected, a return to an earlier style, in which he had excelled. In the chorus of the song can be found some attributes directly comparable to Parker's 1891 song, *The Light is Fading Down the Sky*, in which, supporting the primary upper line in the right hand (shadowing the voice), similar, part-harmonizations accompany it, above frequent syncopations in the left hand, over tones always on strong beats of the bar providing the harmonic foundation in the bass. Ives's song might not exist as a mirror image of any by Parker; however, the link to the same, well-demonstrated format survives with distinction from teacher to student.

The 'German' Songs (c.1894–1902)

Set in a similar late-Romantic style, the eighteen so-called 'German' songs likely all were written during Ives's Yale years, and shortly thereafter—between c. 1894–

1902—despite the *post*-dating of some of them by Ives in *114 Songs*. Consistently in the established idiom of the late-Romantic age genre, they have been at the center of much speculation regarding Ives's apparent fondness of the style, even after having abandoned it for more radical musical adventures, or at least works reflecting wholly American-styled content. An obvious comparison may be drawn between the *Prelude* of Parker's Suite Opus 35 and Ives's *In Summer Fields* (No.82 in *114 Songs*), and *Weil' auf mir* (No.80 in *114 Songs*); the flowing up-and-down arpeggiations of the piano part, although not precisely matching, seem strongly related in the overall sense of the medium. A similar arpeggiated bass line can be found, too, in the first system on the last page of Parker's song, *Evening*, which, at least, confirms the common pianistic idiom.

A similar pacing and spread can be found in the accompaniment in Parker's song, *Morning*, and Ives's *Chanson de Florian* (No.78 in *114 Songs*), characterized by triplet groupings of triadic motion. The even-paced eighth-note five-voice chordal pulse that characterizes the opening of the third movement, *Romance*, of Parker's Trio appears in much the same manner in *The Old Mother* (No.81 in *114 Songs*). In Ives's *Rosamunde* (No.79 in *114 Songs*), again, much can be found in common rhythmically with the accompaniment of the last page of Parker's *Morning*, in which the pulsing, tied triplet chords maintain the character and motion. Such shared attributes are far from unusual, of course, in any music of the period, although it remains always intriguing to look for clues to the evolution of Ives's remarkable musical language along the evidentiary trail.

Verdict: The fact that it remains so challenging to find direct correlations between Ives's and Parker's piano writing—from roughly the same time period—demonstrates just how fast and far Ives shifted musical development in America, with virtually no obvious single precedent. So significant in music, it cannot be stressed too much. Additionally, other than through esthetic considerations, even purely musical, Ives also stretched piano technique, in virtual defiance of all previously accepted norms of virtuosity. Even the flashy and highly demanding works of Gottschalk do not cross these borders, Ives's expansion of the genre being particularly noteworthy through its rhapsodic freedom that imposed entirely new technical and rhythmic demands. With the quantum leap in American music seeming, even now, inconceivably daring, we can only speculate what might have been its greatest trigger. Despite the original spirit of both George Ives and his son, should we, therefore, credit primarily the wild pianist at Poli's—George Felsberg—as the only possible explanation for Ives's apparent sudden realization of the potential possibilities awaiting him on the piano? Even outside the obvious links to Ragtime, Ives's composing style seems to have been forever impacted by

193

the rhapsodic freedom generated by Felsberg's wild syncopated Ragtime rhythms. There is nothing else in any surviving source that offers other explanation.

Because good technical writing for the piano—or any instrument—is the product of training, familiarity of past composers' work, and the sheer practical expedience necessitated by having only two hands with only five fingers on each, its literature can be expected to reflect these considerations. There can be no doubt that Parker did influence Ives in this respect, although it is not possible to gauge to what degree. Regardless, and for whatever reason, overall pianistic resemblances between Parker's and Ives's piano writing, if not always demonstrated in specific examples, are evident, too, in some of Ives's song accompaniments of his Yale years and shortly thereafter—even at time in songs from later years. However, other aspects lead the trail away from Parker, who was primarily an organist, not a pianist. Ives was *both*, and, thus, perhaps Ives was frustrated by Parker's attitude toward things he considered he already knew—and perhaps, even better. Maybe it coincides, too, with Ives's sentiments in *Memos* about his theory classes, in which Parker made him cover materials he had studied under his father—even from the same texts.[379]

More links between Parker and Ives: the Choral works

by Ives: *Three Harvest Home Chorales* (1897–1902; reconstructed before 1912)

by Parker: *The Legend of Saint Christopher* (1897)

In the space of six short years between 1893–99, Ives was not the only composer to make strides. Parker's more radical side could not be constrained forever. Nevertheless, the difference in language between *Hora Novissima* (1893) and *The Legend of Saint Christopher* (1897), written before Ives had departed from New Haven, is substantial, including its design, breadth, chromaticism, extravagant melodic lines, even the color and imagination in his orchestration, which features large segments for orchestra alone; Parked had become aware of its vast potential to contribute to his choral music. The very aspect so modestly featured in virtually all of Parker's earlier musical essays suddenly had germinated, bloomed and come of age.

---

[379] Ives, *Memos*, 49.

Ives, too, was reaching simultaneously into new territory, while consolidating the old. His largely conventional compositions, such as the First Symphony (1897–1902) and *'Adeste Fideles' in an Organ Prelude* (1898), coexisted with the more dissonantly radical *Interludes for Hymns* (1898) and *Postlude for a Thanksgiving Service* (1897), written for services at Center Church on the Green—and certainly not subject to Parker's scrutiny. Rather than comparing only Parker's and Ives's work from roughly the same time—those few years at the end of the nineteenth century and crossing into the twentieth—evidence survives of the lingering residual of their shared Yale years, even as Ives had stepped fully into the future, wholly independent of Parker. However, it is only reasonable to examine Parker's music close to the time Ives was his student—the last point at which Ives would have been exposed to, and potentially influenced by his work to any substantive degree. The fact that the *Three Harvest Home Chorales* appear to have their roots during the late nineteenth century years offers an even better opportunity to look for more direct links between both composers' later, more adventurous choral writing. Although Parker's oratorio (admittedly, an infinitely larger-scale work than Ives's) was completed in the year following Ives's departure from Yale, Ives was surely well aware of his teacher's evolving style, as represented in *The Legend of Saint Christopher* and, perhaps, more than a casual familiarity with some of the content.

Because a complete analysis of the *Three Harvest Home Chorales* may be found in the writer's text, *Charles Ives's Musical Universe*,[380] it is not necessary to repeat it here. In relation to the more conventional attributes common to both works, the first of the chorales features, essentially, traditional four-part block writing for the chorus. Entirely typical throughout much *The Legend of Saint Christopher*, this particular clear reflection of teacher in student seems clear enough. Harmonically, however, Ives's music already has taken a dramatic turn, the vague and transient sense of tonality only maintained by the gravitational scalic pull of the organ part, its descending and ascending parallel harmonies throughout always having a starting and ending point. Although nothing so unconventional appears anywhere in Parker's oratorio, the actual *approach* to writing for four-part chorus is closely matched, 'correct' baroque practice.

A closer examination of both works immediately illustrates not only some striking similarities, but also their radical differences. Of the former, throughout Parker's entire output, i the constraints of convention, and his place in society, always crimped the potential of his more adventurous instincts. Nevertheless, his consistently fine and workmanly scoring, and his solid, if characteristically stolid,

---

[380] Cooke, *Charles Ives's Musical Universe*, 39–51.

style is striking. The very strengths of his disciplined writing, however betray a greater weakness in his creativity than they do his constraints, in which a certain ritual of composing to a well-considered, long existent methodology always stands in the way of breaking real, new ground. Quite impressive, nonetheless, it is eminently musical, proportioned, and never flagging in its narrative. Of the latter consideration, it is only when turning to the rapidly evolving and maturing language of Ives, however, is the chasm between the two figures suddenly obvious. If Parker's genteel culture ultimately limited him, Ives was liberated by many of his own cultural experiences.

The homage to traditional practices also can be observed in the manner that Ives compounded the staggered (though not necessarily imitative) choral entrances in the *First Chorale*. It is not unlike what can be found in Act II, Scene I in *The Legend of Saint Christopher* at Rehearsal No.76. Parker's work, however, remains constrained and 'by the book.' Closer in mutual spirit, perhaps, both Ives and Parker—briefly—set up multiple speeds. Parker, never one to cause too large a ripple, neatly placed four beats against six, before Rehearsal No.81 in Act II, Scene II. Ives took the idea to greater extremes, however, in his second chorale, establishing three, four-and-a-half, and five in the time of four, respectively. Quite aside from the rhythmic aspects, there are certain resemblances in melodic style between these two examples. Parker, always seeming to fall back on imitative baroque counterpoint, relying upon canonic, as well as fugal subjects and answers throughout his oratorio. (See, for example, the fugato in Act II, Scene II, starting on p.134; it features even an augmented appearance in the last bar of p.136 in the lowest voice.) No less tied to traditional counterpoint, Parker included a segment near the conclusion (p.179) that suggests a fugal stretto. However effective such writing might be, one senses that even the adventurous Parker only could go so far; even in a work such as *The Legend*, one constantly is surprised by its reliance on traditional imitative language.

Ives, however, still maintaining the essence of the old forms, infused his *Harvest Home Chorales* with a much wider range of possibilities having their roots in the distant past. In taking the form of 'successive composition,' Ives's *Second Chorale* took another technique that Parker shied away from entirely, despite likely introducing it to his music history class. If the influence was from Ives's studies with Parker, rather than a familiarity with old musical forms prior to attending Yale, Parker, himself, preferred not to incorporate such methods in his own music—again, restricting himself to the mainstream of musical thought— represented by the music from Bach's time up until Beethoven's, and extended, at least in part, into his own time by exposure to mainstream contemporary figures.

196

A good case in point is well illustrated by the examples of staggered imitative choral entries in both works. Out of numerous instances in Parker's oratorio, one of the most starkly defined occurs in Part III, Scene II (at the key change to B major). Briefly unconventional, Parker outlined a minor seventh with the opening notes of his three primary canonic entrances, but soon thereafter, the writing devolves into block harmony, followed by fairly traditional flowing counterpoint. In comparison, Ives's *Third Chorale* commences with four primary canonic entries that outline a G major chord over C, dominant and tonic together being one of Ives's frequent key blends. The chorus threatens to move, similarly, to standard four-part harmony, even as the stark melodic and polytonal aspects indicate that little about it is conventional. Gradually, as in the example by Parker, the chordal writing is freed into counterpoint, only now, Ives's totally independent parts defy convention, through their building of a mirror image between the bass and soprano lines, set against another musical opposite in-between the tenors and altos. Ultimately challenging, while undermining final unification, the work ends with tonic ($C^{(\#4)}$) and subdominant (F) now coincident.

Ch. 7 How Ives's Mature Music Reflects His Influences

Chapter 8
Conclusions

*F*or anyone looking for an indisputable roadmap to the evolution of Ives's musical language, the search, ultimately, is likely to be long, and as frustrating as it is difficult to be certain of anything. The roadmap is, however, not without any prospect of at least some discovery, though we always can be certain that much will remain forever shrouded by the mysteries of creative genius. Parker, too, once a rebellious youth, found out quickly that even long after his reputation was thoroughly established, asserting his musical independence would be met with resistance, even outright rejection. Parker, though hardly an unappreciated musical prophet, was obliged to find a means to survive from his musical labors, rather than starve. Ives, of course, solved the problem another way, though it cost him his health, and also effectively ended his most productive years—though not before he had more than made his mark in two arenas. Parker, too, might have paid the larger price, having staked his traded most of his independence to live among the more privileged elite social and cultural class, to which he owed his very being, and consequently, the dictates of his creative style. Parker's audience and benefactors were hardly of a mindset that was ready to embrace anything that might challenge their own secure culture at the pinnacle of upper crust American society.

Ives's many influences reflect a high level learning aptitude, an ability to soak up virtually everything that entered his experience, to process them and set them free as something new, each influence playing a formative part in the total. It is not possible, therefore, to dismiss anything that might have entered his consciousness, any more than it is possible to downplay anything bequeathed by George Ives or Horatio Parker. What does seem clear is that Charles Ives's Danbury years *were* largely responsible for defining his unique musical brand. By the time he attended Yale, the primary benefits of his time with Parker fueled the impetus to compose large-scale musical structures, professionally-hewn in construction. Through Parker's disciplined teaching, and the requirements of writing within defined formats on demand, Ives would begin to think in terms of creating major works for the concert hall, examples of which began with works such as the First String Quartet, First and Second Symphonies, and *The Celestial Country*, emerging either from his college years, or shortly thereafter. The sudden shift into major compositions was likely Parker's most significant influence.

The importance, thus, of Ives's Yale years overrides Ives's mixed impressions and reservations about Parker's guidance. Likely, even Ives remained unaware of precisely what catapulted him toward such dramatically expanded horizons. The regrettable undue distrust of Ives common in present-day American musicology reflects a bias, and worse, a denial of a larger reality that, perhaps, only an 'outsider' can see. Any group can develop a mindset from tunnel-vision—one that, in many ways, reminds the writer of Parker's dilemma, as a 'member' of an elite social set that unknowingly stood in his way to attain more as an original musical innovator.

Diametrically opposite in nature, Ives's innovations, which became primary to his large musical structures, all were first undertaken within miniature musical forms, and hark back almost entirely to Danbury or New Haven. Gradually evolving and refined into organized methodologies, Ives could utilize them at will as foundations in those monumental works that have cemented Ives's place, at least, outside the cloistered halls of musicology, as the first 'Great American Composer.' The term, in itself, is somewhat problematic, because, despite the plethora of prominent and influential figures in the modern American music world, how realistic is it to suppose that there has been a stream of 'great' American composers to follow in Ives's wake, in the mold of, say, a Mahler, Ravel, or Stravinsky? In this sense, the mold is the pure 'art' music figures, as traditionally defined and accepted. Although Ives certainly belongs in the 'great' category, as so defined, how often can the term be applied to others in America after Ives looked beyond accepted horizons? Undoubtedly, Aaron Copland and George Gershwin fit the profile fairly closely, if not, perhaps, so profoundly. Even the creators of jazz, such as Louis Armstrong or Duke Ellington, and even more diffusely connected figures, those composers who pioneered the 'American musical,' such as Jerome Kern, Richard Rogers or Cole Porter, who were great within their own realms.

However, one can trace a unique lineage: the full list continues the progression and is, in fact, very long. From the pure art forms, often blended through a wide and complex range, it ranges all the way to the popular and generic. Just how many of these figures can be classified in the same breath as in the original meaning of the term is *where American music left the old Western forms behind*. The starting point in any such assessment surely takes into account the universe of differences between highly talented 'tunesmiths'—uniquely gifted persons able to create musical 'hooks' that define a 'hit'—and the true composer who builds almost endless large structures out of small motivic fragments into monumental works of musical architecture. Ives, himself, was inspired by popular sources and drew from them extensively; indeed—so did Mahler! The difficulty has been in knowing where and how to 'draw the line' in determining what American music constitutes, though surely, we must be careful not to confuse entertainment and entertainers with art and artists, as has become increasingly common.

In attempting to discover as much as can be gleaned about Ives's evolution as a composer, not all the answers can be determined with any more certainty than for any composer, although it can be demonstrated convincingly, however, that Ives definitely was early to discover his methods, even his larger guiding influences. He was similarly early to learn the classics and advanced music theory; moreover, his progressive ideas were hardly the result of exposure to Horatio Parker, nor a captive of some constraining method, from which, few great composers can emerge. Many of the greatest composers triumphed, of course, despite less than stellar circumstances, their talents and will to succeed so great that failure was never a prospect. The frequent lack of recognition in their own time sounds just like Ives's story. Even towering figures such as Mahler and Wagner, for example, knew all too well the constant drumbeat of critics who assured them they were pursuing the wrong ends. Even Ives's friends and relatives caused him often to think he might "have his ears on all wrong."

We have learned that Ives's background, precisely because of it was so unlikely, it was the catalyst for everything he did; even its very provincialism acted as a powerful component, because it kept the social musical elite at arm's length. If Ives entered Yale far better equipped than has been allowed, he did gain insights and expertise from Parker, namely, the ability to conceive and execute large musical structures. Parker's hard-nosed, uncompromising approach, too, gave Ives the professional perspective—mere brilliance and aptitude being only the start.

Ives's world, however, is difficult to realize in actual performance. His orchestration, frequently criticized, is often unconsciously confused for his *instrumentation* and sheer awkwardness, which often is highly impractical, even when his orchestrations are standard. Performers, too, need to understand something of the relative importance of each part (especially because Ives was notoriously lax in providing specific indications in his music), and its relationship to their own. Additionally, Ives's incorporations of 'vernacular' elements in his major art works continue to be widely misunderstood and misrepresented, his own mature melodies being typically far more diffuse and structurally complex than his quotes, so their role often is missed or misconstrued. At other times, such as in many of his songs, Ives reveals himself as every bit the melodist of a traditional calling; *The Greatest Man,* and *Charlie Rutlage* show his melodic gift. However, the real revelation of this examination reconfirms George Ives as the seminal influence in his son's life and work. Without him, there is little reason to believe that the phenomenon of Ives's music would have taken place, the world being much the poorer for the loss.

A loose categorization of Ives's primary influences

From George Ives:
- A grounding in harmony and counterpoint
- Strong guidance, support and encouragement
- Openness to all possibilities
- A continual search for the best teachers when unable to provide the requisite tuition himself
- Encouragement of Ives's experiments, including chordal stacking, wedges, polytonal counterpoint, polyrhythms, perhaps, too, metric juxtapositions
- Exposure to band tunes and revival hymns, especially those from the Civil War
- Questioning the status quo about music theory
- Dodecaphony
- Multiple tunings and scales
- Awareness of sounds external to musical
- Spatial sounds
- Awareness of listening to *music*, rather than refined sound
- Awareness of symphonic literature (from attending concerts in New York City), through organ transcriptions of symphonic works, as well as the music of the popular "organ composers."
- Minstrel music
- Transcendentalism and Congregationalism

From his local surroundings:
- The music and flavor of local patriotic festivals, and the uniquely American local culture of the era
- The hymns of local churches, in which he served as organist
- The solitude and peace of other locations in the Adirondacks (such as Elk Lake) that can be heard in *The Unanswered Question*, for example
- Detachment from the big city cultural elite
- His political leanings and sympathetic attitude toward the working man (from direct contact with the plight of Danbury's hatting industry workers), ultimately reflected in his music (e.g., *Majority*)
- The perspective of being a first-rate instrumentalist

202

From Horatio Parker:

- A disciplined approach to all matters in the art of composition
- Exposure to music and forms Ives might otherwise have avoided
- Models for many modes of composition
- Increased knowledge of music history and its evolution
- Exposure to the mindset and critical thinking of a professional composer

From Ives's non-academic background at Yale and New Haven:

- Exposure to extreme piano ragtime (George Felsberg at Poli's Theater)
- Independent compositions related to Ives's position as organist at Center Church on the Green
- Fraternity songs and culture

From New York:

- A broadening of a more worldly existence, reflected in later compositions such as the Fourth Symphony, *Second Orchestral Set,* Universe Symphony
- Incorporations of sounds of the big city in his music (*Scherzo: Over the Pavements*, Fourth Symphony)

From nature:

- Sounds of life (e.g., the thrushes on the woods at the rear of his 16-acre estate in West Redding that he featured in the finale of the Fourth Symphony, the sounds of insects in the still summer air in *Central Park in the Dark*, the sounds of music carried through the air over the running waters of the Housatonic
- The sense of 'grand vista'; depicted, perhaps most notably, that in the Adirondacks in the *Universe Symphony*, and its portrayals of the cosmos
- The quest for solitude and peace, as found at such destinations in the Adirondacks as Elk Lake, and heard in *The Unanswered Question*, for example; Ives had visited and discovered their lure the year before he wrote this work.

Bibliography

Christopher Ballantine, "Charles Ives and the Meaning of Quotation in Music," *The Musical Quarterly*, 65, 2 (April 1979), 167–84

Carol K. Baron, "Dating Charles Ives's Music: Facts and Fictions," *Perspectives of New Music* (Winter issue, 1990): 20–56

———, "Efforts on Behalf of Democracy by Charles Ives and his Family: Their Religious Contexts,," *The Musical Quarterly*, 87, 1 (2004): 6–43

———, Review, J. Peter Burkholder, *All Made of Tunes: Charles Ives and the Uses of Musical Borrowing* (New Haven, CT: Yale University Press, 1995): 437–44

———, "George Ives's Essay on Music Theory: An Introduction and Annotated Edition," *American Music* (Fall, 1992) : 239–88

———, "At the Cutting Edge: Three American Theorists at The End of The Nineteenth Century," *International Journal of Musicology*, 2 (1993)

Stephen Budiansky, "Ives, Diabetes, and His 'Exhausted Vein' of Composition," American Music, 31, 1 (Spring, 2013): 1–25.

J. Peter Burkholder, *All Made of Tunes: Charles Ives and the Uses of Musical Borrowing* (New Haven, CT: Yale University Press, 2004)

———, *Charles Ives: The Ideas Behind the Music* (New Haven, CT: Yale University Press, 1985

———, The College Music Symposium, "Ives and Yale: The Enduring Influence of a College Experience," online, *Scholarship and Research*, 39, (October, 1999)

———, "Ives and the Nineteenth-Century European Tradition," in *Charles Ives and the Classical Tradition*, ed Burkholder, Geoffrey Block (New Haven, CT: Yale University Press, 1996)

———, "Ives and the Four Musical Traditions," in *Charles Ives and His World*, ed. Burkholder (Princeton, NJ: Princeton University Press, 1995)

205

Elliott Carter, "The Case of Mr. Ives," *Modern Music* (March-April, 1939): 172–76

Antony Cooke, *Charles Ives and his Road to the Stars*, second edition (W. Conshohocken, PA: Infinity, 2015)

———, *Charles Ives's Musical Universe*, (W. Conshohocken, PA: Infinity, 2015)

———, "The Mercurial Ailments of Charles Ives and his Family," awaiting publication as of September 8, 2020.

Henry & Sidney Cowell, *Charles Ives and His Music* (London: Oxford University Press, 1955)

Alison Matthews David, "Mercurial Styles, Persistent Toxins: Materiality, "Mad" Hatters, and Mercury Poisoning in the Felt Hatting Trade," *Russian Fashion Theory: The Journal of Dress, Body and Culture*, 21 (Autumn 2011): 13–38

Stuart Feder, *Charles Ives: "My Father's Song," a Psycho-Analytical Biography* (New Haven, CT: Yale University Press, 1992)

Constantin Flores, *Gustav Mahler: The Symphonies* (Portland, OR: Amadeus Press, 1985)

Kyle Gann "Poisoned Musicology": *PostClassic*, Kyle Gann on music after the fact, 24 March, 2014, arts.journal.com

H. Wiley Hitchcock, *Ives: A Survey of the Music* (London: Oxford University Press, 1977)

Charles E. Ives, *Essays Before a Sonata* (New York: Knickerbocker Press, 1921)

———, *Memos*, ed. John Kirkpatrick (New York: Norton, first pub. 1972)

———, *The Universe Symphony, realized by Johnny Reinhard*, (New York: American Festival of Microtonal Music, 1995)

Timothy A. Johnson, *Baseball and the Music of Charles Ives: A Proving Ground* (Lanham, MD: Rowman & Littlefield, 2004)

William K. Kearns, *Horatio Parker, 1863–1919: His Life, Music, and Ideas* (Metuchen, NJ: The Scarecrow Press, 1990)

John Kirkpatrick, *A TemporaryMimeographed Catalog of The Music Manuscripts and Related Materials of Charles Edward Ives 1874–1954* (New Haven, CT: Irving S. Gilmore Library, Yale University School of Music, 1960)

———, "Preface" to the score, *Charles Ives : Symphony no. 4* (Associated Music Publishers, Inc., 1965)

Philip Lambert, *The Music of Charles Ives* (New Haven, CT: Yale University Press, 1997)

Gayle Sherwood Magee, "Charles Ives and 'Our National Malady,'" *Journal of the American Musicological Society,* 54, 3 (Fall, 2000): 555–84.

———, *Charles Ives: A Research and Information Guide* (NY: Routledge, 2010)

———, *Charles Ives Reconsidered* (Urbana, IL: University of Illinois Press, Music in American Life Series, 2008)

———, "Questions and Veracities: Reassessing the Chronology of Ives's Choral Works," *The Musical Quarterly*, 42, 1 (1989): 209–18

Drew Michael Massey, "An Unobtrusive Minister of Genius: John Kirkpatrick and the Editing of Contemporary American Music," Ph.D. diss., Harvard University, 2010

Vivian Perlis, *Charles Ives Remembered* (Urbana, IL: University of Illinois Press, 1974)

Tom C. Owens, *Selected Correspondence of Charles Ives* (Berkeley, CA: University of California Press, 2007)

Johnny Reinhard, , *The Universe Symphony, realized by Johnny Reinhard*, (New York: American Festival of Microtonal Music, 1995)

Frank R. Rossiter, *Charles Ives & His America* (New York, W. W. Norton & Company (February 11, 1975)

Eric Salzman, *Twentieth-Century Music: An Introduction*, ed. 3 (Englewood Cliffs, NJ: Prentice Hall, 1988)

Ann Besser Scott, "Medieval and Renaissance Techniques in the Music of Charles Ives: Horatio at the Bridge?", *The Musical Quarterly*, 78, 3 (autumn 1994)

Isabel Parker Semler, *Horatio Parker: A Memoir for his Grandchildren compiled from Letters and Papers* (New York: G.P. Putnam's Sons, 1942)

Tom Service, "Symphony Guide: Mahler's Ninth," *The Guardian*, 29 July 2014. (Also available at:

https://www.theguardian.com/music/tomserviceblog/2014/jul/29/mahlers-ninth-tom-service-symphony-guide)

Bryan R. Simms, "The German Apprenticeship of Charles Ives," *American Music*, 29, 2 (Summer, 2011): 139–67

James B. Sinclair, *A Descriptive Catalogue of The Music of Charles Ives*, (New Haven, CT: Yale University Press, 1999)

———, Preface: Charles E. Ives, *First Symphony* (New York: Peermusic, 1999), iv.

David Stanley Smith, "A Study of Horatio Parker," *The Musical Quarterly*, XVI, 2 (April 1930)

Maynard Solomon, "Charles Ives: Some Questions of Veracity," *Journal of the American Musicological Society*, 40, 3 (Fall 1987): 443–70

Jan Swafford, *Charles Ives: A Life with Music* (New York: W.W. Norton, 1996)

Nicholas E. Tawa, "Ives and the New England School," in *Charles Ives and the Classical Tradition*, ed. Geoffrey Block & J. Peter Burkholder (New Haven, CT: Yale University Press, 1996)

———, *Serenading the Reluctant Eagle: American Musical Life, 1925–1945* (New York: Schirmer, 1985)

Laurence Wallach, "The New England Education of Charles Ives," Ph.D. diss., Columbia University, 1973

Keith C. Ward, "Ives, Schoenberg, and the Musical Ideal," in *Charles Ives and the Classical Tradition*, ed Burkholder, Geoffrey Block (New Haven, CT: Yale University Press, 1996)

Thomas Warburton: "Charles Ives and His Four Ragtime Pieces," of 1983, in Donna Coleman, "A Source Study of the Fifth Movement of Charles Ives's First Piano Sonata: Toward a Critical Edition," Ph.D. diss., Eastman School of Music, 1987)

Richard Whightman Fox, "The Culture of Liberal Progressivism, 1875–1925," *Journal of Interdisciplinary History*, 23, 3 (Winter 1993)

Victor Fell Yellin, *Chadwick, Yankee Composer* (Washington, D.C., Smithsonian Institution Press, 1990)

Index

Quartal harmony (early), 76, 92
Quintal harmony, 76, 92
Quotes (functions), 14, 27, 46, 48–50, 78, 118, 139, 177, 204

Raasch, Hans, 39
Ragtime, 34, 41, 62, 70–74, 158, 164, 176, 183–84, 188–90, 196, 205
  Characteristics of, 73–74
Ravel, Maurice, 105, 182, 200
  Jeux d'Eau, 180–81
  Ondine, 181
Recitals, church, 43, 62
Reger, Max, 181
Rheinberger, Josef, 23–24, 99–103, 108, 120, 151
Relevance today, 102
Reinecke, Carl, 99
Rhythm of St. Bernard de Morlaix, monk of Cluny, on the celestial country, The 148
Roberts, George, 169
Robinson, Edward, 108
Robinson Fur Cutting Company, 32
Romanticism, 99–100, 152
Root, George F., 50
Rorick, William C., 97
Rossiter, Frank R., 4, 14, 18, 42
'Rules' adjustments of the, 171–74

Saint-Saëns, Camille, 146
Santayana, George, 108
Salzman, Eric, 49
Satie, Erik, 73, 102
  Le Fils Des Étoiles, 76
Schenkerian analysis, 177
Schoenberg, Arnold, 5, 38, 93, 101
Schubert, Franz, 65, 135, 140, 146, 191
  Eighth Symphony ('Unfinished'), 140–41
Schumann, Robert, 49, 146
Scott, Ann Besser, 75–79, 175
Semler, Isabel Parker, 98, 100, 102–04
Serebrier, José, 15
Sessions, Roger, 97–98, 138
Shadle, Douglas, 11
Shakespeare, William, 63
Shelley, Percy Bysshe, 63
Shelley, Harry Rowe, 63
Sherwood, Gayle, 8, 12

Shining Shore, The, 59, 80, 140, 156, 171
Shirley, Wayne B., 26
Simms, Byron R., 68–69
Simrock, N., 138
Sinclair, James, B., 12–13, 135–36, 140, 152
  A Descriptive Catalogue of the Music of Charles Ives, 8, 64, 87, 89–90, 114–117, 119, 126, 150, 160, 181
  Unsupported assertions of composers featured in Parker's class, 139
Slonimsky, Nicolas, 4, 52, 33, 180
Smith, David Stanley, 98–100, 106, 130, 210
Solomon, Maynard, 7, 13–14, 46, 569, 86, 90, 117, 137, 156
Something for Thee, 153
'Spellings,' note, 167
Stevenson, Robert Louis, 64
Stokowski, Leopold, 15
Strauss, Richard, 49, 101, 109
Stravinsky, Igor, 5, 101, 117–18, 200
'Stride,' 70, 72–74, 164–65, 188–89, 197
Study in Europe by American composers, 47, 68, 100
'Successive composition,' 76–77, 173, 199
Syncopations, 70, 72–74, 176, 187, 189, 195
Systemized methodology, 38, 89, 152, 170, 173
Swafford, Jan, 9, 18–22, 26, 31, 39–42, 45–47, 60, 77, 96, 122
'Take-Offs', 80–81

Tawa, Nicholas, 9–10, 24–25, 35–36, 49–50, 53, 66–68, 144, 152–57
Tchaikovsky, Peter Ilyich, 50
  Sixth Symphony, (*Pathetique*), 50
Tempered pitch, 57, 93, 167
Tennyson, Alfred Lord, 63
Thayer, Eugene, 62
  Variations on the Russian National Hymn, Op. 12, 62
There is a Fountain, 35, 76,
Thoreau, Henry David, 45
Toscanini, Arturo, 179
Training, musical, in Europe, 34, 100
Transcendentalism, 9, 31, 44–46, 52–53, 118, 139, 204
Tuning, 57, 93–94, 137, 167, 204
Twichell (Ives), Harmony, 46

Verdi, Guiseppe, 123,
Vernacular elements, 34–35, 37–38, 43, 50, 61–62, 67–68, 75, 78, 141–42, 203

215